INTRODUCTION TO MACRO-ECONOMICS

By the same author

*

ELEMENTARY ECONOMICS
INTERMEDIATE ECONOMICS
THE BRITISH CONSTITUTION (with L. Bather)
HOW BRITAIN IS GOVERNED
PRODUCING AND SPENDING (with M. Harvey)
MODERN ECONOMICS
(Second Edition)
MODERN ECONOMICS: STUDY GUIDE
AND WORKBOOK (with M. K. Johnson)
(Second Edition)
INTRODUCTION TO MACRO-ECONOMICS:
A WORKBOOK (with M. Johnson)
MULTIPLE CHOICE QUESTIONS FOR
INTERMEDIATE ECONOMICS
GOVERNMENT AND PEOPLE (with M. Harvey)

INTRODUCTION TO MACRO-ECONOMICS

J. HARVEY, B.SC.(Econ.)
Lecturer in Economics, University of Reading

and

M. JOHNSON, B.A.
Formerly Lecturer in Economics, Hatfield Polytechnic

M

First edition 1971
Reprinted 1973, 1975, 1977

Published by
THE MACMILLAN PRESS LTD
London and Basingstoke
Associated companies in New York Dublin
Melbourne Johannesburg and Madras

ISBN 0 333 12509 6 (hard cover)
0 333 12511 8 (paper cover)

Printed in Great Britain by
UNWIN BROTHERS LIMITED
The Gresham Press, Old Woking, Surrey

CONTENTS

TABLES

PREFACE

THIS book is intended to bridge the gap between the general coverage of macro-economics in the basic textbooks on economic theory and the advanced treatment of the more specialised books on the subject. It should therefore be useful for first-year university students specialising in economics; first- and second-year students following wider courses in which economics figures prominently, e.g. degrees in business studies, government, sociology and estate management; students taking professional examinations in banking, public administration, company secretaryship, surveying, accountancy, transport and hospital administration; and sixth-form pupils reading economics to G.C.E. 'A' and 'S' level.

The book begins with the basic theory of modern macro-economics. This theory is then used to discuss economic policy, particularly with regard to the current problems of the United Kingdom – full employment, inflation, balance of payments equilibrium, growth, etc.

The main obstacle to a statement of modern macro-economics is the lack of complete uniformity of view. This 'Introduction', therefore, first explains the fundamental Keynesian ideas and then proceeds to show how they have been developed by later economists or modified in the light of post-war experience and research.

To explain and illustrate the theoretical analysis, the authors have relied mainly on simple diagrams and graphs; in all there are over 90 diagrams. It is recognised, however, that modern macro-economics makes considerable use of mathematical techniques and that even an introductory text should allow the student a glimpse of how mathematics can be applied in this field. Where appropriate, therefore, some simple mathematical models have been introduced (chiefly in the appendices) in order to whet the student's appetite. These models only put the argument in a different form, and the standard of mathematics required is no higher than 'O' level.

'Suggested reading' at the end of each chapter contains complementary references and some, marked with an asterisk, which are more advanced. The books selected are those most readily available to students in a college or local library. To encourage students to be accurate in what they attribute to Keynes, the appropriate references in the *General Theory* have been included.

CHAPTER 1

INTRODUCTION

I. THE SCOPE OF MACRO-ECONOMICS

The economic problem

THE economic problem arises because, in comparison with all the things we want, our resources are limited. But, although limited at any one time, these resources have two important characteristics: (*a*) they are capable of alternative uses; (*b*) they can be increased over time. The first enables us to make the most of what we have; the second allows us to improve our lot. We can illustrate the situation as follows.

Suppose that, during a year, a country can, with all its resources fully employed, produce the following alternative combinations of agricultural produce and manufactured goods (in unspecified units):

Agricultural produce	+	*Manufactured goods*
100		0
80		25
60		40
40		45
20		48
0		50

These various combinations can be plotted on a graph (FIG. 1).

We call the resulting curve a 'production possibility curve'. It shows the various combinations of agricultural produce and manufactured goods open to our country with its limited resources. The alternative combinations lie on a curve which is concave to the origin. This is because factors of production are not equally suited to producing agricultural produce and manufactured goods. It can be seen from the table that as more resources are transferred to producing manufactured goods, an ever-smaller quantity of manufactured goods is received for each 20 units of agricultural produce given up. In short, both manufactured goods and agricultural produce are produced under conditions of diminishing returns.

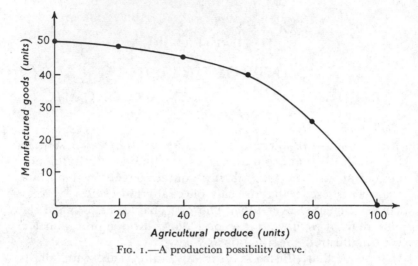

Fig. 1.—A production possibility curve.

Let us examine the economic problem with the aid of the production possibility curve. Scarcity means that economics is concerned with:

(1) *The allocation of resources.* Because resources can be used in alternative ways, it is necessary to choose between manufactured goods and agricultural produce. The particular combination chosen should be the one which yields maximum satisfaction.

(2) *The full employment of resources.* While it is impossible to produce a combination of agricultural produce and manufactured goods which lies to the right of the curve, any assortment on the origin side means that the country is not maximising its output because some resources are idle. A combination of goods on the production possibility curve can be obtained only if there is full employment.

(3) *The growth of resources.* Over time, the production possibility curve must be pushed further from the origin, so that a larger assortment of both agricultural produce and manufactured goods can be obtained.

Micro- and macro-economics

Until the 1930s, economics concentrated mainly on the first problem – the allocation of a given quantity of resources between different uses. The economy was divided into a number of comparatively small parts, and a study was made of how each small part functioned – the demand of consumers in a particular market, the behaviour of the firm, the amount of a commodity being offered for sale in a market at different periods of time, the price of a commodity in the market, and so on. Such a study is known as '*micro*-economics', after the Greek word *mikros*, meaning 'small'. Thus, if we ask ourselves what forces determine the price of potatoes, the rent of an acre of land in London, the dividend on a particular equity, or the wage of a Nottingham bus driver, we are dealing with micro-economic questions.

In contrast, problems of full employment and growth are concerned with the economy as a whole. They give rise to a series of 'general' questions: How do fluctuations in the overall level of employment occur? How can overall demand in the economy change? How do firms in general respond to such a change in demand? What brings about changes in the general level of prices? Such questions are the concern of *macro*-economics, from *makros*, meaning 'large'.

II. THE METHOD OF MACRO-ECONOMICS

Because micro- and macro-economics differ in the type of subject they study, their methods of analysis also differ. A simple analogy will explain why.

We can investigate the working of a motor-car by examining its different parts in isolation from one another. Thus we look at the wheels, then the gearbox, the engine, the carburettor, the electric fuel-pump, and so on. In this way we can find out how each part of the car works in detail.

Now while such an examination is very important and useful, it has its limitations. This is because we just spotlight one component and see how it operates, *ignoring the rest of the car*. It will not enable us to predict what will happen if, for instance, we replace a one-litre engine by a two-litre engine. We cannot assume that, 'other things being equal', the larger engine will make the car run faster. There will be certain 'feedbacks' on the other parts of the car which will affect its running efficiency as a whole. Thus the larger engine may be too powerful for the gearbox; the carburettor may be unable to supply sufficient fuel; the suspension may not be capable of withstanding higher speeds; and so on. It is not enough to examine how one part of the car works in isolation; we have also to consider how the various components are interrelated, and the relative importance of each.

The same applies when we study how an economic system works. The micro approach will only take us so far, for it merely examines how small parts of the economy operate in isolation. Changes which are simultaneously taking place in other parts of the economy and in the level of activity in general are ignored by inserting the phrase 'other things being equal'. So are the repercussions – the feedbacks – which may result from the single change being analysed.

Now this is legitimate enough if we are analysing a comparatively insignificant part of the economy, for example a small industry. Thus if we wish to discover the effects of an increase in the demand for pencils, we are unlikely to make serious errors by assuming 'other things equal', for such a change is unlikely to cause repercussions on the economy as a whole.

But what if we are examining the effects of a considerable increase in the demand for cars? The car industry is a significant part of the whole economy, and so we cannot merely analyse the effects in isolation, stopping at the point where the price of cars rises or the wages of car workers increase. To indicate the full economic results, we shall have to consider: (a) possible 'feedbacks' on the demand for cars; (b) repercussions on the economy as a whole – which in turn can produce further feedbacks. For one thing, we shall have to know the level of employment in the economy. If this is low, the increased demand for cars may lead to a considerable expansion of activity throughout the economy, leading to a further increase in the demand for cars. On the other hand, if the economy is already running at full employment, the increased demand may merely cause higher prices.

Simplifying by aggregating

Although, when dealing with changes in the economy as a whole, we cannot assume 'other things being equal', we still need to simplify if we are to build up a satisfactory model. This we do by 'aggregating' variables into a few broad groups.

The main aggregates we examine in macro-economics are national income, national output and national expenditure. But we can also deal with sub-aggregates and analyse the factors that determine these. Thus, in analysing national expenditure, we examine consumption spending, investment spending, government spending, export receipts, spending on imports, etc. Similarly, when looking at national income, we consider wages, rent, interest and profits. Aggregating in this way enables us to handle all the different variables so that we can bear in mind the effects which a change in any one of them will have on the other groups and upon the level of activity as a whole.

The economic system

What we have said so far must not be taken to imply that particular markets and the economy as a whole are mutually exclusive. To return to our analogy of the car, all the parts of a car are 'ticking over' when the car is running. Each bit of the carburettor and gearbox, and the way each is functioning, affect the overall running of the car. And how the car is driven will influence the performance of the individual parts – the engine, the suspension, the wheels, and so on. So it is with the economy. The millions of independent decisions made by individual firms and consumers affect the overall functioning of the economy. Each decision of an individual firm regarding alterations to its factory, plant or stocks affects the amount of investment spending which the economy as a whole is undertaking. And the firm's decisions will also be influenced by the price of its product – which in its turn depends upon the demands of individual purchasers.

We need, therefore, both micro- and marco-economics to understand how the whole economy functions. We need to know the results of an increased demand for one good, and the results of an increased demand for all goods simultaneously.

We need to know how the structure of relative prices is determined at any one time; but we also need to know what determines the level of prices as a whole.

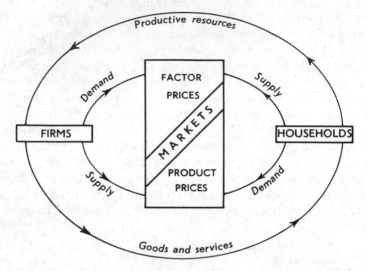

FIG. 2.—The allocation of products and resources through prices in the market.

Figure 2 illustrates the basic economic processes in an economy which, for simplicity, has no government and no relationships with other economies. The fundamental economic process is visualised as one in which the productive units (firms) create a flow of output for the consuming units (households). (The term 'production' is used in a wide sense to include any activity which contributes towards the satisfaction of a want.) In any economy there will be millions of economic units acting as 'firms' (from a rag-and-bone man to Imperial Chemical Industries Ltd.) and millions of economic units acting as consumers. We assume that the behaviour of firms is governed by the desire to maximise profits, and that the behaviour of households is governed by the desire to maximise satisfaction from limited incomes.

The flow of goods and services from firms to households is a flow of 'final' products, that is, a flow of finished goods and services ready for sale to the consumer. It does not include intermediate products and raw materials, for these are utilised in final products. Thus a car is included in the flow, but the steel and other materials which went into the car are not counted as well (*see* p. 27).

In order to produce the flow of final output, firms must hire factors of production and purchase raw materials. We regard the flow of productive resources as going from households to firms. The diagram therefore shows two *real* flows: (1) goods and services; (2) productive resources.

Micro-economics is concerned with the centre of the diagram – an examination of a particular market and of the connection between one market and another, e.g. pencils and pens. But it does not analyse the relationship of anyone market to the system as a whole. This is covered by macro-economics, which examines the two outer flows of goods and services and of factors of productions.

III. SOME PRELIMINARY NOTES ON TERMS AND THE NATURE OF THE ANALYSIS

The meaning of 'full employment'

Broadly speaking, unemployment arises for two main reasons: (1) the immobility of labour; (2) a lack of total spending on goods and services. Casual, seasonal, frictional and structural unemployment are all basically caused by some form of immobility; general unemployment results from deficiency in overall spending.

It is the latter type of unemployment which we are chiefly interested in. In this book, therefore, full employment means that there is sufficient spending power to activate all factors able and willing to work.

Regarding this definition, certain points should be noted:

(1) Even when there is full employment in the above sense, there will always be some unemployed workers in the first category, probably about 2 per cent of the working population.

(2) 'Factors able and willing to work' tends to be elastic. A high level of demand itself leads to overtime working and attracts more workers, particularly married women, into the labour force.

(3) The actual level of full employment aimed at depends upon the importance which the government attaches to other objectives of economic policy, e.g. price stability, the balance of payments, growth.

It follows, therefore, that there is no unique definition of full employment. We can either, like the 1944 White Paper, speak in general terms of 'a high and stable level of employment', or we can adopt a pragmatic approach, regarding full employment as the figure which the government deems politically acceptable.

The difference between stocks and flows

Macro-economics, as we have seen, is concerned with aggregates. All the aggregates we have mentioned so far have been *flows*, that is, they have a *time dimension*. Thus national income is the total sum of incomes generated in an economy *over a period of time*. In this respect it is like the speedometer of a car which shows so many miles *per hour*.

Flows may be contrasted with *stocks*, which represent the quantities of things in existence *at a particular moment of time*. The number of houses in the U.K. on 1 January 1971, for example, is part of the total stock of capital in the U.K. on that date. It is similar to the petrol gauge which shows the stock of petrol in the car at any moment of time.

In macro-economics, we have frequently to distinguish flow concepts from stock concepts, and to examine the relationships between them. The basic relationship between stocks and flows can be illustrated by the diagram of a water tank (Fig. 3).

Suppose both taps are closed and the tank contains a stock of

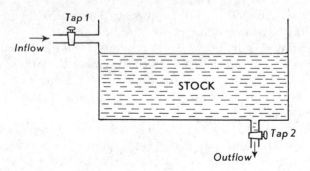

FIG. 3.—Stock and flow relationships.

water, e.g. 10 gallons. If the outlet, tap 2, is opened, water will flow out of the tank say at the rate of 2 gallons per minute. This will affect the stock left in the tank: at the end of one minute, 8 gallons will be left; at the end of three minutes, 4 gallons. Suppose now that tap 1 is opened, allowing water to flow in at the rate of 1·5 gallons per minute. The net outflow is therefore reduced to 0·5 gallons per minute.

A parallel example in economics is that of the stock of capital. Unless the rate of gross investment (new capital goods produced and additions to stocks of goods held) at least equals the rate of deterioration, the capital stock will decrease.

It is particularly important to distinguish between stock and flow concepts when dealing with money, liquidity, etc. It is essential, for example, to realise that the stock of money in existence at a particular moment of time is very different from money income, which is a flow of wealth over a period of time.

Intentions and realisations

Students of micro-economics will already be familiar with the difference between the *intended behaviour* of an economic unit and the *actual behaviour** carried out by that unit. For example, a demand schedule for apples shows the quantities of apples which consumers will be prepared to buy in a given period of time at certain hypothetical prices. But only one price can rule in the market at any one time; consequently, the intended purchases which some consumers were going to make at prices lower than the actual market price will be frustrated. Only what was sold at the ruling market price will be actual purchases.

This distinction is of great importance in macro-economic analysis. For example, we shall soon meet the proposition that an individual's saving depends primarily on his income. If a person expects an income of £1,000 a year and he usually saves 0·1 of his income, he will expect to save £100 in the coming year: intended savings are £100. But if he is unexpectedly unemployed for part of the year, so that his income is reduced to £800, he will only be able to save £80: this is his actual saving.

* The intended behaviour of an economic unit is referred to in some textbooks as his *ex ante* behaviour, while his observed behaviour is termed *ex post*.

The use of mathematics

Modern macro-economics makes considerable use of mathematical techniques. We recognise that this can make the subject
difficult for some students. On the other hand, we feel that an
'introductory' text should not duck the problem, but contain
an introduction to the application of mathematics in the field of
macro-economics. We promise the reader, however, that the
mathematics included goes no further than solving simple
equations, the notion of a 'function', and the concept of a 'rate
of change'. The following notes should set the reader's mind at
rest.

If we have two equations and two unknowns, we can obtain
the value of the two unknowns. Thus, from the equations
$10x - y = 20$ and $x + y = 24$, we obtain the values $x = 4$, $y = 20$.
Similarly, if there are three equations, we can solve for three
unknowns. This approach can be applied to many macro-
economic problems. Suppose that full employment requires a
national income of Y, and that national income is related to
consumption and investment spending; then, provided we have
three equations defining this relationship, we can determine the
amount of both consumption and investment spending which
will produce Y. Provided we can obtain *sufficiently accurate*
equations, such predictions will be of considerable help to the
government in formulating a full employment policy.

The relationships we have referred to above need not be
expressed precisely in equations. Instead we can refer to one
thing as simply being *dependent* upon another. For example,
we may not know that the circumference of a circle is exactly
equal to $2\pi r$, but we may believe that it is dependent upon its
radius. Later investigation may determine the precise relationship. Another way of stating that one thing is dependent upon
another is to say that it is a 'function' of the other. Our hypothesis that the circumference of a circle is a function of its
radius can be written: circumference $= f$ (radius). The same
idea can be transferred to macro-economics. For example,
consumption spending $= f$ (income). Once again, as with the
equations, if we have as many independent functions as we have
variables, there is the *possibility* of obtaining the value of each
variable. It is what is known as a 'closed system'.

Finally, we often wish to know the rate at which one variable is changing relative to another variable. This rate may be constant; for example, the circumference of a circle bears a fixed relationship to its radius. We thus have $C = 2\pi r$, the graph of which would be a straight line. In many cases, however, the rate of change is not constant. Thus the proportion of income spent can vary according to the level of income. This means that the graph of consumption with respect to income will be curved, and its rate of change at any one point will be equal to the slope of the tangent at that point. Usually we do not need to know the rate of change *at a point*; the rate of change between two distinct points is sufficient. For example, $\Delta C / \Delta Y$ measures the change in consumption (ΔC) due to a change in income (ΔY) expressed as a fraction of ΔY.

The importance of macro-economic theory for government policy

Few economies nowadays are *laissez-faire*; on the whole, we are accustomed to 'mixed economies', in which the government plays an important part. Not only does the government interfere in the normal processes of the market economy (for example, by subsidising farmers or controlling rents); it is itself a consuming and producing unit. Moreover, besides purchasing goods and services for consumption purposes (e.g. desks and books for schools, food and boots for the Forces), it controls directly about 40 per cent of all investment in the U.K. (e.g. in coal, gas, electricity and local authority building). Above all, the government is responsible for the overall level of activity. Not only must it maintain a high and stable level of employment, but it is also expected to promote economic growth without too high a rate of inflation, and to ensure stability of the balance of payments.

These ends require essentially macro-economic policies (although the government may supplement them by micro-economic measures). Macro-economic theory, therefore, lies behind all the government's attempts to 'steer' the economy. In this book, we first outline the theory and then proceed to show how it can be applied.

SUGGESTED READING

* G. Ackley, *Macroeconomic Theory* (Macmillan, New York, 1961) ch. 1.
F. S. Brooman, *Macroeconomics*, 4th ed. (Allen & Unwin, 1970) ch. 1.
S. G. B. Henry, *Elementary Mathematical Economics* (Routledge & Kegan Paul, 1969).
D. C. Rowan, *Output, Inflation and Growth* (Macmillan, 1968) chs. 1–2.

CHAPTER 2

THE MEASUREMENT OF THE NATIONAL INCOME

MACRO-ECONOMICS, as we have seen, is concerned with the full employment and growth of resources. It is necessary, therefore, to have some means by which we can measure the current level of production, for this will allow us to compare actual output with potential output, and present output with past output. The first will indicate to what extent resources are unemployed; the second, whether the rate of growth is acceptable. Such a measurement is usually referred to as the 'national income' – the toal money value of all the goods and services produced by a country during the year. How do we carry out this measurement?

I. THE CONCEPT OF NATIONAL INCOME

The nature of national income measurement

Before describing the principle upon which national income is measured, it is necessary to emphasise two important points:

(1) Income is, as we have seen, a *flow* concept. Hence we are trying to measure the flow of wealth produced in an economy in a year as opposed to the *stock* of wealth at a given moment of time.

(2) When we are *measuring* national income we are dealing with a *realised* flow; that is, we are measuring things which have already occurred. Since we are not attempting to *predict* anything, there is no reason why, in principle, we should not obtain reasonably reliable figures. In practice, statistics are incomplete, and national income figures are subject to a certain margin of error.

And, as we shall see, they deliberately exclude some activities which, in principle, should be included.

The principle of national income calculation

We can obtain the value of national income by measuring (a) output, (b) income, or (c) expenditure. A simple example will make this clear. Let us imagine a closed community (such as a desert island) in which there are three people who specialise, and barter their products. A rears 20 pigs in the year; B makes 100 loaves; C brews 50 gallons of beer. In real terms, national output $= 20p + 100l + 50b$.

Now suppose the following exchanges occur. A sells 7 pigs to B in return for 35 loaves, and 8 pigs to C in return for 20 gallons of beer. Then A's income $= 5$ pigs retained $+ 35$ loaves $+ 20$ beer.

B has exchanged 35 loaves for 7 pigs, and he also sells 40 loaves to C for 20 gallons of beer. Hence B's income $= 7$ pigs $+ 25$ loaves retained $+ 20$ beer.

Finally, C, who retains 10 gallons of beer, has an income of $8p + 40l + 10b$ retained.

What is the total income? Adding the incomes of A, B and C, we obtain $20p + 100l + 50b$, which is the same as the national output of the island. Thus we obtain the relationship:

$$\text{Output} \equiv \text{Income}.$$

This is true by definition; it is an accounting identity, indicated by the sign $\equiv$.

It is clear that we can also total A's spending of his output. He sells 7 pigs to B and 8 pigs to C. He also retains 5 pigs, 'selling' these to himself. Similarly for B and C. Here again, by totalling expenditure, we have:

$$\text{Output} \equiv \text{Expenditure}.$$

To sum up, therefore, the complete identity is:

$$\text{Output} \equiv \text{Income} \equiv \text{Expenditure}.$$

The same identities hold if, instead of a barter economy, we have an 'exchange' economy, where money acts as the common denominator for the millions of different goods and services produced. In this case, we measure the economy's flow of output in a year by using the current market price of each product.

Our first task is to define exactly what to include in output, and what to exclude. Let us take a simple example.

Suppose the owners of a forestry plantation sell rough timber to a timber merchant for £500. The timber merchant cuts, planes, and treats the wood, and sells it to a furniture factory for £700. The furniture factory uses the timber to make chairs and tables to the value of £1,000. What is the value of the output of these three productive units?

The answer is found by concentrating on *final demand* – the final flow of output bought by consumers. In our example, this is the chairs and tables to the value of £1,000. Obviously, we would be *double-counting* if we also included the value of the rough timber and the value of the cut timber, for these values are incorporated in the final value of the chairs and tables. The rough and cut timber are both *intermediate* products, and are not sold to final demand.

To avoid double-counting, therefore, we can add up total output in either of two ways:

(1) include only *final* values, ignoring all intermediate transactions; or

(2) add up the *values added* by each stage of production

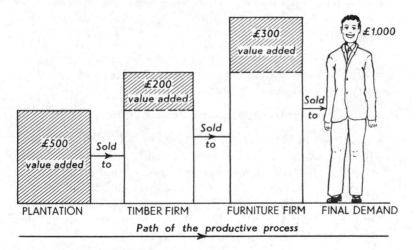

FIG. 4.—Value of final product equals sum of values added.

as the good approaches its final form. The two methods are shown in Fig. 4.

By method (1), the final value of output is that paid by the consumer, £1,000. By method (2), the final value is the sum of the 'values added' at each stage, £(500 + 200 + 300) = £1,000.

What we are really doing is to label an area of the economy as 'productive', and to define as national output *everything which leaves that area*. Activities and transactions which occur *within* this area are, by definition, intermediate transactions, and are therefore excluded. The basic idea is represented in our outline of the economic system in Fig. 2 where we have a productive area (firms), and an area which receives the final output (households). Figure 5 shows that the intermediate transactions from *P*, the plantation, to *T*, the timber firm, to *F*, the furniture factory, all take place within the boundaries of firms, the productive area.

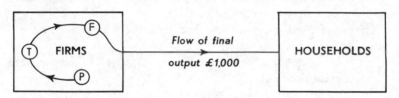

Fig. 5.—Intermediate transactions take place within the productive area 'firms'.

It should be noted that the final value of output (method (1)) is really the same as final expenditure. Thus again we have the identity:

$$\text{Total output} \equiv \text{Total expenditure.}$$

We can go further. Value can only be added by factors of production – labour, land, capital and entrepreneurship – which are paid money rewards, respectively wages, rent, interest and profit. Profit, however, is a residual, the difference between what is received by the firm for the product and what is paid out in wages, rent and interest. Thus, by definition, value added equals the sum of factor payments. That is:

$$\text{Total output} \equiv \text{Total income.}$$

Table 1, which gives the expenditure of firms on labour and on inputs of raw materials and intermediate products, also shows the above relationships. Income ≡ output because profits are defined as the excess of receipts of firms over their expenditure on labour, raw materials and intermediate products.

TABLE 1

RECEIPTS AND COSTS OF FIRMS PRODUCING FURNITURE ($£$)

(1) Firm	(2) Value added (3) − (4)	(3) Receipts	Costs		(6) Profits (3) − (4 + 5)	(7) Income (5) + (6)
			(4) bought in	(5) labour		
Plantation	500	500	0	450	50	500
Timber	200	700	500	175	25	200
Furniture	300	1,000	700	260	40	300
Total	1,000	2,200	1,200	885	115	1,000

II. THE MEASUREMENT OF NATIONAL INCOME

The identity of realised flows

The above identities hold for any economy provided our terms are correctly defined. Consider Fig. 6 which shows the *recorded* flows which have occurred over a period of time in an economy with no government activity or international transactions.

We assume that all output comes from firms. Corresponding to this flow of output is a flow of factor incomes paid to households. (This assumes that all profits are distributed as dividends.) The income received by households is either spent on consumption or saved. Savings can be regarded as flowing into the capital market ('banks'), from which firms borrow funds for investment – that is, spending on new capital goods or additions to stocks.

We must stress once again, however, that the flows in Fig. 6 are *realised* flows – actual flows which can be measured. (A similar diagram which uses *intended* flows is developed in Chapter 3.)

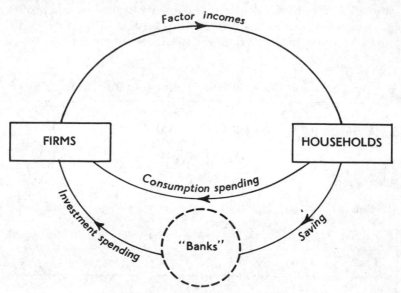

Fig 6.—Money flows in a simple economy.

Investment and saving will always be equal when we are referring to measured flows. The reason is that if actual consumption spending by households and intended investment spending by firms do not together equal the income firms have paid out, there will be a change in stocks – 'unintentional' investment or disinvestment, as the case may be.

Thus the diagram does *not* indicate that the economy is in equilibrium. This will only occur where *intended* investment equals *intended saving*; that is, there is no unintended investment (or disinvestment). We shall analyse this important point in more detail in Chapters 3 and 7.

Summary

The national income is the national output – the total value of all goods and services produced by the country during the year. We can regard it as:

(1) Income: the cost of the national output expressed as the earnings (wages, rent, interest, profit) of all the factors of production combining to produce it.
(2) Expenditure: the total amount spent on final goods and services for consumption and investment purposes during the year.
(3) Output: the total of the values added by the various firms and public authorities during the year.

Before we proceed to examine in more detail the actual process of measuring these three identities, it is convenient to consider some of the general difficulties which arise and how they are overcome.

General difficulties

Difficulties arise in calculating the national income through:

(1) Arbitrary definitions

(a) *Imputed payments.* In calculating the national income, only those goods and services which are paid for are normally included. Because calculations have to be made in money terms, the inclusion of other goods and services would involve 'imputing' a value to them. But where would we draw the line? If we give a value to certain jobs which a person does for himself – growing vegetables in the garden, cleaning the car, painting his house – then why not include shaving himself, cleaning his shoes, driving to work, etc.?

On the other hand, excluding what a person does for himself may distort national income figures. As the division of labour develops and the number of market exchanges consequently increases, a country's national income can rise although there may have been no addition to real output!

The rule has been made, however, that output is excluded if no corresponding money payment takes place. This has the advantage of convenience, but it does mean that very important categories, e.g. housewives' services, are excluded from national output.

The main exception to the rule is owner-occupied houses. Here the rateable value provides a basis for an imputed value. Including a notional rent keeps owner-occupied houses in line with property owned for letting (income shown as rents or profits of companies) and prevents the national income falling as more people become owner-occupiers!

A money value is also given for certain payments in kind which are recognised as a regular part of a person's earnings, e.g. goods produced and consumed by a farmer; food, etc., of the Forces and of domestic servants.

(b) *Government services*. Education and health services provided by the State are obviously no different from similar services for which some persons pay. Consequently, they are included in national income at cost. But how should we view the work of persons maintaining law and order and defence? A policeman, for instance, when helping children to cross the road is providing a consumer service. But at night his chief task may be guarding banks and factories against theft, and in doing so he is contributing an intermediate service, like that provided by Securicor. Thus the value of his output is already included in the value of the final product. Strictly, therefore, to avoid double-counting, this part should be excluded from output calculations. Nevertheless, because in practice it is impossible to differentiate between the two activities, all the policeman's services, and indeed all government services (including defence), are included at cost in the national output.

(2) *Inadequate information*

The sources from which data are obtained were not specifically designed to provide information for national income calculations. Thus not only do income-tax returns fail to cover the small-income groups, but they err on the side of understatement. Similarly, the Census of Production and the Census of Distribution are only taken at three- and ten-year intervals respectively. The result is that many figures are simply estimates based on samples.

Information, too, may be incomplete. Income-tax returns do not show income from State-owned property or profits of public corporations.

But it is *depreciation* which presents the major problem. As production takes place, so capital wears out. Resources have to be employed in maintaining it, and ultimately it must be replaced if the capital stock is to be kept intact.

In order to obtain a true picture of the *net* flow of wealth produced in a year, therefore, we must deduct from the total or gross value of output the amount by which capital deteriorates each year. This is called capital consumption or depreciation. Thus net output = gross output − depreciation.

For example, suppose in year 1 a machine is manufactured of value £1,000. This will be part of the flow of output (capital investment) in year 1. As the machine is used, it deteriorates. It is difficult, if not impossible, to estimate how much we should deduct each year for depreciation; in practice, a rule of thumb is adopted, often a *straight-line* depreciation. For example, if the machine's life is five years, we then write off £200 a year. Suppose the value of the final output produced by the machine each year is £500, then the net flow of output will equal £300.

Since the practical measurement of depreciation is so difficult and arbitrary, it is usual to deal in terms of gross output (that is, gross national product) rather than net output (that is, net national product).

(3) *The danger of double-counting*

Apart from the inclusion of *intermediate products* (p. 27) and transfer incomes (p. 36), double-counting can occur through stock appreciation. Stock appreciation refers to an increase in the value of stocks resulting purely from a rise in prices (or to a decrease in value due to falling prices), as opposed to a change in the physical volume of stocks. Suppose, for example, that stocks of copper in an economy consist of 10,000 metric tons valued at £5 million at the end of year 1. At the end of year 2, stocks are still 10,000 tons but because of a rise in the price of copper, they are valued at £6 million. Since there has been no addition to physical stocks, we must exclude £1 million of stock appreciation from the total value of 'increase in stocks'.

Similarly, we must ignore transactions in *financial* assets and in *second-hand goods*.

If a firm sells one million £1 shares at par to the public, those shares cannot be regarded as 'output'. The firm will usually employ the money it has raised to build a capital asset such as a new factory, and the factory is then part of output: it will be classed as capital investment, and regarded as a *final sale* of a capital good to the firm which has bought it. We should be double-counting if we included the £1 million sale of securities as well as the £1 million sale of the factory. And if the firm merely retains the cash as a liquid resource, no output has been produced at all. It is even clearer that, when old securities are resold on the Stock Exchange, this transaction must be excluded.

Second-hand goods are dealt with similarly. If a house is actually built in 1970, it counts as part of national output in 1970. But if houses already in existence change hands, no new output is produced: a second-hand asset is simply transferred from one owner to another.

It should be noted in passing that there are *some* productive activities associated with financial and second-hand asset transactions. Brokers, jobbers, estate agents, second-hand car salesmen, etc., are helping to satisfy final demand, and *the value of their services* (but *not* any capital gains made by the original owners of the assets) count as output.

(4) *Complications arising from relationships with other countries*

National income calculations must take into account the effects of international trade and international indebtedness.

(*a*) *Trade.* British people spend some of their income on foreign goods, while foreigners buy British goods. In calculating *national expenditure*, therefore, we have to deduct from domestic expenditure the value of goods and services imported (since they have not been produced by Britain) and add the value of goods and services exported (where income has been earned by factors in Britain).

(*b*) *Indebtedness.* If a father increases his son's pocket-money, he does not increase the family income: he merely redistributes it, the father having less and the son more. But if the boy's income is suddenly augmented by a wealthy aunt who makes him a regular allowance, then the family income is increased. Similarly with the nation: while internal transfer incomes do not increase national income, payments by foreigners do. These payments arise chiefly as interest and dividends from loans and and investments made abroad. They can be regarded as payments to factors owned by British people but situated abroad, e.g. factories of the Bowater Paper Corporation in Canada and the U.S.A. Similarly, interest and dividends have to be paid to foreigners who have invested in Britain. If, therefore, we wish to consider the value of *national* output as opposed to *domestic* output, we must include the net flow of property income from abroad. This may be positive or negative; and large or small relative to national income. In the case of the U.K., it is positive because of the capital investments made

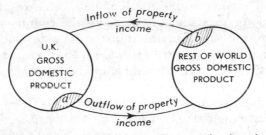

Fig. 7.—Gross domestic product and gross national product.

abroad during past years, but fairly small; in countries like Kuwait and Venezuela, there is a large net outflow. In Fig. 7 the left-hand circle represents the gross domestic product of the U.K. If we want gross national product, we must deduct *a* and add *b*.

III. CALCULATION OF THE UNITED KINGDOM'S NATIONAL INCOME

Calculations of the national income are now given in the National Income and Expenditure Blue Book, published each autumn. The figures are broken down in different ways, and all the sub-aggregates analysed later in this text are estimated and included.

Here, however, we shall confine our discussion to the overall national income figure and its calculation by the three different methods. The results are not identical, because information is not complete, but the proportionate error is small. In practice, the expenditure figure is taken as the datum, and the difference between this and the income and output figures is treated as a residual error.

In deciding whether an item should be included in the

calculations, the student should remember the basic principle: does it represent income earned by, expenditure on, or output of, goods and services produced by the factors of production of the United Kingdom during the year?

(1) *National income*

National income is the total money value of all incomes received by persons and enterprises in the country during the year in return for current contributions to output. Such incomes may be in the form of wages, salaries, rent, or profit.

In practice, income figures are obtained mostly from income-tax returns, but estimates are necessary for small incomes. Two important points should be noted:

(*a*) *Transfer incomes are excluded by the definition.* These are incomes which are received without any corresponding contribution to the output of goods and services, e.g. through unemployment insurance benefit, retirement pensions, students' grants, interest on the national debt, and gifts of money (such as an allowance to a relative) from one person to another. These are merely *transfers* of income within the nation – from the income of productive workers to the recipient. The income is counted once when the productive worker earns it: we should be double-counting if we counted it again when it was transferred. Although such incomes are normally included in income-tax returns, they must be deducted for national income purposes.

(*b*) *Income earned by government activities must be included.* Personal incomes and the profits of companies can be obtained from tax returns. But the government also receives income from its property and may make a profit from such sources as the public corporations. Similarly, local authorities may show a surplus on their trading activities – water supply, passenger transport, harbours and docks, etc. Income earned in these various ways by public authorities must be added in.

(2) *National expenditure*

National expenditure is the total amount spent on consumer goods and services and on net additions to capital goods and stocks in the course of the year.

Figures for calculating national expenditure are obtained

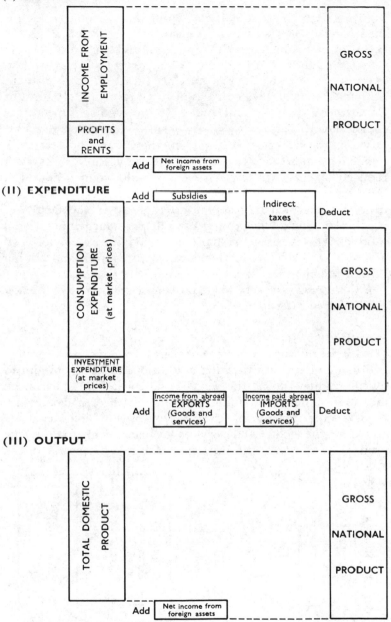

FIG. 8.—Summary of gross national product calculations.

from a variety of sources. The Census of Distribution records the value of shop sales; the Census of Production gives the value of investment goods produced and the additions to stocks. But these censuses are not taken every year, and so estimates have to be made which are based on data from the National Food Survey, statistics of retail sales collected by the Department of Trade and Industry, the Family Expenditure Survey, etc.

Many market prices collected in these ways, however, are swollen by indirect taxes (e.g. on petrol, cigarettes, cars) or reduced by subsidies (e.g. on welfare milk, council housing). What we are trying to measure is the value of the national expenditure which corresponds to the cost of the factors of production (including profits) used in producing the national product. This is known as 'national expenditure at factor cost' and is obtained by deducting indirect taxes from and adding subsidies to national expenditure at market prices.

Adjustments necessary for exports and imports have already been referred to (*see* p. 34).

(3) *National output*

National output is the total of consumer goods and services and investment goods (including additions to stocks) produced by the country during the year. As shown in Fig. 4, it can be measured either by totalling the value of the *final* goods and services produced during the year or by totalling the value added to the goods and services by each firm, that is, the production of every enterprise from the sole proprietor to the

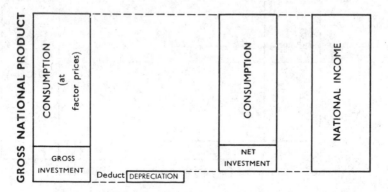

FIG. 9.—Gross national product and national income.

TABLE 2
CALCULATION OF THE NATIONAL INCOME OF THE U.K., 1969

A. INCOME

	£m.
Income from employment	27,174
Income from self-employment	3,009
Profits of private companies and public enterprises	6,523
Rent	2,601
Total domestic income	39,307
less Stock appreciation	-815
Residual error	-342
Net property income from abroad	451
GROSS NATIONAL PRODUCT	38,601
less capital consumption	-3,694
NATIONAL INCOME	34,907

B. EXPENDITURE

Consumers' expenditure	28,618
Public authorities' current expenditure on goods and services	8,118
Gross capital formation (investment) at home, including increase in stocks	8,221
Total domestic expenditure at market prices	44,957
plus Exports and income from abroad	11,986
less Imports and income paid abroad	-11,318
less taxes in expenditure	-7,868
plus subsidies	844
GROSS NATIONAL PRODUCT AT FACTOR COST	38,601
less capital consumption	-3,694
NATIONAL INCOME	34,907

C. OUTPUT

	£m.
Agriculture, forestry, and fishing	1,197
Mining and quarrying	678
Manufacturing	13,346
Construction	2,559
Gas, electricity, and water	1,364

Transport	2,348
Communication	930
Distributive trades	4,193
Insurance, banking, and finance (including real estate)	1,250
Public administration and defence	2,391
Public health and educational services	1,987
Other services	5,073
Ownership of dwellings	1,991
Total domestic output	39,307
less Stock appreciation	−815
Residual error	−342
Net property income from abroad	451
GROSS NATIONAL PRODUCT AT FACTOR COST	38,601
less capital consumption	−3,694
NATIONAL INCOME	34,907

government. Net property income from abroad has to be included, for this can be regarded as the net output of British capital (fixed or liquid) based abroad (Fig. 8).

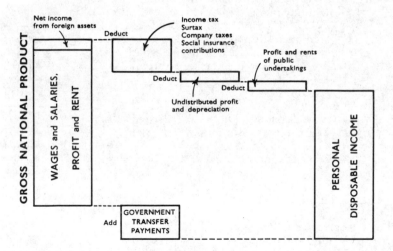

FIG. 10.—The relationship of gross national product and personal disposable income.

Personal disposable income

For some purposes, e.g. an indication of people's current living standards, a measurement of personal disposable income, that is, what people have to spend after various adjustments have taken place, is more significant. The necessary adjustments to gross national product to obtain personal disposable income are shown in Fig. 10.

SUGGESTED READING

W. I. Abraham, *National Income and Economic Accounting* (Prentice-Hall, 1969) ch. 2.

W. Beckerman, *An Introduction to National Income Analysis* (Weidenfeld & Nicolson, 1968) chs. 1–3.

F. S. Brooman, *Macroeconomics*, 4th ed. (Allen & Unwin, 1970) ch. 2.

Central Statistical Office, *National Income and Expenditure Blue Book* (H.M.S.O., London, yearly).

R. Stone, and G. Stone, *National Income and Expenditure*, 8th ed. (Bowes & Bowes, 1966).

CHAPTER 3

THE 'CLASSICAL' THEORY OF FULL EMPLOYMENT

In this chapter, we shall outline a theory of the economy which is essentially derived from the partial equilibrium approach of micro-economics. In doing so, we shall reveal the problems which this analysis cannot handle. Our version is a simplified summary of the ideas of pre-Keynesian economists; what we are really doing is setting up an Aunt Sally, which can be knocked down and replaced by a superior model. Like Keynes, we shall refer to these earlier economists as the 'classical economists'.

The classical economists tended to assume that, if prices (and particularly wage-rates) were flexible, there was a built-in tendency for the economy to function at full employment. Discussion of the level at which the economy as a whole was operating was therefore largely overlooked. Instead, their attention was concentrated upon explaining how this given total of resources was allocated between competing firms and how the resulting output was allocated between households. As Professor D. Dillard puts it, classical economics is simply 'a study of the alternative uses of a given quantity of employed resources' (*The Economics of John Maynard Keynes*).

Their acceptance of full employment was based on two main assumptions:

(1) An aggregate deficiency of demand can never occur because 'supply creates its own demand' (Say's Law).
(2) The operation of the free-market price system automatically removes any unemployment which may occur.

Let us examine these assumptions in more detail.

Say's Law
The French economist, J. B. Say (1767–1832), held that any

42

general unemployment brought about by the overproduction of goods was unlikely to persist for long because 'supply creates its own demand'. His argument can be followed by looking at the money flows in an economy based on the following simplifying assumptions:

(1) All income received by households is immediately spent on consumption goods and services – there is no saving and no hoarding of money.

(2) There is no government activity if any nature, e.g. no government expenditure, taxation, subsidies, price control.

(3) It is a 'closed' economy, that is, it has no relationships with other economies.

Figure 11 shows the money flows which correspond to the real flows of productive resources and goods and services in Fig. 2. Firms pay for factor services in money – wages, rent, interest and profit – which is the income of households. House-

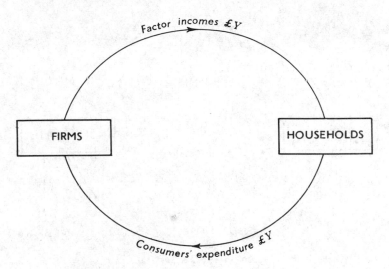

FIG. 11.—Money flows in a 'Say's Law' economy.

holds spend their income on goods and services. There is thus a circular flow of money from firms to households and from households to firms.

Suppose firms incur factor payments (including normal

profit) of £Y in the production of goods and services. If, as we have assumed, there is no saving, all these factor incomes will be spent. Spending equals £Y. Thus, what the firms have spent on factor services is exactly covered by what they receive when they sell the goods and services.

Say's Law with saving

The assumption that all income is spent is, of course, unrealistic. Does it make any difference to the pre-Keynesian analysis if we relax assumption (1) and now assume that some income is *not* spent? The answer depends on what happens to the unspent income. Suppose we have an economy which has been in equilibrium with income = £1,000, and consumers' expenditure = £1,000. Households now decide to save 0·1 of their income. Immediately, firms' receipts fall to £900. Profits will fall, and firms will tend to react by reducing output and there reducing employment and income.

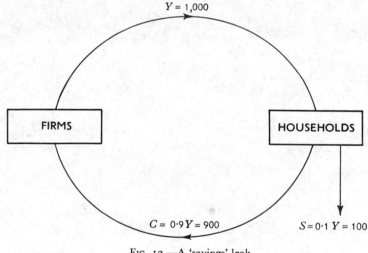

FIG. 12.—A 'savings' leak.

But what if some entrepreneurs borrow the unspent income in order to purchase capital goods? So far, we have tacitly assumed that firms only produce consumption goods and services; the analysis becomes more realistic if we assume that they also invest in factories, machinery and stocks of raw materials and unsold goods. Provided that firms wish to borrow and spend exactly the same amount that households wish to save, the circular flow of income can be maintained, and so can employment. This is shown in Fig. 13, where savings are channelled to firms through intermediary institutions, 'banks'.

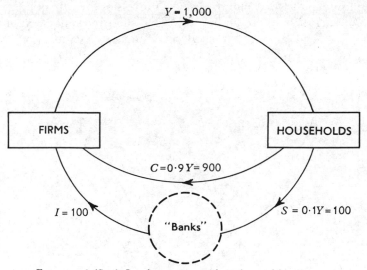

FIG. 13.—A 'Say's Law' economy with saving and investment.

Is there any reason why investment should equal intended saving? Since investors and savers are different people, why should their intentions match? The answer lies in the classical assumptions about the role of the rate of interest in the economy and the flexibility of prices.

The function of the rate of interest

Because investment is profitable, entrepreneurs are prepared to pay a price, a rate of interest, to secure investible funds. With a diminishing marginal productivity of capital, the number of profitable investment projects increases as the rate of interest falls. There is thus a downward-sloping demand curve

(D) for funds (Fig. 14). Loanable funds are supplied by saving – refraining from present consumption. The greater the reward, the more will people save. There is thus an upward-sloping supply curve (S) for funds. As with other markets, the two flows, investment and saving, are brought into line by price – the rate of interest. Thus in Fig. 14, given the curves D and S, the market rate of interest will be i. If the willingness of households to save increases at all levels of the rate of interest (S_1), the rate of interest falls (i_1). As a result, investment expands (to OM_1), where once again saving equals investment.

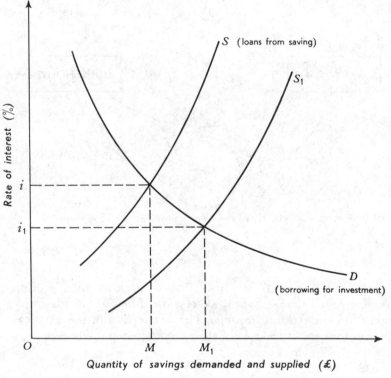

FIG. 14.—The classical interest-rate mechanism.

Therefore, according to the classical economists, the function of the rate of interest is to bring saving and investment into equality. Flexibility of the rate of interest maintains the circular flow of income. Moreover, since the classical economists assumed that there are virtually unlimited opportunities for investment, the economy can always function at full employment irrespective of what people desire to save, that is, no matter how far the saving curve shifts to the right.

The role of flexible prices and wage-rates

What will happen if general unemployment temporarily develops? The classical economists' answer is that, provided all prices (including wage-rates) are flexible, market forces will cause wage-rates to fall until the unemployed labour has been re-employed.

In Figure 15, with OM labourers seeking work, a wage-rate of OW_1 and a marginal revenue product curve MRP, MM_1 labourers- are unemployed. Unemployment, however, leads

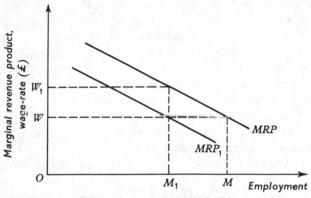

FIG. 15.—Full employment through flexible wage-rates.

to competition for jobs in the market, and this will force the wage-rate down to OW. Here there will be full employment (OM) because firms engage labour according to its marginal revenue productivity and the wage-rate.

Similarly with the other factors of production. And so, because equilibrium obtains in individual markets (particularly the labour and capital markets), there is *general* equilibrium with full employment.

Conclusion

The classical economists had no separate theory for dealing with the level of activity. Market forces ensured that it always tended towards a full employment equilibrium because:

(1) There could never be a deficiency of demand;

(2) competition and flexible prices in product and factor markets quickly and automatically removed any dis-equilibrium.

If unemployment persisted in the real world, it must be due to market imperfections – stickiness of wage-rates (through trade union power), monopoly price-fixing, restriction of credit by banks, or loss of confidence which reduced the willingness of firms to invest.

Their explanation of equilibrium does not merely apply to the restricted case of a closed economy without a government. If the economy is 'open', spending on imports will represent another leak from the circular flow. But this can be rectified if foreigners spend an equal amount on the economy's exports. Again it is the function of the price system to bring imports and exports into equality. Should the economy have a balance of payments deficit (and it maintains a fixed exchange rate, as with the nineteenth-century gold standard), the level of income will fall, causing unemployment and lower wage-rates. Exports thus become cheaper, with the result that demand for them expands. Other countries which have developed surpluses will experience a decreased demand for their own exports as their wage-rates rise. This process continues until the balance of payments disequilibrium has been removed.

Similarly, taxation by the government represents yet another leak. But since it was a fundamental canon of financial policy to balance the budget, government expenditure would auto-matically equal tax revenue and thus pump back into the circular flow what had been withdrawn.

One final point in passing. What determined the general level of prices? This, the classical economists held, was depend-ent purely on the supply of money – the Quantity Theory of Money.

If the quantity of money was increased, prices would rise; if it was reduced, prices would fall (*see* Chapter 15).

SUGGESTED READING

* G. Ackley, *Macroeconomic Theory* (Macmillan, New York, 1961) chs. 5–8.

D. Dillard, *The Economics of John Maynard Keynes* (Crosby Lockwood, 1958), ch. 2.

M. G. Mueller (ed.), *Readings in Macroeconomics*, No. 1 by E. E. Hagen (Holt, Rinehart & Winston, 1969).

J. Pen, *Modern Economics* (Penguin, 1965) ch.2.

M. Stewart, *Keynes and After* (Penguin, 1967) chs. 2 3.

CHAPTER 4

THE KEYNESIAN APPROACH

WITH the advantage of hindsight it is easy to criticise the classical economists. But it must be remembered that they were writing in the nineteenth century before the experience of the inter-war depression. Nor were their assumptions so unrealistic as they appear to us today. For one thing, when the typical business unit was the sole proprietor (farmer, shopkeeper or manufacturer), there was a greater identity between saving and investment. For another, there was then greater flexibility of wage-rates, for trade unions were far less strong than they are today.

But in the twentieth century, the full employment hypothesis of the classical economists did not stand up to testing by experience. Cyclical fluctuations increased in length and intensity. More important, unemployment persisted even in years of comparative prosperity. In 1937, for example, unemployment in the U.K. was almost 1½ million although this was a peak year of activity.

I. KEYNES'S CRITICISMS

Hence in his *General Theory of Employment, Interest and Money* (1936), Keynes attacked the old views. His main point was that an economy could be in equilibrium at *any* level of employment: *full employment was merely a special case.* This was because both the assumptions of the classical model were unrealistic:

    (1) Savings and investment were not brought into equilibrium by the rate of interest, and hence a level of aggregate demand sufficient to generate full employment could not be assumed.

(2) Market prices were not flexible downwards – particularly
    wage-rates.

Let us deal with each in turn.

The savings-investment relationship

Keynes criticised the classical economists for accepting Say's
Law and thereby failing to examine the level of aggregate
demand. Supply does not necessarily create its own demand;
saving decisions and investment decisions are taken by two
sets of persons – households on the one hand, firms on the other
– and for different reasons. Nor are they brought into line by
the rate of interest. In particular, Keynes emphasised that the
rate of interest has only a marginal effect on the desire to save,
so that an upward-sloping supply curve of savings with respect
to the rate of interest cannot be assumed. The chief determinant
of people's desire to save is their income (*see* p. 65).

Aggregate demand, therefore, cannot be taken for granted;
investment, for instance, may be less than intended saving. If
so, it is not the rate of interest that brings them into equilibrium,
but a fall in the level of income (that is, output and employment).
Moreover, the level of income which produces this equilibrium
may be *less than that required for full employment*. Thus, in the
Keynesian model, the distinction between investment and
intended saving is crucial. Keynes believed that investment plays
the dominant part and that it is liable to fluctuate because the
expectations of entrepreneurs are volatile.

The flexibility of prices, particularly wage-rates

In the classical model, wage-rates, like other prices, were
assumed to be flexible, downwards as well as upwards. Unemployment, therefore, was eliminated, as explained on p. 47,
by a fall in money wage-rates. Keynes disagreed with this on
both practical and theoretical grounds.

In practice, any reduction in wage-rates was difficult to
achieve because of the opposition of organised labour. If
unemployment was widespread throughout the economy, the
whole spectrum of wage-rates would have to be lowered, and
while this might have been conceivable in the early nineteenth
century, it was quite impracticable in the twentieth with the
growth in the power of trade unions. Keynes argued that wor-

kers would fight much harder to prevent a reduction of money wage-rates (at constant prices) than they would to prevent a reduction of real wages brought about by a rise in the general price level (at constant money wage-rates). Workers, he implied, suffered from a 'money illusion'. Consequently, the aim of reducing *real* wage-rates in order to stimulate employment could be achieved more easily by allowing prices to rise than by attempting to force down money wage-rates. But in order to raise the price level, aggregate demand would have to be increased.

His objection on theoretical grounds was more fundamental. Even if money wage-rates could be forced down, it would not provide the solution to unemployment in the way the classical economists predicted. Their mistake was to apply partial equilibrium analysis to a macro-economic problem. When we are studying employment in the whole of the economy (as opposed to a particular industry or occupation), we cannot make the simplifying assumption 'other things being equal'. But the classical economists' interpretation of Fig. 15 does this implicitly; it assumes that cutting wages generally will not affect the position of the marginal revenue productivity curve.

If wages in general are cut, however, people will have less purchasing power. Reducing money wages means, therefore, less spending. As a result, prices fall, the receipts of firms fall, and there is thus no increase in employment. In terms of Fig. 15, the fall in product prices pushes the MRP curve leftwards. If it falls to MRP_1, employment will not increase as a result of a wage-rate cut from OW_1 to OW.

II. THE KEYNESIAN ARGUMENT

Aggregate demand and aggregate supply

Having rejected the classical economists' assumptions, Keynes was faced with two main problems:

(1) What is the mechanism by which equilibrium is achieved in the economy?

(2) In what circumstances, if any, will equilibrium be at that full employment level?

He outlined his argument as follows.

Entrepreneurs produce in order to make a profit. In perfect

competition they will employ factors up to the point where they maximise profits. But since production is in advance of sales, entrepreneurs' decisions are largely based on expectations. Thus their actions can be viewed as a function of (*a*) the receipts which they *expect to obtain* from the sale of any given output, and (*b*) the actual costs of producing that output.

If any given level of output is to be maintained, actual receipts must cover costs, including normal profit.

The receipts which entrepreneurs as a whole *expect to obtain* can be termed *aggregate demand*; their costs, the receipts that they *must obtain* if they are not to reduce output, can be termed *aggregate supply*. It is possible to take different levels of output and to show aggregate demand and aggregate supply at each level. As with demand and supply in particular markets, we then obtain aggregate demand and aggregate supply schedules. The corresponding curves are shown in Fig. 16.

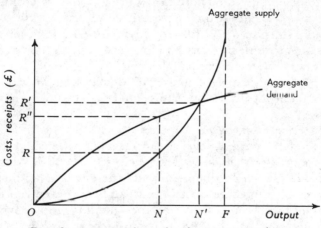

FIG. 16.—Aggregate demand and aggregate supply.

The aggregate demand curve shows the receipts which entrepreneurs expect to receive from any given level of output. Thus at an output *ON*, expected receipts are *OR"*; at *ON'*, they are *OR'*. For the economy as a whole, aggregate demand is, of course, the same as the expected expenditure of the community. This expenditure is likely to increase as output, and therefore incomes, increase. Thus the aggregate demand curve

rises with output. However, as we shall see (Chapter 5), when
income increases, people tend to spend a smaller proportion
of income. In other words, as output increases, aggregate
demand rises but at a diminishing rate – and thus the slope of
the curve diminishes.

The aggregate supply curve shows the costs of producing any
given level of output, that is, the minimum receipts which must
be obtained if that level of output is to be maintained. Thus an
output ON costs £OR, while ON' costs £OR'. The shape of the
curve depends upon technical conditions of production – the
extent to which a given addition to employment increases costs.
For our purposes we can accept these technical conditions as
given, and here simply mention three important points: (1)
because marginal costs are bound to be positive, the aggregate
supply curve will slope upwards as employment increases;
(2) if, as output increases, less efficient factors of production
have to be employed or bottlenecks are encountered, diminishing returns set in and the aggregate supply curve will start to
rise more steeply; (3) at full employment, OF, any increase in
costs cannot result in extra employment, and so the aggregate
supply curve becomes vertical.

In Figure 16, expected aggregate demand equals aggregate
supply at output ON'. How is this equality to be interpreted?

(1) *The equilibrium output*

Suppose the current level of output is ON. Expected receipts
OR'' are greater than necessary receipts (costs) OR. Abnormal
profits are expected to be made, and there will be an incentive
for entrepreneurs to increase output, and for new entrepreneurs
to begin production. On the other hand, if the economy is
operating at output OF, aggregate costs exceed expected
aggregate receipts, and entrepreneurs will tend to reduce
output. The output ON' will therefore be the equilibrium output, for only at ON' are there no forces in operation to cause
entrepreneurs to increase or decrease output: expected receipts
and necessary receipts are equal.

(2) *Expected receipts and actual receipts*

The argument in the preceding paragraph, however,
tacitly assumes that entrepreneurs *anticipate demand correctly*;

that is, that actual aggregate demand turns out to fulfil their
expectations. This may not be so. Figure 17 shows the expected
aggregate demand curve D as before, and also the curve of
actual aggregate demand, D'. In our example, expectations
are not fulfilled. This will cause entrepreneurs to revise their
expectations; they will not be so optimistic as they were before.

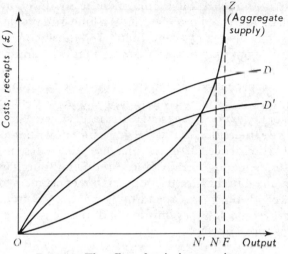

FIG. 17.—The effect of revised expectations.

Since their expectations are based primarily on the current
level of demand, we can assume that they will continually
revise their expected receipts until they equal actual receipts,
that is, the expected aggregate demand curve will be lowered
from D to D'. Output will therefore fall from ON to ON', and
employment will decrease accordingly.

Full employment and aggregate demand

Figures 16 and 17 show that equilibrium can be attained at
any level of output. (In practice, there is a lower level below
which output will not fall corresponding to minimum consumption demand.) This equilibrium is determined simply by
the relationship between the aggregate demand curve and the
aggregate supply curve. If, when there is less than full employ-

ment, the relative position of the curves is altered, the equilibrium level of output will be altered. To expand employment, we need either to lower the aggregate supply curve or to raise the aggregate demand curve.

Let us first consider the aggregate supply curve. This can be lowered by increasing productivity. But, when men are unemployed, there is little point in emphasising increased productivity (although at full employment it is a different matter). In any case, increased productivity is a long-run phenomenon.

Policy for unemployment, therefore, must concentrate on raising the aggregate demand curve; that is, it must persuade entrepreneurs to become more optimistic. But, as we showed above, entrepreneurs' expectations are based primarily on the current situation; actual aggregate demand determines the position of the expected aggregate demand curve.

It follows, therefore, that if the government wishes to improve business confidence it must increase the current level of aggregate demand. For instance, reducing purchase tax or relaxing hire-purchase restrictions enable consumers to increase their expenditure. As expenditure rises, entrepreneurs will tend to become less pessimistic, and the aggregate demand curve will move upwards.

Summary

(1) The equilibrium level of output depends upon the relationship between the aggregate demand curve and the aggregate supply curve.

(2) There is no automatic tendency for the equilibrium output to coincide with the full employment output. If full employment is desired, its attainment must be a conscious act of policy.

(3) In seeking to attain full employment, the government will have to operate upon aggregate demand rather than upon aggregate supply.

(4) The position of the aggregate demand curve is determined by entrepreneurs' expectations which depend mainly on the level of current aggregate demand. Thus a full employment policy consists largely of maintaining an adequate level of aggregate demand.

We must therefore study in more detail what determines the

level of demand at different levels of employment. It will be the main theme of this book.

We shall begin by considering a very simple economy with no government or external economic relations. This basic model is shown in Fig. 13. Our next two chapters will answer the questions: What determines the level of consumption spending? What determines the level of investment spending? We shall then proceed to explain changes in the equilibrium level of income, gradually relaxing our assumptions to allow for government activity and foreign trade.

To simplify the argument, we shall assume throughout that employment varies in direct proportion to the level of output. In practice, this relationship does not hold exactly:

(1) As full employment is approached, less and less efficient labour is hired and 'bottlenecks' develop, so that a given increase in labour produces decreasing increments of output.

(2) An increase in output may occur through better use of capital equipment rather than increased employment of labour.

SUGGESTED READING

D. Dillard, *The Economics of John Maynard Keynes* (Crosby Lock-wood, 1958) ch. 9.

M. Fleming, *Introduction to Economic Analysis* (Allen & Unwin, 1969) ch. 24.

A. H. Hansen, *A Guide to Keynes* (McGraw-Hill, 1953) ch. 1.

*J. M. Keynes, *The General Theory of Employment, Interest and Money* (Macmillan, 1936) chs. 1–5, 14, 19.

M. Stewart, *Keynes and After* (Penguin, 1967) ch. 1.

A. W. Stonier and D. C. Hague, *A Textbook of Economic Theory*, 3rd ed (Longmans, 1964) chs. 17, 19.

CHAPTER 5

CONSUMPTION EXPENDITURE
I. INTRODUCTION

Definition of consumption and saving

THE reader is asked to refer back to Fig. 11. This depicts a very simple economy in which all income received by households is spent on the consumer goods and services produced by firms. Whatever the level of income (Y), consumption expenditure (C) is equal to income. Mathematically, the functional relationship between consumption expenditure and income is: $C = Y$.

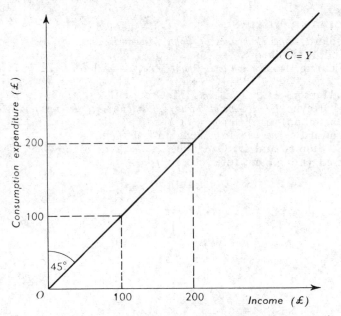

FIG. 18.—The consumption function when all income is consumed.

This relationship can be shown graphically by a straight line passing through the origin at 45° to the axes (Fig. 18).

By the geometry of an isosceles triangle, if income equals 100, consumption equals 100; if income =200, consumption = 200, etc. (In general, the 45° line can be regarded as the locus of all points for which *expenditure* (on the vertical axis) equals *income* (on the horizontal axis). This graphical device will be used considerably in later chapters.)

We proceeded to consider a more realistic case in which only a part of income is consumed (Fig. 12). Unspent income is defined as saving (S); that is, $S = Y - C$.

It is important to note that this definition of saving does not correspond with the idea in ordinary speech, where people are only said to 'save' when they put money in banks, buy shares, etc. The reason is that we are concentrating on *expenditure* because of the effect this has on maintaining the circular flow of income. If a person spends part of his income, that *spending* becomes someone's else's *income*, and contributes to the circular flow of income. If income is *not* spent, it is withdrawn from the circular flow. Whether the person hoards the unspent income in a stocking, or puts it into a deposit account, is of secondary importance. The crucial point is that money income has been withdrawn from the circular flow; it is a 'leak'.

Consumption and disposable income

So far we have related consumption to income in a rather loose way. In practice, spending by households on consumer goods and services takes place out of *disposable income* (Y_d). As we saw on p. 40, disposable income (Y_d) equals:

National income   − Direct taxes
                     − National Insurance
                       contributions
                     − Undistributed profits
                     + Transfers.

Our early examination of consumption will be with reference to disposable income. Later we shall relate it to national income (Y).

The importance of consumption

Spending on consumer goods is important in a number of

TABLE 3

CONSUMPTION EXPENDITURE IN THE U.K., 1959–69

Year	(1) Personal disposable income (£m.)	(2) Total domestic expenditure at market prices (£m.)	(3) Consumption expenditure (£m.)	(4) = (3) ÷ (1) Average propensity to consume	(5) = (3) ÷ (2) Consumption as a fraction of total domestic expenditure
1959	16,931	24,017	16,106	0·95	0·67
1960	18,150	25,872	16,909	0·93	0·65
1961	19,536	27,341	17,810	0·91	0·65
1962	20,486	28,626	18,906	0·92	0·66
1963	21,740	30,444	20,125	0·93	0·66
1964	23,290	33,513	21,493	0·92	0·64
1965	24,891	35,627	22,865	0·93	0·64
1966	26,401	37,768	24,236	0·92	0·64
1967	27,445	40,049	25,339	0·92	0·63
1968	29,140	42,769	27,065	0·93	0·63
1969	30,929	44,957	28,618	0·93	0·64

respects. First, it accounts for about two-thirds of total expenditure (Table 3). Second, even small relative changes in consumer spending can have significant effects on the level of employment. If, for instance, consumption falls by only 3 per cent, the immediate effect on total expenditure will be 2 per cent. Given a multiplier of only 2 (*see* Chapter 7) the ultimate result will be a drop in national income by 4 per cent. For Britian, provided there is no excess aggregate demand, such a fall will produce some extra 700,000 persons unemployed. Third, whereas investment spending can be nil, consumption provides a floor below which national expenditure cannot fall: people must spend in order to live.

The long- and short-run consumption functions

Table 3 indicates that, comparing one year with another, there is a fairly definite relationship between consumption and disposable income. In the U.K., consumption is approximately 92 per cent of disposable income (or 75 per cent of national income). Thus the long-run (secular) consumption function can

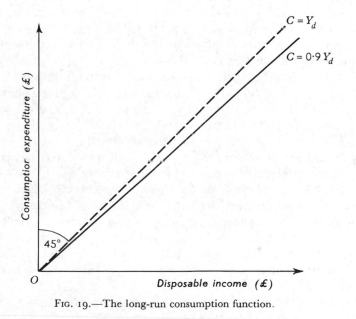

FIG. 19.—The long-run consumption function.

be shown as a straight line through the origin whose slope is approximately 0·9 (Fig. 19).

We must emphasise, however, that this graph relates long-run consumption to long-run *disposable* income, whereas we are primarily interested in explaining *short-run* fluctuations in *national* income. To do this, we must consider the factors which influence consumption in the short period. We shall first consider an individual's expenditure and from this derive the aggregate household consumption function out of disposable income. For analytical purposes, this will then be transposed into consumption out of national income.

The method of analysing the short-run consumption function

We can approach the analysis of spending out of income in the same way as, in micro-economics, we deal with demand. We say that the quantity of a good demanded depends upon (a) the price of the good; (b) the conditions of demand – tastes, income, the distribution of income, etc.

In practice, however, the conditions of demand are fairly stable; it is price which is likely to have the greatest effect on quantity demanded in the short period. We therefore treat the conditions of demand as 'parameters', concentrating our analysis on the relationship of quantity demanded to price.

Similarly with consumption; the level of consumption spending is dependent upon:

(a) the level of income, factors in (b) remaining unchanged;
(b) the overall factors which determine how much of income is consumed irrespective of the particular level of income.

Since, as we shall see, short-term variations in the level of consumption spending are chiefly the result of changes in the level of income, it is realistic to relate consumption to the level of income and treat the other factors as parameters. Then, as with demand, the parameters fix the position of the consumption curve within the axes, whereas the relationship of consumption to income fixes its shape. In Figure 20, for example, a movement of the curve from C to C_1 represents a fall in consumption due to a change in a parameter (say through increased thriftiness). Consumption at a level of income OY falls, therefore, from OE to OE_1.

For convenience, we deal first with the overall factors (the parameters), assuming for the time being that consumption increases with an increase in income.

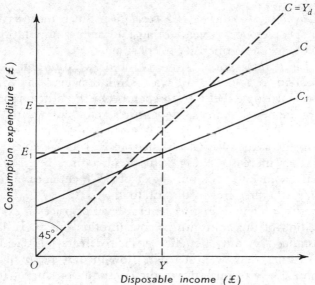

FIG. 20.—A shift of the short-run consumption function.

II. FACTORS OTHER THAN INCOME AFFECTING CONSUMPTION

Factors which affect how much people spend out of disposable income are, in Keynes's terms, both objective and subjective.

(1) *Objective factors*

(*a*) *The distribution of wealth and income in the community.* Since poorer people are inclined to spend more of their income than rich people (especially the very rich), a more equal distribution of wealth and income may increase consumption.

(*b*). *The size and nature of assets held.* Liquid assets can be spent at any time. But the possession of even illiquid assets (e.g. a house) may increase consumption, either because they can be used as security for credit or simply because owners feel that, in an emergency, they can realise them. Consumption can therefore be regarded as dependent, not only on income, but on total resources (income + borrowing power). On the other hand, liabilities, such as mortage repayments, reduce consumption.

(c) *The age-distribution of the population.* Since most saving is done by people over 35 years of age, an ageing population will tend to reduce the propensity to consume.

(d) *The level of prices.* Inflation and deflation may affect consumption in a variety of ways. Inflation leads to windfall gains which people feel free to spend. On the other hand, the value of money balances, debentures, etc., falls with rising prices. People holding these feel worse off and, in order to maintain the value of such balances in real terms, spend less – that is, they increase saving. This is sometimes referred to as the 'real balance' or 'Pigou' effect of price changes, after the economist who first drew attention to it.

Secondly, a change in the general level of prices may affect the position of the community consumption curve. Inflation, for instance, would benefit profit-receivers (high-income people) rather than wage-earners (low-income people). Thus inflation is likely to push down the consumption curve (in real terms), deflation to raise it, particularly at the higher income levels. It must be remembered, too, that inflation pushes people into higher income brackets and so more is taken by progressive taxation in real terms.

(e) *Expectations.* People may anticipate changes in the future prices of goods (e.g. the budget) or shortages (e.g. through import control), and thus bring forward or delay spending.

(f) *'Private sector' influences on spending.* Advertising and the introduction of important new consumer goods (e.g. colour television, central heating) affect the level of consumption. While some of these goods will be bought out of 'saving', many will be obtained through hire-purchase. Periodic relaxations of credit restrictions allow people to go on 'spending sprees', thereby bunching such expenditure. If we assume that such goods have a life of five years, a 'hire-purchase cycle' may result.

Saving, too, depends partly on the outlets provided by institutions such as insurance companies, building societies, banks and unit trusts. But the influence of the rate of interest is doubtful. Most saving is contractual, e.g. mortgage repayments.

(g) *Government policy.* This affects *spending* (e.g. through variations of hire-purchase terms and restrictions on bank lending) and *saving* (e.g. through propaganda, taxation, social security, and the facilities provided by the National Savings Bank, Premium Bonds, etc.).

There is evidence of a time-lag before consumption actually responds to the above changes, probably because it takes time to readjust spending habits (*see* p. 70).

(2) *Subjective factors*

'Subjective' factors which, according to Keynes, affect people's spending include: foresight in providing for the future (e.g. to cover unemployment, illness, old age, children's education), pride and ostentation, the desire for independence or power, avarice, habit, the desire to bequeath an estate or fortune to children, and the wish to provide for an enlarged future income from yields on capital investments.

The above analysis suggests that, apart from abnormal changes in an objective factor (e.g. through war or strikes) or from sharp changes in government policy (e.g. through hire-purchase controls), shifts in consumption out of a given level of *disposable* income are not likely to be of great importance in the short run. (*Note:* Shifts in consumption out of *national* income are likely to occur through changes in taxation and credit policy.)

Our next task, therefore, is to see what happens to consumption as incomes varies, the other factors affecting consumption (the parameters) remaining unchanged. That is, we look at the *shape* of the consumption curve, assuming its position remains unchanged.

III. CONSUMPTION AS A FUNCTION OF INCOME

The shape of the consumption function of a single consumer or household

The most reasonable assumption to make is that, at low levels of income, the household will not be able to save out of its income. In fact, it will probably dissave, either by drawing on past savings, by selling or mortgaging assets, or by borrowing. Thus, in Fig. 21, if income actually sinks to zero in the short run, consumption will still remain at a positive level, *OA*. An equivalent amount of dissaving *OB* must occur in order to finance it.

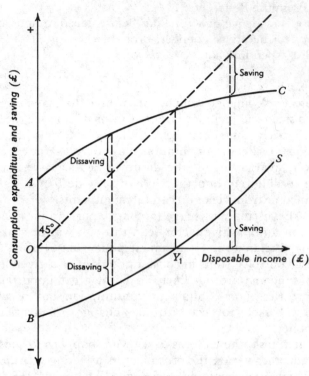

FIG. 21.—Consumption and saving out of disposable income.

Thus saving takes place only when an individual has attained what he considers to be a satisfactory standard of living; until that position is reached, he will probably raise his living standards by borrowing or by spending out of past savings.

The marginal propensities to consume and save

If income increases, we should expect that, after a certain income level, the amount consumed out of any given addition to income will progressively diminish. Correspondingly, the amount saved will progressively increase. The effect on the shape of the consumption curve is shown in Fig. 21.

These relationships between a change in income, ΔY, and a change in consumption, ΔC, and a change in saving, ΔS, are usually expressed by the concepts of marginal propensity to consume, c, and the marginal propensity to save, s. Let us take a simple numerical example.

Suppose an individual's annual income, consumption and saving are as follows:

Income ($\pounds$)	1,000	1,500	2,000	2,500
Consumption ($\pounds$)	900	1,300	1,600	1,850
Saving ($\pounds$)	100	200	400	650

As income rises by $\pounds500$ (ΔY), the corresponding increments of consumption (ΔC) are $\pounds400$, $\pounds300$ and $\pounds250$. We define the marginal propensity to consume, c, as $\Delta C/\Delta Y$. Thus, in the above example, as income rises, the marginal propensity to consume falls from 0·8 to 0·6 to 0·5.

The corresponding increments of saving (ΔS) are $\pounds100$, $\pounds200$ and $\pounds250$. We define the marginal propensity to save, s, as $\Delta S/\Delta Y$. Thus, as income increases, the marginal propensity to save rises from 0·2 to 0·4 to 0·5.

Note that, since any increment of income, ΔY, must be divided between the increment of consumption, ΔC, and the increment of saving, ΔS, we have:

$$\Delta C + \Delta S = \Delta Y$$

$$\frac{\Delta C}{\Delta Y} + \frac{\Delta S}{\Delta Y} = 1$$

$$c + s = 1.$$

Thus, in our example, when income rises from $\pounds1,000$ to $\pounds1,500$, $c = 0·8$ and $s = 0·2$.

We can now express the conclusions reached earlier in a more precise form. As income increases, the marginal propensity to consume will tend to fall and the marginal propensity to save will tend to rise. This is shown in Fig. 22, where ΔY_1, ΔY_2, ΔY_3, etc., represent equal increments of income, and ΔC_1, ΔC_2, ΔC_3, etc., corresponding increments of consumption. Since the increments of consumption get progressively smaller, the consumption function is represented by a curve which grows progressively flatter. Evidence confirms this sort of shape.

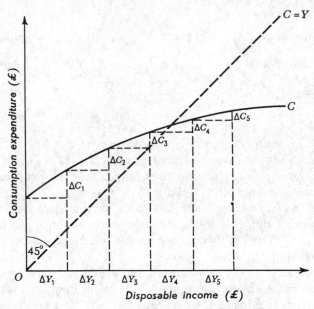

FIG. 22.—The diminishing propensity to consume.

Graphically, we can measure the marginal propensity to consume at a particular income (that is, where the change in income is infinitely small) by the slope of the tangent at that particular point. Thus, in Fig. 23, the marginal propensity to consume at A equals AB/BD, the slope of the tangent at A.

The *marginal* propensity to consume must not be confused with the *average* propensity to consume. If, at any given income Y, consumption is C, the average propensity to consume is C/Y.

Similarly, the average propensity to save is S/Y. In Figure 23, the average propensity to consume at Y equals AY/OY, that is, the gradient of the line OA.

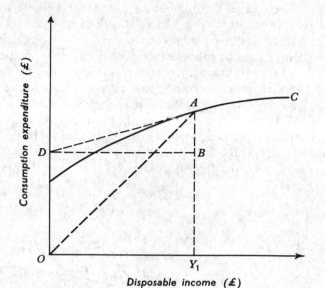

Fig. 23.—The average and marginal propensities to consume at a particular income.

Refinements of the simple consumption function

The Keynesian consumption function outlined above is based on three main assumptions:

(1) Consumption is a function of current income, that is,

$$C_t = f(Y_t).$$

(2) The consumption function is reversible with respect to income; if income falls, people will lower their consumption along exactly the same path as they increased it when income was rising.

(3) Consumers' spending patterns are determined autonomously; they do not depend on the expenditure of other consumers.

All three assumptions are challenged by Professor J. S. Duesenberry in his *Income, Savings and the Theory of Consumer Behaviour* (Harvard, 1952).

Let us start with (2). When its income rises to a new level which is regarded as 'permanent', a household will eventually adjust its consumption to a higher standard of living. This is shown by the secular consumption curve C_L (Fig. 24). If, for instance, the long-run propensity to consume of the household is 0·7, it will consume \$4,900 out of a disposable income of \$7,000, and \$6,300 if income rises to \$9,000. Suppose now that income reverts to \$7,000. Duesenberry argues that the household will not cut consumption back to \$4,900. Instead it will attempt to maintain, as far as it can, the standard of living to which it has become accustomed.

We can show this diagrammatically (Fig. 24). Suppose a

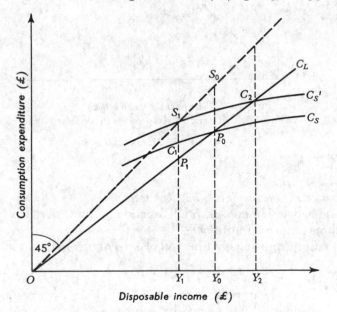

FIG. 24.—Short-run and long-run responses of consumption to changes in the level of income.

person has Y_0 income, and consumption $P_0 Y_0$. Now income drops to Y_1. Instead of cutting consumption to $P_1 Y_1$, the consumer moves backwards along the C_s curve to $C_1 Y_1$ trying to maintain his standard of living by cutting back on what his saving would otherwise have been, S_1P_1, had he started with an income of Y_1. If his income rises again to Y_0, he will first try to regain his previous saving level, S_0P_0, by cutting back on the extra consumption he could have enjoyed. If his income continues to increase to Y_2, he will eventually move up the C_L curve to consume C_2, having a new short-run consumption function, C_s.

This explanation suggests that we can reconcile the short-run function and the long-run function (which shows consumption to be fairly steady at 92 per cent of disposable income) by picturing the latter as being made up of a series of short-run curves (Fig. 25).

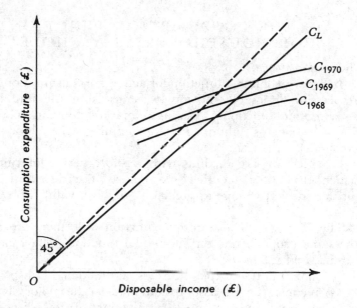

FIG. 25.—The relationship between the short- and long-run consumption functions.

Duesenberry's argument means that assumption (1) must also be amended. Consumption is not simply a function of current income; it is also a function of the highest level of income previously attained. To quote Duesenberry: 'The peak year's consumption sets the standard from which cuts are made (provided the peak did not represent a mere spurt in income). The higher the peak consumption the more difficult will it be to reduce consumption to any given level.'

Finally, with regard to assumption (3), Duesenberry referred to figures showing that Negroes in their own neighbourhoods tend to save about three times as much as whites in their districts at corresponding income levels, He argues, therefore, that household consumption is not merely a function of the autonomous tastes of that household (if these could be identified), but of the tastes of other consumers in the same and higher income brackets. People attempt to 'keep up with the Joneses', an attitude which is fostered by intensive advertising campaigns.

IV. THE CONSUMPTION FUNCTION FOR HOUSEHOLDS AS A WHOLE

Aggregate consumption

In order to obtain a function for aggregate consumption with respect to disposable income, we must sum the individual consumption functions (just as a market demand schedule for a good is obtained by summing the individual demands).

Provided we are dealing with a short period of time in which the 'other factors', particularly the distribution of income, do not change appreciably, this is a valid theoretical idea.

The aggregate consumption function will therefore have the same properties as the individual function. These can be summarised as follows:

(1) Consumption expenditure is a function of disposable income. (On the assumptions made at the end of Chapter 3, *real* consumption is a function of *real* disposable income.)

(2) The marginal propensity to consume is positive, but less than 1.

(3) The marginal propensity to consume diminishes as income rises.

(4) Factors other than income affect the *position* of the consumption function.

V. CONSUMPTION AS A FUNCTION OF NATIONAL INCOME

So far we have related consumption to disposable income (Y_d) since this is what household spending comes from. But to analyse national income (Y), it is essential to show consumption as a function of national income. This necessitates certain adjustments in both the position and shape of the consumption function on account of:

(1) *Government taxation*

When we allow for government activities, it is necessary to consider the kind of taxes imposed, their yield and other effects. An increase in direct taxation will reduce disposable income at all levels of income. As a result the absolute level of consumption will fall at all levels of income. In Fig. 26(*a*) the curve moves from $C_{(Y_d)}$ to $C_{(Y_d)}$.

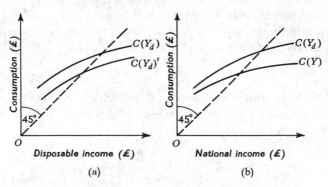

FIG. 26.—The effects of taxation on consumption.

More than that, with progressive taxation, as income increases a greater proportion of it goes in taxes, leaving a smaller proportion as disposable income. Whereas consumption out of disposable income will be curve $C(Y_d)$ in Fig. 26 (*b*), consumption out of national income after an increase in direct taxation will be shown by the curve $C(Y)$.

(2) *Retained profits*

Retained profits are likely to increase at a greater rate than increases in income. Not only will entrepreneurs be optimistic regarding investment possibilities but there will be induced investment to meet the increase in demand. Thus, as the proportion of business saving increases as income increases, a smaller proportion of profits will be distributed. Again this will tend to lower the consumption curve relative to income as income increases.

(3) *Any change in the distribution of income as income increases*

Does more of the extra income go to profit-receivers or to wage-earners? In the former case the propensity to consume will tend to fall at higher incomes; in the latter, it will rise.

APPENDIX
THE MATHEMATICAL EXPRESSION OF DIFFERENT CONSUMPTION FUNCTIONS

(*a*) On the assumption that consumption is a function of income, we can write $C = f(Y)$.

Alternatively, assuming that consumption is a function of disposable income Y_d, we can write

$$C = f(Y_d).$$

(*b*) A consumption function in which consumption is a constant proportion of income at all levels of income can be written:

$$C = cY \text{ (Fig. 19)}.$$

This is the form of the long-run function discussed earlier, where it was suggested that, in the U.K., the value of $c = 0.9$. (The average propensity to consume in this case also equals c.)

The corresponding savings function is:

$S = sY$, where s is the marginal propensity to save

$$\therefore S = (1 - c) Y.$$

The slope of the savings function is thus (1 – the slope of the consumption function). It should be noted that the maximum slope of either function is unity; if $c = 1$, $s = 0$, and vice versa. This maximum slope is $45°$. In practice, this simple idea may not hold; in the short run, consumption may exceed income as people decide to spend out of liquid resources.

(*c*) A simple linear function which allows for autonomous consumption (Fig. 27) can be written $C = a + cY$, where c is the marginal propensity to consume (the gradient) and a is autonomous consumption taking place even when income is zero (the intercept on the C-axis).

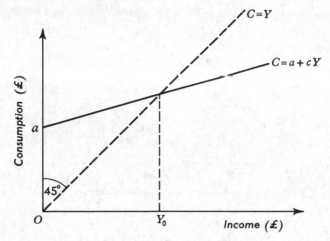

Fig. 27.   A linear consumption function with autonomous consumption.

The 'break-even point' is at the income Y_0, where all income is consumed.

The corresponding saving function is:

$$S = -a + (1 - c)Y.$$

(*d*) Figure 28 illustrates the sort of consumption function obtained if the function is of the form:

$$C = a.Y^n,$$

where a is a constant and n is positive but less than one. The function passes through the origin, since when $Y = 0$, $Y^n = 0$.

This function can easily be modified to yield one in which there is a positive level of consumption even at zero income:

$$C = k + a.Y^n.$$

(*e*) We can allow for a time-lag in adjusting consumption to a new level of income. Where consumption in the current period t is a function both of current income and of income in the previous period, $t - 1$, a simple linear function would be:

$$C_t = a + b.Y_t + d.Y_{t-1},$$

where a, b and d are constants.

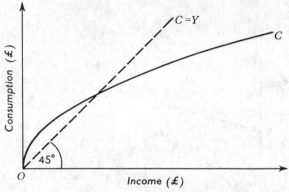

FIG. 28.—A consumption function of the form $C = a.Y^n$

SUGGESTED READING

*G. Ackley, *Macroeconomic Theory* (Macmillan, New York, 1961) chs. 10–12.

F. S. Brooman, *Macroeconomics*, 4th ed. (Allen & Unwin, 1970) ch. 5.

D. Dillard, *The Economics of John Maynard Keynes* (Crosby Lockwood, 1958) ch. 5.

J. S. Duesenberry, *Income, Saving and the Theory of Consumer Behaviour* (Oxford U.P., 1967).

A. H. Hansen, *A Guide to Keynes* (McGraw-Hill, 1953) chs 3–4.

*J. M. Keynes, *The General Theory of Employment, Interest and Money* (Macmillan, 1936) chs 8–10.

CHAPTER 6

INVESTMENT EXPENDITURE
I. INTRODUCTION

Definition of 'investment'

INVESTMENT is defined as a flow of expenditure over a given period of time on new fixed capital goods (e.g. houses, factories, machinery) or on additions to stocks (e.g. raw materials, unsold consumer goods).

Strictly speaking, this definition refers to *gross* investment. Some of the new goods will be required to maintain existing capital intact (depreciation). Others will represent a *net addition* to fixed capital goods or stocks (net investment). We have, therefore:

Gross investment = Net investment + Capital consumption
(depreciation).

This is shown in Fig. 9.

If gross investment is only sufficient to maintain capital stock intact, net investment will be zero. If gross investment is not even sufficient to cover capital consumption, net investment will be negative; that is, the actual stock of capital is declining. Such a decline sometimes occurs in war-time, when the economy is geared to the maximum output of consumer goods (including weapons), and the stock of houses, transport, factory equipment, etc., is allowed to deteriorate.

Normally an economy will aim at a positive net investment because 'roundabout' methods of production using capital equipment are more productive.

As we saw in Chapter 2, depreciation is difficult to measure, the rate at which firms write off their capital equipment being guided by considerations of prudence, future sales prospects, tax concessions, etc. Hence investment is often quoted as a *gross* annual flow.

Warning: In ordinary speech, the word 'investment' is used to denote the purchase of securities: a person who has bought shares in the British Leyland Corporation is said to have 'invested'. This is *not* the sense in which economists use the term.

Private and public investment

Investment takes place in both the private and public sectors. Of gross investment in 1967, 48 per cent was in the private sector and 52 per cent in the public.

The distinction is important. Since private investment is motivated solely by the profit motive, the level of private investment in a depression is likely to be low just when it is most desirable for it to be high. Furthermore, without direct controls, the government is limited to influencing the level of private investment through monetary and fiscal measures designed to persuade firms that expectations should be revised upwards (*see* Chapter 3). Over public investment, however, the government has direct control. Consequently, this can be used to make good any deficiency in the private sector, although the respective merits of the particular schemes will also be important.

The discussion which follows relates primarily to private investment. Although we shall conclude that its level is mainly determined by the size of current and expected income, we first of all discuss the influence of the rate of interest.

II. INVESTMENT AND THE RATE OF INTEREST

The difficulties of measuring the yield on investment spending

We obtain total private investment expenditure by aggregating the investment expenditures of each individual business. These individual expenditures are undertaken for profit; each entrepreneur expects the yield of the investment to exceed its cost.

However, difficulties arise in calculating the yield on a capital good. In the first place, because capital goods are usually durable, yields on them are spread over a number of years. Any calculation of yield, therefore, must allow for the fact that a given sum to be received in *x* years' time is worth less than the same sum received now. Secondly, since the future is always uncertain, all yields are really only estimates based on expectations.

Here we deal with the first problem – how yields spread over a number of different years can be made comparable. The second – expectations – will be dealt with later.

Methods of comparing the profitability of investment projects

We can calculate either (1) the present value of the capital asset, or (2) the discounted rate of return.

(1) *The present value of the capital asset*

An entrepreneur can decide whether to invest or not by comparing the 'present value' of the assest – obtained by discounting expected future yields at the market (or a 'target') rate of interest – with its actual supply price (the cost of its replacement as new). If the present value, V, is greater than the supply price, C, it will pay to invest.

Suppose I expect to receive £133·1 in three years' time and the rate of interest is 10 per cent per annum. What is the value now of this amount? The answer can be found by working backwards. At the end of the second year, its value will be $\frac{£133·1}{1·10} = £121$. At the end of the first, $\frac{£133·1}{(1·10)^2} = £110$. Hence, its present value is $\frac{£133·1}{(1·10)^3} = £100$.

In general, if P_n is the sum to be received in n years, and i is the rate of interest:

$$V = \frac{P_n}{(1+i)^n}.$$

Example: A machine which has a life of two years yields £121 each year. Its present cost is £200 and the current rate of interest is 10 per cent. Is it profitable to invest in the machine?

Answer: The present value (V) of the machine is:

$$V = \frac{121}{1·1} + \frac{121}{(1·1)^2}$$

$$= 110 + 100$$

$$= 210.$$

Since $V(\pounds 210) > C(\pounds 200)$, this investment is profitable.

In general, $V = \dfrac{A_1}{1+i} + \dfrac{A_2}{(1+i)^2} \cdots \dfrac{A_n}{(1+i)^n}$

and the investment is profitable if $V > C$.

(2) *The rate of return*

Alternatively we can calculate r, the rate of return over the supply price of the asset, and compare this rate with the current market (or 'target') rate of interest, i. We discount the gross yields (that is, they include depreciation) throughout the life of the asset so that the sum of these discounted yields just equals the supply price or replacement cost, C. The rate of discount, r, which has to be applied to these gross yields to reduce them to the supply price is the expected rate of return over cost.

Suppose, for instance, that the yield in the first year is A_1, in the second A_2, ... and in the nth, A_n. We then have:

$$C = \sum_0^n A \text{ discounted}$$

$$= \frac{A_1}{1+r} + \frac{A_2}{(1+r)^2} \cdots \frac{A_n}{(1+r)^n},$$

where r is the expected rate of return on this item of capital.
Thus, if we know C, A_1, A_2, ..., A_n, we can find a unique value for r which will satisfy the equation.

Example: A machine whose life is two years costs $\pounds 110$. In each year of its life its yield is $\pounds 72$. What is the expected rate of return on this particular machine?

Answer: From (3) above, we have:

$$110 = \frac{72}{1+r} + \frac{72}{(1+r)^2}$$

$$\therefore 110(1+r)^2 = 72(1+r) + 72$$

$$110 + 220r + 110r^2 = 72 + 72r + 72$$

$$110r^2 + 148r - 34 = 0,$$

which gives $r = 0 \cdot 2$

= 20 per cent (*Check*: Yields are 60 and 50 discounted.)

Thus, with these yields and supply price, investment in the asset is profitable if the cost of borrowing is less than 20 per cent. If the supply price was higher, then the expected rate of return on this particular asset would be lower. For example, if the supply price was £120, the rate at which the same yields would have to be discounted would be about 11 per cent, giving approximate discounted yields of £64 and £56.

The marginal efficiency of investment

What happens to the expected rate of return as the number of machines possessed by a firm increases?

In the short period, such machines represent a variable factor applied to fixed factors. The marginal physical product eventually falls, therefore, and so the expected rate of return on each additional unit falls. It is a simple case of a falling marginal revenue product curve (Fig. 30). But even in the long period we should get a similarly shaped curve. Increasing investment means that a larger proportion of a firm's assets are dependent on estimated future yields. The risk is therefore greater if things should go wrong, and so a larger allowance must be made for risk as investment increases. This will reduce expected future yields for each additional unit as investment expands. This 'marginal' expected rate of return is termed by Keynes the 'marginal efficiency of capital'. It is the expected rate of return over its supply price of *one more unit* of the capital asset, that is, of one unit of new investment. From now on we shall talk entirely in terms of the marginal efficiency of *investment* (MEI), signifying additions to capital.

When we consider the industry as a whole, we have further grounds for assuming that the marginal efficiency of investment will fall as investment expands. In the first place, additional output of the product will be likely to cause the price to fall. Prospective yields are therefore lower. Secondly, increased demand for factors of production as investment expands means that the prices of these factors rise. As a result, the supply price of the investment also rises. Smaller prospective yields and a higher supply price both have the effect of reducing the expected rate of profit. Thus the marginal efficiency of investment falls as output expands.

For the MEI of the economy as a whole, what we are really

interested in is the marginal efficiency of the *most worth-while* capital assets not yet produced.

The cost of investment

To determine the level of investment which will actually take place, we must look at the decisions of individual firms. A firm will expand its investment so long as the MEI (the expected rate of return from an additional machine) is greater than the cost of purchasing the machine. This cost is represented by the market rate of interest. (Even if the purchase is to be made out of internal finance, there is still an opportunity cost, e.g. what could be obtained on a government bond or the share of another company.) The level of investment will be

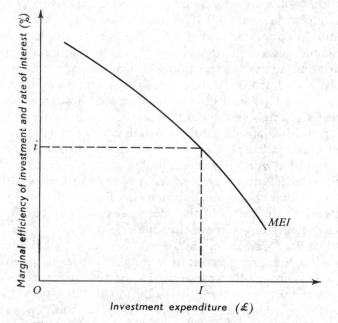

FIG. 29.—The investment demand curve with respect to the rate of interest.

determined by the intersection of the MEI curve and the rate of interest (Fig. 29). Thus with a rate of interest Oi, investment will be OI. A higher rate of interest will contract investment, a lower rate will expand it. Similarly for the economy as a whole. We can thus draw up a schedule showing the amount of investment which will take place at different rates of interest. This is the investment demand schedule, from which we can plot the demand curve for investment.

III. CRITICISMS OF THE INVESTMENT – INTEREST RELATIONSHIP

The Keynesian view

Keynes stressed the long-term rate of interest as the factor which, with his marginal efficiency of capital, determined the level of investment. Investment would be carried to the point where the MEI equalled the rate of interest.

But it had always been recognised that the rate of interest was ineffective towards the extreme ends of the trade cycle. In a depression, the existence of excess capacity prevents a fall in the rate of interest from stimulating investment; in a boom, expectations are so high, especially in inflationary conditions, that a rise in the rate of interest fails to choke off investment.

In recent years, and more especially since the Radcliffe Report (1959), economists have thrown doubt on whether the rate of interest is a major factor in determining investment at *any* stage of the trade cycle. There are three main criticisms of the Keynesian approach.

First, it suggests that the level of investment is responsive to changes in the rate of interest; that is, that the MEI curve is interest-elastic. As we shall see, there are good grounds for concluding that this is not the case.

Secondly, it is only useful to relate the level of investment to the rate of interest if the parameters remain relatively stable. We may once again draw a parallel with the construction of a demand curve in micro-economics. Here it is legitimate to emphasise the dependence of quantity demanded upon price. Not only is price the determinant most likely to vary in the short period, but demand is often price-elastic. Such a situation does not hold, however, with the MEI curve. Its position is determined mainly by expectations – and these are subject to frequent change.

Finally, the rate of interest does not always represent the real cost to firms of investment. We shall find that various institutional considerations affect the relationship.

Let us consider each of these criticisms in turn.

(1) *The shape of the MEI curve*

The reasons why entrepreneurs may not adjust their investment spending to changes in the rate of interest can be summarised as follows:

(a) *Investment projects usually have a short 'pay-off' period.* Because of uncertainty – chiefly through the possibility of a machine becoming obsolete – firms tend to invest only if the cost can be recovered within four to five years. Such short-term capital projects are much less susceptible to changes in the rate of interest than long-term projects. The reason is that the rise in the rate of interest affects longer-yielding assets more than the shorter-yielding ones because the higher rate has to be applied to yields for a longer time. Hence only those comparatively few projects where the yield extends far into the future (e.g. housing) have a tendency to be interest-elastic.

(b) *Investment decisions are the result of long-term planning.* Current investment is often part of a programme stretching far into the future. Any present reduction would throw the whole programme out of phase.

Even where investment is not part of a programme, it may take a long period to complete. When the rate of interest rises, firms do not drop the project but borrow short to finance it in the hope that the long-term rate will fall in the future.

(c) *Investment in stocks is influenced by considerations other than the rate of interest.* It is unlikely that investment in stocks, is elastic with respect to the rate of interest for the following reasons:

(i) Stocks are held for convenience, and this will decide the quantity held. Even if the rate of interest rises, stocks cannot be reduced below a certain minimum; conversely, there is little point in increasing them if the rate of interest falls. In fact, it is not the rate of interest but the level of output and sales which is the chief influence on the size of stocks held.

(ii) The rate of interest is only a small part of the cost of stock-holding. The main costs are fixed, e.g. warehousing, and will be incurred irrespective of short-term changes in the rate of interest.

(2) *The position of the MEI curve*

In the preceding section, we referred to the MEI as if there were a unique investment demand curve at any time. However, it would be more correct to picture the MEI as an *area*, as in Fig. 30, rather than as a single curve, as in Fig. 29. For reasons

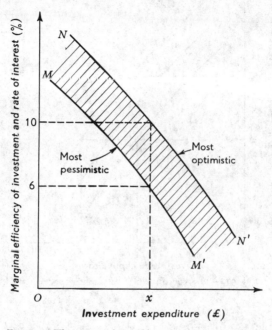

FIG. 30.—The uncertainty of investment expectations.

outlined below, firms are uncertain of the exact yield of any marginal unit of investment; they may estimate the yield of the *x*th unit as lying between, say, 6 per cent and 10 per cent. If the rate of interest rises from 6 per cent to 10 per cent, the investment in the *x*th unit will still take place. The lines MM^1 and NN^1 therefore constitute the area covered by uncertainty about the MEI.

Alternatively we can picture this area as arising because the MEI curve is volatile (Fig. 31). Its position fluctuates in the short run, although it is unlikely to shift to the right further than NN^1 or to the left further than MM^1. Thus a fall in the rate of interest from 10 per cent to 6 per cent will, given the curve NN^1, lead to a rise in investment from x_1 to x_2. But if, simultaneously, the MEI curve shifts to the left to MM^1,

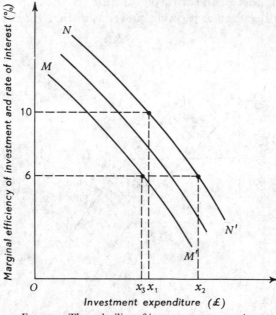

FIG. 31.—The volatility of investment expectations.

investment actually *falls* to x_3. To conclude, the MEI curve is often so volatile that the rate of interest is a *minor* influence upon investment decisions.

This area of uncertainty arises because of market imperfections and the fact that yields are based on expectations.

As regards the first, most large manufacturing firms face a downward-sloping demand curve, and each has to estimate what consumers will pay for its product at a given output. These estimates are subject to error, which can offset changes in the rate of interest.

As regards estimated yields, the entrepreneur has to look into the future to assess the likely demand for his product. He has to ask: Will competitors introduce a better product? Will new methods of production enable competitors to undersell him? Will a recession cause incomes to fall?

In making these estimates, he has little definite to go on (though information is gradually improving). An estimate of the earning power of an asset, say over five years, can only be very tentative, and the entrepreneur will have to allow a margin of error according to the confidence he has in the accuracy of his estimates. The most important factors which he may consider are:

(a) *Current demand for his goods.* Since the entrepreneur has little definite upon which to work, his expectations are likely to be influenced by his most recent experience. If current demand for his goods is buoyant, and has been so for some time, he will be optimistic, although he will take into account the extent to which existing capacity can deal with any increase in demand. But, if present demand is flagging, he will be reluctant to increase productive capacity.

(b) *Long-term considerations.* The further into the future an entrepreneur plans, the more uncertain are his estimates of 'yield' – the MEI area becomes larger. But there are specific factors he will bear in mind:

(i) *The future price level.* Generally speaking, inflation is likely to stimulate investment, for there is the possibility of windfall profits, which makes it cheaper to bring forward investment.

(ii) *The future rate of interest.* The possibility of a future fall (rise) in the rate of interest may induce an entrepreneur to postpone (bring forward) investment.

(iii) *Political stability.* An entrepreneur will weigh up the political situation, both internal and external. Can the government maintain a balance of payments equilibrium and avoid 'stop–go'? Will its fiscal measures penalise profits? What is its general attitude to private enterprise? Similarly, international developments may affect profitability, e.g. war, tariff barriers.

(iv) *The rate of technical progress.* The possibility of an invention which will render his machine obsolete or of new products or competitors will cause the entrepreneur to take a less optimistic view of the future. The

less he knows about his rivals' plans, the more uncertain will his estimates be.

(v) *Conditions in the labour market.* What changes can be
expected in the level of wages? Will the future be free
of strikes? Higher future wages will probably increase
the relative yield on capital and encourage the manufacturer to invest in labour-saving capital equipment.
Industrial strife, however, is likely to dissuade an
entrepreneur from incurring charges on capital which
might stand idle for long periods.

(vi) *The course of Stock Exchange prices.* In making his decisions
regarding the future, an entrepreneur can easily be
caught up in current moods of optimism or pessimism,
especially those prevailing on the Stock Exchange. Apart
from general sentiments, an entrepreneur will be unlikely to extend his factory, etc., if the Stock Exchange
values similar businesses unfavourably. In any case,
such a valuation makes it more difficult to raise capital.

Keynes emphasised, however, that such a valuation
may not reflect the long-term earning capacity of a
business, but simply the opinion of speculators seeking
to make a profit out of the short-term price movements
of the shares by estimating what other people are
likely to think they will do! Since moods on the Stock
Exchange are contagious and reinforced by self-
justified expectations, price swings are magnified, and
'the capital development of a country becomes a by-
product of the activities of a casino' (Keynes).

(3) *The rate of interest as a real cost*

Chiefly for institutional reasons the long-term rate of interest
does not always represent the real cost of investment.

(*a*) *High rates of corporation tax reduce the real cost.* Higher interest
charges can be claimed by companies as costs for tax purposes.
They are thus partly offset by lower tax charges, the Exchequer,
as it were, paying a part of the additional burden.

(*b*) The rate of interest on stocks held does not increase if
such stocks are financed by trade credit, for the rate charged on
this does not usually change with changes in the long-term rate.

(*c*) *Funds for investment may be allocated by 'rationing' rather than through the price system.* When entrepreneurs are very optimistic, only sharp increases in the rate of interest may deter investment. High rates have serious disadvantages (*see* p. 193), and the government therefore puts pressure on banks and other financial institutions not to raise their rates but to discriminate in favour of certain types of customer. Thus investment is regulated, not by the rate of interest, but by rationing – the ability to obtain funds by negotiation rather than by the price offered.

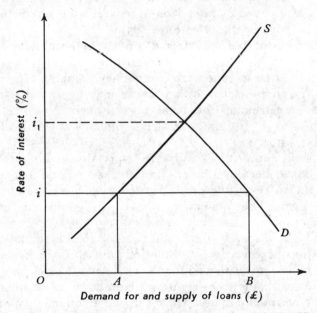

FIG. 32.—The results of keeping interest rates below the market equilibrium.

In Figure 32, the rate of interest is 'controlled' at Oi. Here demand exceeds supply by AB. Not until the rate of interest has risen to Oi_1 does it take over from 'rationing' in allocating investment finance. Thus the rate may move within fairly wide limits without affecting investment.

Conclusion

(1) Expectations are the largest single determinant of the level of investment, and these depend on a number of diverse factors.

(2) Generally, it is doubtful whether the rate of interest is an important determinant of the level of investment. We can, however, point to certain instances when investment may be responsive to changes in the rate of interest:

(a) a capital project may have yields which stretch far into the future;

(b) a small firm's investment decisions may be interest-elastic because:

(i) it may already be working to tight margins, and there is not the scope for increasing prices through market imperfections, etc.;

(ii) a shortage of internal funds may necessitate greater reliance on external borrowing;

(iii) there is less forward investment planning;

(iv) interest charges on stocks may represent a higher percentage of total cost in certain small firms, e.g. furniture, retailers, wholesalers (Radcliffe Report);

(c) local authority investment (especially in housing) may be cut because higher interest charges would involve a rate increase, and this is disliked for political reasons.

(3) Even allowing for (2) above, it is probable that the greatest impact of a change in the rate of interest on investment is through its psychological impact on expectations – as an indication of government intention and through the uncertainty of how it will affect a firm's customers.

(4) Because the rate of interest cannot be relied upon as a direct determinant of investment, its use as a monetary weapon must be for other reasons, chiefly (a) *external* – to attract funds from abroad and to restore international confidence; (b) *internal* – through its psychological effect on businessmen, usually as part of a 'package deal' of measures (*see* p. 196).

(5) Since the level of private investment is subject to such frequent change, aggregate demand can be stabilised only if the government succeeds in controlling private investment, or uses other 'compensatory' measures. That is, there must be some government 'regulation' to maintain aggregate demand at the full employment level without inflation.

IV. THE INVESTMENT DEMAND FUNCTION

Introduction

Of all factors which are likely to influence the level of investment, the one that is most likely to change in the short run is expectations. Since expectations are closely related to the current level of income, it is better to relate investment to income rather than to the rate of interest. First, however, we must distinguish three different types of investment.

Gross investment can be divided into:

(*a*) *Replacement investment*, which depends upon the rate at which capital equipment wears out or becomes obsolete. We can regard this as a function of the current rate of consumption. If the propensity to consume rises, output will be increased as soon as practicable, and since the capital stock cannot be adjusted in the short run, the existing capital will wear out more quickly.

(*b*) *Autonomous investment*, which is an increase in investment resulting from the invention of new goods (e.g. colour television), a change in the pattern of consumer demand, or a new way of producing a good (e.g. electricity from atomic power). This investment is determined independently of the level of income.

(*c*) *Induced investment*, which is a change in investment resulting from a change in consumption or income. As we shall see later, induced investment is linked not so much with absolute changes as with relative changes.

When we relate investment to the level of income, we are faced, as with the consumption function, with two problems:

(1) *The position of the investment curve*

Here we are asking how much will be spent on investment at any given level of income. In other words, what are the comparatively long-term influences on investment which we can take as our parameters?

As we have seen, the chief of these are: the propensity to consume, the existing stock of capital assets, estimates of the future price level and rate of interest, political stability, the rate of technical progress, conditions in the labour market, the size and age structure of the population, and so on.

These are factors, other than the level of income, influencing investment. Investment resulting from them is therefore autonomous investment.

(2) *The shape of the investment curve*

If all investment were autonomous, the level of investment would be unaffected by the level of income. The investment curve would be the horizontal straight line *AA* in Fig. 33. But we also have to consider induced investment.

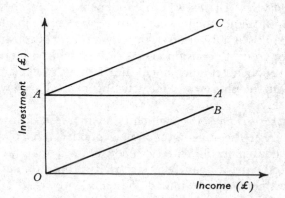

FIG. 33.—Autonomous and induced investment.

It would be convenient to postulate a direct relationship between the level of investment and the level of income – that any change in income would 'induce' a proportionate change in investment. We should then have the straight-line investment curve *OB* (Fig. 33). The constant slope of the curve indicates a constant 'marginal propensity to invest'. Total investment would be obtained by adding vertically *AA* and *OB*, to produce curve *AC*.

Unfortunately this is far too simple. Nor does it help a great deal if we pursue the analysis further along these lines and investigate the possibilities of a 'diminishing' or an 'increasing' propensity to invest. The reason is that any change in consumption – whether autonomous or through a change in income – is likely to produce a disproportionate change in the level of investment. We cannot assume a static position for the investment curve as consumption changes.

The situation is dynamic because much investment spending is related to the *rate at which consumption changes* rather than to the *abolute level* of consumption. We can see this more clearly by examining what is usually known as the 'acceleration principle'.

V. THE ACCELERATION PRINCIPLE

Example

Suppose that:

(*a*) 1,000 machines are fully employed in producing carpets;

(*b*) the life of each machine is 10 years;

(*c*) each machine can produce 100 carpets a year;

(*d*) the demand for carpets in the current year (year 0) is 100,000.

If demand remains at this figure, 100 carpet machines will have to be replaced each year, and so the capacity of the carpet-machine-making industry will be 100 machines a year.

Now suppose the demand for carpets increases by 10 per cent, that is, to 110,000 carpets a year. Extra machines are now needed to cope with this increased demand equal to 10,000/100, that is, 100 machines. Altogether then in year 1, 200 carpet-making machines are required. In other words, a 10 per cent increase in the consumption demand for carpets has produced a 100 per cent increase in the investment demand for machines. Investment has doubled in this particular industry.

Let us imagine now that the demand for carpets increases again by 10,000 per annum. In year 2, therefore, 100 new machines are required in addition to those for replacement purposes. But the capacity of the machine-making industry is already 200. Hence, there is no need for this industry to increase in size. And, provided that the demand for carpets increases by 10,000 each year, there is no need for it to decrease.

But suppose that in year 3, demand for carpets expands by only 5,000. This will mean that only 50 machines are required in addition to the replacement demand. There has thus been a contraction in investment *although consumption demand has continued to expand*!

If, in year 4, the demand for carpets remains at the same figure as in year 3, no extra machines will be required, and the capacity of the machine-making industry will be back to the replacement requirement of 100 machines.

We tabulate our findings in Table 4.

TABLE 4

THE EFFECT OF CHANGES IN CONSUMPTION OR INVESTMENT

MACHINES REQUIRED

Year	Demand for carpets	Replacement	Additional	Total
0	100,000	100	—	100
1	110,000	100	100	200
2	120,000	100	100	200
3	125,000	100	50	150
4	125,000	100	—	100

Conclusions from this example

(1) Changes in the rate of consumption produce a change in investment on a magnified scale.

(2) Where the rate of increase in consumption falls, the absolute amount of induced investment declines. Hence, to keep investment at 200 machines, the *rate of increase of consumption must be maintained* at 10,000 carpets per annum. (After 10 years, replacement demand will justify this size of machine-making industry.)

(3) 'Induced' investment depends upon changes in the *rate of consumption*, rather than on absolute changes in consumption. In fact, a study of the U.K.'s G.N.P. suggests that current investment is induced (in so far as it is not autonomous) by *past* changes in income – a time-lag is in evidence.

(4) Swings in the level of activity are likely to be much greater in the producer goods industries than in consumer goods.

(5) The longer the life of a machine, the greater will be the change in the capacity of the producer goods industry. If, for instance, the machines above had had a life of 20 years, a 10 per cent increase in the demand for carpets would have tripled the capacity of the machine-making industry.

(6) A single change in the level of consumption can lead to a

'bunching' of investment replacements in later years. There is thus to some extent a built-in cyclical mechanism. Too much, however, should not be made of this. When we are considering investment as a whole, bunching tends to be reduced because different machines have different lengths of life.

Notes

(1) The measurement of the accelerator should be in money terms. That is, it should show the number of pounds worth of machinery necessary to produce one pound's worth of output – often referred to as the capital–output ratio, or the capital coefficient. Thus, if the 100 carpets are each worth £100 and a machine costs £20,000, the accelerator is $\dfrac{20,000}{100 \times 100} = 2$.

(2) In practice, induced investment may result from an increase in investment demand elsewhere as well as from an increase in consumption because machines are needed to make the new machines. Thus the accelerator depends upon the rate of change in income rather than simply on the rate of change of consumption.

(3) The accelerator may also work through changes in stocks as a result of changes in demand.

Criticisms of the accelerator theory

(1) *It contains implicit assumptions which are either contradictory or unrealistic*

(*a*) The analysis assumes that there is no excess capacity in the production of carpets, but that there is plenty in making the carpet-machines. Thus a 10 per cent increase in the demand for carpets *has* to be met entirely from new machines. This involves a doubling of the machine-making capacity – which is achieved!

But there are alternatives: (i) it may be possible to produce the extra carpets by using idle machines or by double-shift working, in which case the accelerator does not operate; (ii) there may be no surplus capacity in the machine-making industry, in which case investment cannot increase immediately, and the increased demand for carpets finds its outlet in higher prices.

(*b*) It assumes that none of the existing machines can be used for more than 10 years!

(2) *It makes no allowance for the expectations of entrepreneurs*

Entrepreneurs do not invest on the basis of a single year's increase in sales. Hence: (*a*) the increased demand may be met from stocks or excess capacity because it has been anticipated; (*b*) new machines may not be ordered because the change in demand is thought to be only temporary. As soon as we bring in expectations, we have to recognise that induced investment, like autonomous investment, is subject to a variety of factors which we can sum up as the 'economic climate' – confidence, the political scene, international developments, stock market changes, and so on.

(3) *It does not allow for physical limitations*

(*a*) There may be a period of gestation before new investment can be produced. If, for instance, this period is three years, the full impact of induced investment will not be felt in one year but will be spread over three. This is important in period analysis.

(*b*) Increased demand requires increased stocks in addition to increased fixed capital. Firms which are unable to borrow the full amount or have insufficient internal funds may have to postpone ordering some fixed equipment.

(*c*) Existing management can only cope efficiently with limited additions to plant and capital equipment. This again will lead to a more gradual introduction.

Conclusion

For the above reasons, the acceleration principle is not likely to work with mechanical precision. A firm will try to increase production by overtime, shift working, etc. Whether or not it orders new equipment will depend partly on the extent to which its costs rise as existing equipment is worked more intensively and partly on the extent to which it thinks the increased demand is likely to persist. Where there is a significant rise in costs and increased demand looks like continuing, induced investment is likely, but not in rigid proportions. In any case, orders for extra capital are likely to be phased over time, so that investment expenditure does not rise and fall so violently as the acceleration theory suggests.

It should be noted, however, that the qualifications above are less applicable to investment in stocks. Unlike plant and equipment, stocks can be adjusted fairly quickly to sales changes. Such investment, therefore, tends to follow the accelerator pattern more closely than investment in fixed capital.

Keynes did not introduce the accelerator into his *General Theory*, although he knew about it. He emphasised expectations which, as we have seen, can, and probably will, modify the mechanical operation of the accelerator. As a rough generalisation, we can say that there is some functional relationship between investment and income; that is, $I = f(Y)$. For purposes of short-run analysis, however, we shall assume that all investment is autonomous; that is, the investment curve will be like AA in Fig. 33.

APPENDIX:
MATHEMATICAL EXPRESSIONS OF THE INVESTMENT FUNCTION

(a) The investment function

In this chapter we rejected the idea that investment is a function primarily of the rate of interest and concluded that investment depends chiefly on the level of income; that is, $I = f(Y)$.

If investment is regarded as a linear function of income, we could, for example, have the function:

$$I = a + i.Y,$$

where a certain level of investment, a, is carried out even at zero income and the 'propensity to invest' is i.

(b) Replacement investment

We divided gross investment into three categories: replacement investment, autonomous investment and induced investment.

We regarded replacement investment, I_r, as a function of the current level of consumption. Hence:

$$I_r = \alpha C, \text{ where } \alpha \text{ is a constant.}$$

(c) Investment as a function of the rate of change of consumption

A shift in the consumption function will induce new investment, I_i. This induced investment depends on the rate of change of consumption over time. Thus:

$$I_i = \beta \frac{dC}{dt}.$$

We can draw certain conclusions from this relationship. Suppose consumption expenditure over time is as shown in Fig. 34. From period t_0 to t_1, consumption is constant at C_0 per month. After t_1, consumption increases and grows at an in-

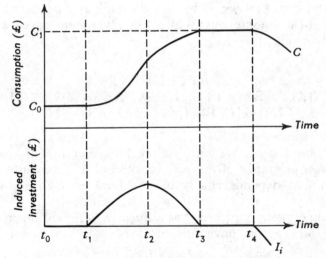

Fig. 34.—The relationship between induced investment and consumption spending.

creasing rate (dC/dt is positive and increasing) until t_2; after this consumption grows, but at a diminishing rate (dC/dt is positive but diminishing), until at t_3 it levels off at the rate of C_1 per month. This level continues until t_3, when consumption falls (dC/dt is negative).

Now induced investment depends on the rate of change of consumption; provided dC/dt is positive and increasing, induced investment will increase. As soon as the value of dC/dt begins to

fall, however, investment will decrease. When dC/dt becomes
negative, I_i becomes negative. These changes are shown in the
lower half of Fig. 34.

It should be noted that the idea of 'negative induced investment' creates a difficulty because it suggests that firms have
deliberately destroyed capital equipment. (For an interpretation, see p. 184.)

(d) The gross investment demand function

The aggregate investment demand function can now be
shown as:

$$I = I_a + I_r + I_i ,$$

where the components are autonomous, replacement and
induced investment. If we assume that autonomous investment
is independent of income, we have:

$$I = I_a + \alpha C + \beta \frac{dC}{dt} .$$

SUGGESTED READING
*G. Ackley, Macroeconomic Theory (Macmillan, New York, 1961)
   ch. 17.
F. S. Brooman, Macroeconomics, 4th ed. (Allen & Unwin, 1970)
   ch. 7.
G. C. Harcourt, P. H. Karmel and R. H. Wallace, Economic Activity
   (Cambridge U.P., 1967) ch. 9.
J. M. Keynes, The General Theory of Employment, Interest and Money
   (Macmillan, 1936) chs 11–12.
M. G. Mueller (ed.), Readings in Macroeconomics, No. 8 by W. H.
   White and No. 9 by A. D. Knox (Holt, Rinehart & Winston,
   1969).
D. C. Rowan, Output, Inflation and Growth (Macmillan, 1968) ch. 10.
R. S. Sayers, Modern Banking, 7th ed. (Oxford U.P., 1967) ch. 9.
A. W. Stonier and D. C. Hague, A Textbook of Economic Theory,
   3rd ed. (Longmans, 1964) ch. 21.

CHAPTER 7

THE BASIC THEORY OF INCOME DETERMINATION

I. INTRODUCTION

In chapter 4 we concluded that output depends on aggregate demand (AD). This idea will now be developed in a simple model to give a basic theory of income determination.

Assumptions

(1) There is less than full employment; that is, we start the analysis at a level of AD which is insufficient to draw all the economy's resources into employment.

(2) Employment $(N) = f(Y) = f(AD)$. Of course, this relationship holds only up to full employment; thereafter, although income may rise in money terms, there can be no increase in employment or in output.

(3) Firms adjust their output in period $t+1$ to equal AD in period t. That is, $Y_{t+1} = AD_t$.

(4) The general level of prices remains constant up to full employment. This allows us to measure Y, C, I, etc., in money terms *and* to use these money figures as expressions of changes in *real* terms.

(5) The money wage-rate remains constant.

(6) There is no government taxation or spending.

(7) Gross profit *less* retentions for depreciation = net profit.

    (a) All retentions for depreciation are actually spent on replacements. Thus when we speak of 'investment' it refers solely to *net investment*, that is, *net additions* to fixed capital and stocks.

    (b) All net profit is distributed to the owners of the risk capital; there is no saving by firms.

Assumptions (6) and (7) mean that all Y is received by households as disposable income (Y_d); that is, $Y = Y_d$.

(8) It is a 'closed' economy – there are no economic connections with the outside world.

Assumptions (7) and (8) mean that the sum of factor payments is equal to national income (Y), which equals national output as defined in Chapter 2.

(9) The relative distribution of income among people with different propensities to consume remains constant at all income levels. Thus changes in Y do not affect the proportion of Y spent.

(10) Investment spending by firms is autonomous; there is no induced investment.

(11) There are no dynamic changes, e.g. in entrepreneurs' expectations.

(12) All unspent income is placed with financial intermediaries termed 'banks'. Thus some saving can be hoarded because it is not re-lent by 'banks' for investment spending, but there is no other form of hoarding.

(13) All figures are in £ million.

Initial position

Let us suppose that, in period 0, $Y = 10,000$, $C = 0.6\ Y_d$ at all levels of income, and $I = 4,000$. This level of income will be an equilibrium one because:

$$AD = C + I = 6,000 + 4,000 = 10,000$$
$$Y = C + S = 6,000 + 4,000 = 10,000.$$

Intended saving equals investment.

Our task now is to follow through what happens when, for some reason, intended saving and investment become unequal.

II. THE EFFECT OF AN INCREASE IN AUTONOMOUS INVESTMENT: THE MULTIPLIER

Suppose that, in period 1, I increases by 2,000 to 6,000. AD is now 12,000; that is, the receipts of firms have increased to 12,000. Stocks of goods decrease and, as a result, entrepreneurs expand production in period 2. Thus factor payments equal

12,000 = Y (period 2). This expansion of Y has come about solely because I is greater than intended S. (Similarly, a contraction of Y will occur if I is less than intended S.)

But this is not the end of the expansion. An increase of Y to 12,000 will mean that more workers are employed, and they too will have income to spend. Thus $C = (0.6) (12,000) = 7,200$; with $I = 6,000$, this gives a new AD of 13,200. Thus, in period 3, Y increases to 13,200. As a result $C = (0.6) (13,200) = 7,920$, which with $I = 6,000$ gives AD = 13,920. Y in period 4 is therefore 13,920 (Fig. 35).

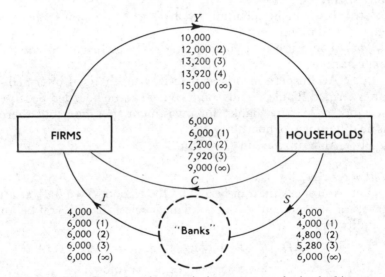

FIG. 35.—The effect of an increase in investment on the level of income.

And so it continues. The process in real life is illustrated in Nevil Shute's *Ruined City*. After years of idleness, the shipyard obtained an order for three tankers:

> The small, returning ripple of prosperity had not passed unnoticed in the district; a shop, long closed, reopened to sell meat pies, cooked meats, black puddings and small delicacies. It did a good trade over Christmas. Small articles began to be sold at the door for the first time for many years; a man who gleaned a sack of holly in the country

lanes disposed of it within an hour, a penny for a spray. A hot roast chestnut barrow came upon the streets, and did good trade.

The expansion of Y will come to an end only when intended $S=I$. Since $I=6,000$ and $S=0.4Y$, Y will have to expand to 15,000. Because now intended $S=I$, this is the new equilibrium level of Y. How the additional flow of saving is created can be seen from Table 5 where, to signify that we are now referring to *changes* in the variables, the symbols are prefixed with Δ.

TABLE 5

THE EFFECT OF AN INCREASE INVESTMENT ON AD, C, S AND Y.

Period	I	2	3	4	5	$\Sigma\infty$
$\Delta AD = \Delta I = $	2,000 +	1,200 +	720 +	432 +	259·2 +	... 5,000 $= \Delta Y$
ΔC	—	1,200 +	720 +	432 +	259·2 +	... 3,000 $= \Delta C$
ΔS	—	800 +	480 +	288 +	172·8 +	... 2,000 $= \Delta S$

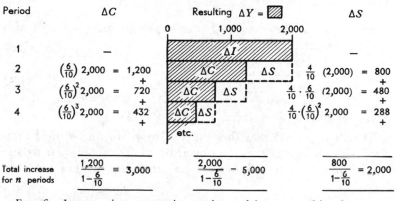

Period	ΔC		Resulting $\Delta Y = $ ▨			ΔS	
			0	1,000	2,000		
1	—			ΔI		—	
2	$\left(\frac{6}{10}\right) 2,000 =$	1,200	ΔC		ΔS	$\frac{4}{10} (2,000) =$	800
		+					+
3	$\left(\frac{6}{10}\right)^2 2,000 =$	720	ΔC	ΔS		$\frac{4}{10} \cdot \frac{6}{10} (2,000) =$	480
		+					+
4	$\left(\frac{6}{10}\right)^3 2,000 =$	432	ΔC	ΔS		$\frac{4}{10} \cdot \left(\frac{6}{10}\right)^2 2,000 =$	288
		+	etc.				+
Total increase for n periods	$\dfrac{1,200}{1-\frac{6}{10}} = 3,000$		$\dfrac{2,000}{1-\frac{6}{10}} - 5,000$			$\dfrac{800}{1-\frac{6}{10}} = 2,000$	

FIG. 36.—Increases in consumption, saving and income resulting from an increase in the level of investment.

Figure 36 can be explained as follows. The initial increase in I leads to an increase in AD and thus in Y. A proportion of these extra factor payments is spent according to the marginal propensity to consume (0·6). The proportion not spent (0·4) is saved.

This extra spending increases AD and therefore Y still further. And so the process is repeated, extra increments of C going to swell the total increase in AD and therefore of Y.

These totals are shown at the foot of each column. Each column is really a geometric progression of the form $a + ar + ar^2 + \ldots$ where r equals the marginal propensity to consume. Now the sum of a geometric progression to infinity, where r is less than 1, equals $a/(1 - r)$. It follows, therefore, that:

$$\text{total } \Delta Y = \frac{2{,}000}{1 - 0 \cdot 6}.$$

In general terms, let the increment of investment expenditure be ΔI, and the propensity to consume, c. Then:

$$\Delta Y = I + c\Delta I + c^2\Delta I + c^3\Delta I + \ldots.$$

This is a geometric progression where, in the notation above, $a = I$ and $r = c$. Thus, summing to infinity, we have:

$$\Delta Y = \frac{\Delta I}{1 - c}. \tag{7.1}$$

Since $1 - c = s$, the marginal propensity to save, we can also write our result as:

$$\Delta Y = \frac{\Delta I}{s}. \tag{7.2}$$

The multiplier

It will be noted that the increase in Y is much larger than the original increase in I. The ratio $\Delta Y/\Delta I$ is known as the 'multiplier' (often written k). Substituting (7.1) above, we have:

$$k = \frac{1}{1 - c} = \frac{1}{s}.$$

Thus the value of k in our example is $\dfrac{1}{1 - 0 \cdot 6} = 2 \cdot 5$.

This can be verified visually from Fig. 36, where the shaded area equals the total increase in Y. If the proportion of income spent fell to 0·5, the shaded area would be smaller. Our analysis points to the reason for this. When the fraction of income consumed falls, a higher proportion is saved. Thus income does not have to expand so much in order to bring intended saving into line with investment.

Hence, the same increment of investment will yield different ncrements of income for different values of c. For example:

Marginal propensity to consume (c)	Multiplier $\left(\dfrac{1}{1-c}\right)$
0.9	10
0.8	5
0.5	2
0.2	1.25

This brings us to the basic difference between saving and investment in the process of income creation. Whereas an increase in investment will, other things being equal, automatically produce an increase in saving, an addition to saving need not lead to an increase in investment. Indeed, when the desire to save increases with no increase in investment, income merely contracts until what is saved from it equals investment.

Diagrammatic exposition of changes in the equilibrium level of income

Employment, we have assumed, varies directly with the level of income, which itself depends upon AD. If AD is equal to income, there is no change in stocks, and entrepreneurs will continue to employ the same amount of labour. If AD is less than income, stocks accumulate and entrepreneurs make losses because they are receiving less than they have paid out. They will therefore reduce output. If total spending is more than income, entrepreneurs more than realise their expectations and they expand output. This is demonstrated in Fig. 37.

The 45° line traces all points where AD is equal to income (the same scale being chosen for both the x- and y-axes). Therefore any point on this line will represent an equilibrium level of income.

The line C is a consumption curve (see Fig. 37) and shows consumption expenditure at different levels of Y. Here $C = 0.6Y$.

To this we have to add investment expenditure of 4,000 at all levels of income. Thus the line $C + I$ is vertically distant 4,000 above the C curve, and gives AD at each level of Y.

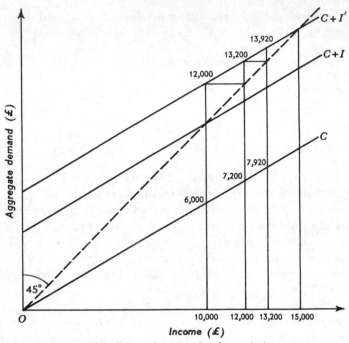

Fig. 37.—The effect on income of a change in investment.

In equilibrium, $Y = AD = C + I$. The only point where this can occur is the intersection of the $C + I$ line with the 45° line. Here $AD = Y = 10,000$.

When I increases to 6,000, the $C + I$ line moves vertically by 2,000 to $C + I'$. AD immediately increases to 12,000, and so does Y in the next period. Of this new income, $C = 7,200$ which, with $I' = 6,000$, means that AD and Y increase to 13,200. This expansionary process continues until AD and Y are equal to 15,000.

III. THE EFFECT OF CHANGES IN CONSUMPTION

A change in the propensity to consume

Suppose now that C decreases from $0.6Y$ to $0.5Y$ at all levels of Y. This means that the C curve rotates downwards about the origin from C to C' (Fig. 38). The equilibrium level of Y is still where $S = I = 4,000$. But since the marginal propensity to save has risen to $0.5Y$, 4,000 can be saved out of a smaller income – 8,000.

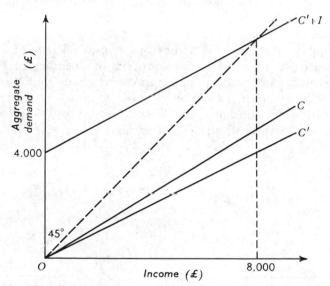

Fig. 38.—The effect on income of a decrease in the propensity to consume.

Similarly, if I now increases by 2,000, the increase in Y will be only 4,000 because a smaller fraction of income is passed on in each period; that is, the value of the multiplier has fallen.

Limiting cases

It should be noted that we have assumed (realistically) that the value of c lies between 0 and 1. Consider what would happen in the limiting cases:

(1) $c = 0$. Here there is no subsidiary flow of income because

it is all saved. Thus an injection of $\varDelta I$ expands income by $\varDelta I$, but by no more.

(2) $c=1$. Here the subsidiary flow is endless – people save nothing. If $c=1$, $c\varDelta I=\varDelta I$; $c^2\varDelta I=\varDelta I$; and so on. Thus any increase in I generates an infinitely large flow of Y. The assumption that $c<1$ is therefore essential for the stability of the process.

An autonomous change in consumption

So far we have assumed that the marginal and average propensities to consume are constant at all levels of income; this means that the consumption function is a straight line passing through the origin.

Suppose now that C increases by 2,000 at all income levels, even when Y is zero. This consumption, independent of Y, can be termed autonomous consumption. It means that the consumption function is $C=2,000+0\cdot6Y$. Although the marginal propensity to consume is still constant at $0\cdot6$, the *average* propensity varies with the level of income.

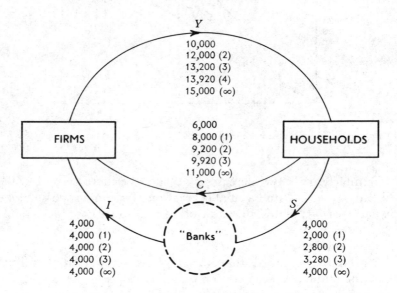

FIG. 39.—The effect of a change in autonomous consumption on the level of income.

Given investment of 4,000, the flows are shown in Fig. 39.

It is clear that an autonomous change in consumption is subject to the multiplier just as a change in investment is. Income rises until it is sufficient to generate savings equal to the level of investment. In terms of Fig. 37, it simply means that the original $C+I$ curve moves vertically upwards by 2,000 with the $C'+I$ curve occupying the same position as the $C+I'$ curve (where autonomous investment has increased by the same amount). Thus Y increases as before to 15,000. (Note that the saving function is $S=-2,000+0\cdot4Y$, giving $S=4,000=I$, when $Y=15,000$.)

The paradox of thrift

But what is the situation when there is an increase in the propensity to save? Here we have what is often called the 'paradox of thrift'.

As we have seen, saving occurs because all income is not spent on consumption; people are limiting their demand for consumer goods. In real terms, the existence of saving frees factors from the production of goods for present consumption so that they can produce capital goods – houses, roads, factories, machinery, etc. The acquisition of capital involves forgoing present consumption; in this respect, thrift is a virtue.

In a primitive economy, producers themselves may reduce their current consumption by devoting some of their time to making a piece of capital equipment, such as a plough. Here saving automatically equals investment. However, in a modern economy, decisions to save and decisions to invest are taken for different reasons by two different sets of persons – households and firms respectively. When intended saving is greater than investment, not all factors released from producing goods for present consumption are used to produce capital goods. Some may remain unemployed. From the community's point of view saving can only be in capital goods or additions to stocks. When factors are unemployed there can be no real saving – what they could have produced is lost for ever.

What happens, as we have seen, is that income falls to that level where intended saving out of income just equals investment. Furthermore, the fall in income may lead entrepreneurs to *cut* investment! Thus, if additional saving is not matched by additional investment, thrift is a curse, not a virtue, for it leads to a reduced standard of living as factors become unemployed and fewer consumer goods are produced.

The effect of a diminishing marginal propensity to consume

So far we have assumed that the marginal propensity to consume is constant at all levels of income. But, as we saw in Chapter 5, the value of c is likely to fall as Y increases. Nevertheless, the principle of the multiplier is the same. The only difference is that the calculations are more complicated because, for each period increment, we have to apply a smaller multiplier, since the marginal propensity to consume diminishes as income increases.

Summary

The level of income and employment depends upon the level of AD – the total amount of money spent on the goods produced. AD fluctuates according to the relationship between intended saving and investment until eventually intended saving equals investment.

(1) AD expands if:
    (a) investment increases but the propensity to save remains unchanged;
    (b) the propensity to save decreases but investment remains unchanged.

(2) AD contracts if:
    (a) investment decreases but the propensity to save remains unchanged;
    (b) the propensity to save increases but investment remains unchanged.

In practice investment fluctuates more than saving. Whereas entrepreneurs' expectations are highly sensitive to new conditions, people's spending habits are fairly stable.

(3) The basic principle of income determination is that income will expand or contract until it is just sufficient to generate a flow of saving equal to the flow of investment. Thus the economy can be in equilibrium at any level of employment depending on the flow of AD. Full employment is a special case.

(4) If full employment is an end of policy, the government may have to take measures to ensure adequate AD. Where there is a diminishing marginal propensity to consume at higher levels of income, the gap to be filled grows larger as income rises.

APPENDIX:
MATHEMATICAL EXPRESSION OF INCOME DETERMINATION

Our simple approach of comparing one equilibrium position with another can be shown mathematically as follows.

(a) *Equilibrium*

Here $Y = C + I$, and $C = cY$.

Therefore $Y = cY + I$. $\hfill (7.3)$

Thus $Y(1 - c) = I$

$$Y = \frac{I}{1 - c} = \frac{I}{s}.$$

Thus the equilibrium size of national income depends upon the level of investment and the marginal propensity to consume.

(b) *An increase in autonomous investment*

Investment increases by ΔI with the result that income increases by ΔY. We have, therefore;

$$\Delta Y = c\Delta Y + \Delta I$$

$$\Delta Y = \frac{\Delta I}{1 - c}. \hfill (7.4)$$

(c) *The multiplier*

The multiplier, k, is defined as $\Delta Y / \Delta I$.

Dividing (7.4) by ΔI gives $k = \dfrac{1}{1 - c} = \dfrac{1}{s}$.

(d) *A change in the propensity to consume*

Suppose the marginal propensity to consume changes from c to c'. We have, therefore,

$$C = c'Y, \text{ and } Y = c'Y + I.$$

Thus $k = \dfrac{1}{1 - c'}$.

(e) *An autonomous change in consumption*

Assume consumption increases by a at all levels of income.

Thus $C = a + cY$

$$Y + \Delta Y = a + c(Y + \Delta Y) + I.$$

But from (7.3) $Y = cY + I.$

Therefore $\Delta Y = a + c\Delta Y$

$$\Delta Y - c\Delta Y = a$$

$$\Delta Y = \frac{a}{1 - c}.$$

That is, an autonomous change in consumption is subject to the multiplier in the same way that a change in investment is.

SUGGESTED READING

*G. Ackley, *Macroeconomic Theory* (Macmillan, New York, 1961) ch. 13.

W. Beckerman, *An Introduction to National Income Analysis* (Weidenfeld & Nicolson, 1968) chs 6–7.

F. S. Brooman, *Macroeconomics*, 4th ed. (Allen & Unwin, 1970) ch. 6.

T. F. Dernburg and D. M. McDougall, *Macro-economics*, 3rd ed. (McGraw-Hill, 1968) ch. 5.

A. H. Hansen, *A Guide to Keynes* (McGraw-Hill, 1953) ch. 4.

*J. M. Keynes, *The General Theory of Employment, Interest and Money* (Macmillan, 1936) ch. 18.

G. L. S. Shackle (ed.), *A New Prospect of Economics* (Liverpool U.P., 1958) ch. 14.

M. Stewart, *Keynes and After* (Penguin, 1967) chs 4–6.

CHAPTER 8

THE DEMAND FOR MONEY

So far our outline of the basic theory of income determination has concentrated on what Professor D. H. Robertson called the 'real forces' of productivity and thrift. But there are also monetary forces at work – forces which arise because of the peculiar nature of money. These influence the rate of interest, which until now has been taken as given. Our immediate task is to consider the nature of money, as a preliminary to showing how monetary forces influence the level of activity.

I. MONEY AND ITS FUNCTIONS

What is money?

In an economy where there is a high degree of specialisation, exchanges must take place quickly and smoothly. Hence we have a 'go-between' – money – a common denominator for all goods. The product of specialised labour is sold, that is, exchanged for money, and this money is then used to buy the different goods and services required.

Anything which is *generally acceptable* in purchasing goods or settling debts can be said to be money. The main forms of money in the U.K. today are coins, notes and bank deposits.

The basis of money is confidence. The paper from which notes are made is comparatively worthless, but people who receive them are confident that others too will accept them. Notes, therefore, possess the essential characteristic of money – general acceptability – even though, since 1931, it has not been possible in the U.K. to exchange notes for gold at the Bank of England.

The fact that the basis of money is confidence, or general acceptability, is obvious when we consider bank deposits, the most important kind of money in a developed economy. A bank deposit consists merely of an entry in a bank ledger, crediting a customer with a stated sum of money. The customer settles debts by writing a cheque, transferring deposits from his account to that of his creditor's. No 'physical' money – coins or notes – changes hands. Because the cheque is accepted, the bank deposits act as money.

It might be objected that the customer will only have bank deposits credited to him if 'physical' money has been deposited – just as though the entry in the bank ledger were backed by an equal quantity of coins or notes in a safe bearing the customer's name. But this is not so and, indeed, is quite unnecessary. Because people accept cheques (which transfer book deposits) as confidently as they accept coins or notes, a bank can, within certain limits, 'create' deposits. As we shall see in Chapter 9, when a customer asks for a loan, it simply credits the customer's account with the agreed amount by making the appropriate book entry. Such a credit is money, just as a bank deposit representing cash paid into the account is money. And the same reason applies – people in general will *accept it without question in payment of a debt.*

The functions of money

Money, it is usually stated, performs four functions:

(1) It is *a medium of exchange*, the 'go-between' which facilitates exchanges in a modern economy.

(2) It is *a measure of value and a unit of account*, making possible the operation of a price system, and automatically providing the basis for keeping accounts, calculating profit and loss, costing, etc. We used money in this way to add up the national income in Chapter 2.

(3) It is *a standard of deferred payments*, the unit in which, given stability in its value, loans are made and future contracts fixed. Without money, there would be no common basis for dealing in debts – the work of such institutions as insurance companies, building societies, banks and discount houses. By providing a standard for repayment, money makes borrowing and lending much easier.

(4) It is *a store of wealth*, a convenient way of keeping any income which is surplus to immediate requirements.

For simplicity, we can classify the first two functions of money as 'exchange' functions, and the last two as 'asset' functions.

II. THE DEMAND FOR MONEY

Money as a liquid asset

We began our discussion of money by considering it as a medium of exchange. As such it would seem to perform a neutral role in the economy, acting as a go-between to facilitate buying and selling – just as the referee in a football match acts impartially between the two sides.

But when we come to consider the part which money plays in the economy as a whole, we are much more concerned with its 'asset' functions. Because money is generally acceptable, people hold it, not only to pay debts, but as a particular form of asset – one which can be converted into other goods without delay, cost or loss. In other words, money is 'perfectly liquid'.

Moreover, no other form of wealth is perfectly liquid. Assets kept in a deposit account at a commercial bank are subject (nominally, at least) to seven days' notice of withdrawal. Equities and bonds have to be sold on the stock market, and this may incur delay, cost (broker's commission, etc.), and perhaps a capital loss if market prices have moved downwards since the securities were acquired. Real goods impose storage costs, and may depreciate in value; moreover, it usually requires time to sell them. The position is summarised in Fig. 40.

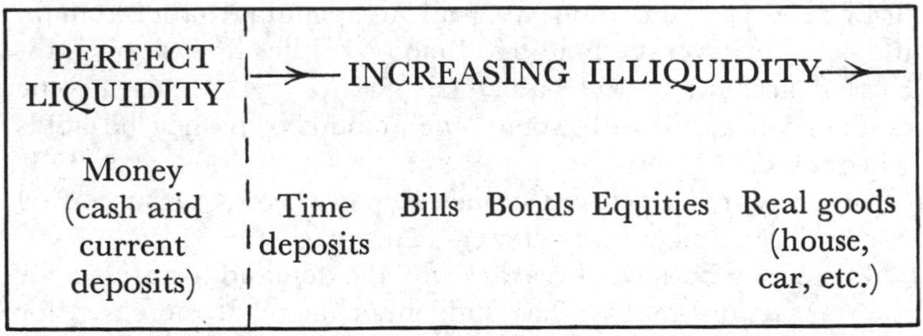

PERFECT LIQUIDITY	⟶ INCREASING ILLIQUIDITY ⟶				
Money (cash and current deposits)	Time deposits	Bills	Bonds	Equities	Real goods (house, car, etc.)

Fig. 40.—The liquidity of money compared with other assets.

To sum up, only with money can we move directly into another form of asset; with all others we must usually first exchange the asset for cash, which involves delay, cost, and perhaps a capital loss.

There is thus a demand for money 'to hold', that is, for assets in the form of cash and current deposits. This demand exerts important influences in the economy as a whole; money has ceased to play a purely neutral role. It is as though the referee in a football match were to take an active part, kicking the ball first for one side and then the other! We will now examine why money behaves in this way.

Why people demand money

In keeping money balances, people are sacrificing the interest they could have obtained by lending it. There must, therefore, be good reasons for holding money. Keynes suggested three.

(1) The transactions motive

Both households and firms hold money to facilitate current transactions. They do so because payments rarely coincide with receipts.

While most households receive the bulk of their income weekly or monthly, payments for food, travel and pleasure have to be made each day. Thus a part of money income has to be held throughout the week or month to cover these everyday purchases. How much on the average will this be?

Suppose that a man is earning £26 a week, all of which is being spent. He receives £26 on the Friday which begins the week, and by the following Friday he will have nothing left. Thus his average holding of money is £13. Should it now be decided to pay him monthly, and his spending habits remain the same, his average holding of money, either in cash or in his current account at the bank, will rise to £52. If his income doubles but is still fully spent, the amount of money he holds will double.

Similarly, firms require money to pay wages, purchase raw materials, and meet other current expenses.

There may be special reasons why the demand for money for the transactions motive may suddenly change. It increases, for instance, at Christmas and holiday periods, or if there is a flurry of activity on the Stock Exchange. It decreases when firms combine, for then money transactions are replaced by internal book-keeping entries. But usually the underlying determinants are fairly stable. For households, these are the length of time between successive pay-days and the level of income and prices; for firms, it is the size of turnover. Thus the community's demand for money transactions purposes will be roughly in proportion to the size of money national income.

It should be noted that the value of transactions for which money is required is much greater than the value of money national income. For instance, if the cost of goods to a shopkeeper (including his shop expenses) is £100, and he sells them for £110, the income he makes from the transaction is £10, whereas £210 in money was required to effect the necessary exchanges. In addition, money is required for what are basically non-income-increasing transactions, e.g. switching securities.

It should also be noticed that the transactions demand for money will increase in inflationary conditions. Although we have assumed that prices will remain constant up to full employment, they will in practice start to rise before full employment is reached. This means that as income approaches full employment, there will be an increasing demand for money to hold for two reasons: first, through the increase in income; secondly, through the general rise in prices (but *see* pp. 122–124).

In what follows, we shall assume that the demand for money for transactions purposes changes proportionately with income. Other factors, such as the rate of interest (which probably has a negligible effect) and the institutional framework (e.g. the times of wage payments) will be ignored.

(2) *The precautionary motive*

Apart from expenditure on regular, everyday purchases, money is held to cover events of a more uncertain nature, for example illness, unemployment, or the possibility of coming across cash bargains. Some kinds of income, too, may be received irregularly (e.g. authors' royalties), and this is likely to affect the precautionary balance held. In general, therefore, the amount held for the precautionary motive will depend on the outlook of the individual and on his income level. It will vary with his optimism or pessimism as regards events or the possibility of borrowing at short notice. Moreover, changes in uncertainty in the economy may cause shifts in the community's propensity to hold precautionary balances. Thus a financial crisis or threat of war may lead people to guard against future contingencies by holding a larger part of their wealth in the form of money.

In normal times, however, we may assume that the amount of money set aside for the precautionary motive is related, like that for the transactions motive, to the level of national income.

The combined sum of balances held for the transactions and precautionary motives Keynes termed *active balances* and labelled M_1. The demand for active balances can be referred to as L_1, and thus $L_1 = f(Y)$. This relationship is shown diagrammatically in Fig. 41; L_1 is directly proportionate to the level of national income.

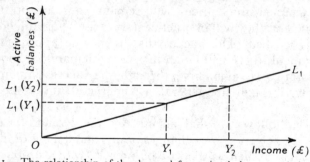

Fig. 41.—The relationship of the demand for active balances and the level of income.

For purposes of future analysis, it is desirable to plot the demand for money with reference to the rate of interest, i. This brings us to a major snag of holding money – *it does not provide a yield*. (In periods of inflation, there is the added disadvantage that the value of money is falling, but we can ignore this complication for the time being.) Furniture, jewellery, works of art, etc., afford pleasure; a house can be lived in or rented out. Shares usually provide a dividend; bonds, a fixed rate of interest. There is thus an opportunity cost of being liquid – the yield forgone. To simplify, let us refer to this yield as 'the rate of interest'.

Thus, while people may desire liquidity, they have also to think of the cost involved. The higher the rate of interest, the greater the cost of remaining liquid. As the rate rises, fewer people will be prepared to pay the 'price'; they economise on active balances. This is depicted in Fig. 42(a).

However, since active balances are held mostly for purposes of convenience, there is not a lot of scope for reducing them as the rate of interest rises. In fact, in future analysis we shall

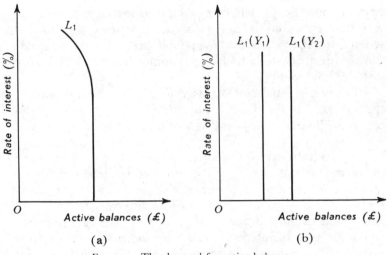

FIG. 42.—The demand for active balances.

ignore the tendency, showing the demand for active balances with respect to the rate of interest as absolutely inelastic (Fig. 42(b)). Here $L_1(Y_1)$ and $L_1(Y_2)$ correspond to different national income levels with $Y_2 > Y_1$.

(3) The speculative motive

People also hold money, says Keynes, in *idle balances* for speculative purposes. Such speculation arises as follows.

On any given day it is quite usual for the prices of some

securities to rise while those of others fall. But there are periods when the prices of almost all securities move in more or less the same direction. To simplify our explanation, we shall concentrate our attention on undated government bonds (fixed-interest-bearing securities); this eliminates time and risk complications.

If people think that the price of bonds is going to rise, they will buy bonds now; if their forecast proves correct, they will make a capital gain. Similarly, if they think that the price of bonds is going to fall, they will sell bonds in order to avoid a capital loss. Now the lower the price of bonds, the more will people expect the next likely move to be upwards. As the price rises, so more people will come round to the view that the price is so high that a fall is likely to occur. It follows, therefore, that when the price of bonds is low, people prefer bonds to liquidity; but as the price of bonds rises, people move out of bonds in order to hold money.

However, the price of bonds varies in inverse proportion to the rate of interest. Thus if the rate of interest is currently $2\frac{1}{2}$ per cent, £100 $3\frac{1}{2}$ per cent War Loan will sell on the Stock Exchange for £$3\frac{1}{2}$/$2\frac{1}{2}$ × 100 = £140, because the annual interest of £3·50 purchased by £140 gives a yield of $2\frac{1}{2}$ per cent, exactly the same as a newly-issued bond. Thus, when people are speculating against the future price of bonds they are also speculating against the future rate of interest. Hence we can restate our original proposition in terms of the rate of interest: when the rate of interest is low (the price of bonds is high), people will prefer to hold money; when the rate of interest is high (the price of bonds is low), people will not wish to hold money. Thus the demand for idle balances (L_2) depends upon the rate of interest. That is, $L_2 = f(i)$. The relationship is shown diagramatically in Fig. 43.

It should be noted that there is nothing sinister about this. Speculation must occur where there is an element of uncertainty and where changes in the market price of a bond are important to the holder. The factors which influence his decision to buy or sell are the current rate of interest, the rate which he expects in the future, the degree of certainty he places on his estimate, and the time he expects to elapse before a change takes place.

Assuming that he is quite certain that a rise in the rate of interest will occur within a year, a wealth-owner who is trying to make as large a gain as possible will compare the interest the bond will earn in the year with any loss he expects on its market value. Suppose the present rate of interest is 4 per cent. This

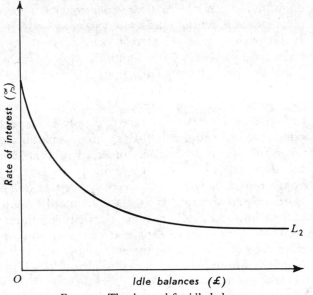

FIG. 43.—The demand for idle balances.

means that he will earn £4 in interest during the year on bonds which he can at present buy or sell for £100. It will obviously not pay him to hold this bond if the price is going to drop to less than £96, for this will mean that, even after receiving interest, he will make a net loss. Now a price of £96 will rule if the rate of interest rises to 4·16 per cent. Thus he will sell the bond if he expects a rise of at least this magnitude, and hold money instead. (This ignores the costs involved in buying and selling bonds, such as brokers' fees. While these complicate calculations, they do not alter fundamental principles.)

Keynes pointed out that when the rate of interest falls to 2 per cent (the level is probably higher today, since the fall in the real value of money debts through inflation has to be allowed for), the demand for money becomes perfectly elastic – any additional money issued by the authorities goes into idle balances. There are two reasons for this 'liquidity trap':

(a) Apart from the loss of liquidity, the process of changing money into bonds involves both cost and inconvenience. Some minimum return (say 2 per cent) is necessary to compensate potential lenders for this.

(b) If the present rate of interest is 2 per cent, a wealth-owner receives only £2 per annum on bonds which cost £100 on the market. Thus it is better to hold money rather than bonds if their price is expected to fall below £98 by the end of the year. This, however, corresponds to a rise in the rate of interest to only 2·04 per cent – both absolutely and relatively a much smaller rise than when the rate is 4 per cent (see above). Wealth-owners are therefore more and more likely to switch out of bonds into money as the rate of interest falls. In other words, when the rate is low, the demand for money is almost infinite. Such a high elasticity of demand for money at 2 per cent means that any government would have difficulty in forcing the rate below this unless some penalty were imposed on holding money (such as taxing bank deposits).

The result is that there is a minimum rate of interest which people generally consider to be the bottom; here the demand for money is perfectly elastic.

The demand for money during inflation or deflation

In practice, speculation does not only affect transactions between bonds and money. It may, for instance, be profitable to switch from bonds to equities. This will bring some adjustment in the demand for money, for it will affect the price of bonds; as the price of bonds falls, so less money is demanded. Furthermore, as we have seen, there may be occasions, e.g. war or a severe depression, when the prices of all securities are under severe pressure. Here people switch into money as a safety measure – though in such a situation the precautionary motive is merging into the speculative.

Other abnormal conditions, such as inflation (or deflation), also affect the demand for money. When the prices of real goods in general are rising (or falling), another form of speculation is possible – between money and goods. If people expect a general price rise, they are likely to bring forward their purchases. Manufacturers, too, will be inclined to stockpile raw materials, wholesalers will stock up, and so on. If such expectations are general, the demand for money will decrease because it will be prudent to hold wealth in the form of goods rather than in money.

The reverse tendency will be likely when prices are falling; people will prefer to hold money, delaying their purchases as long as possible.

Although this motive for holding money is speculative, it differs from the speculative motive described by Keynes. While the latter is concerned only with the future prices of securities, and can occur in condition of stable goods prices, the inflationary and deflationary motives represent speculation against future economic conditions generally.

It is in conditions of severe inflation that such an influence on the desire to hold money is especially important. Money is quickly losing its value, and it is unwise to hold more than the absolute minimum. Consequently any money received will be spent as soon as possible and attempts will be made to hold all wealth in forms whose money values keep pace with the general price rise, e.g. stocks of materials, equities, antiques, real estate, etc. Thus the flight from money is coupled with an unwillingness to hold claims valued in terms of money, such as bonds. The result is that, in spite of the greater risk, the rate of return on first-class ordinary shares may be lower than on government securities. Such a situation, referred to as 'the reverse gap' or the 'cult of the equity', has existed in the U.K. since 1953.

Even in relatively mild inflations, such as that in Britain since the Second World War, some flight from money may occur. Generally speaking, however, we can ignore inflationary and deflationary influences on the demand for money. For short-term analysis, we can regard the demand to hold wealth in the form of money as being dependent on: (1) the transactions and precautionary motives; (2) the speculative motive. In practice, it is impossible to identify what fraction of a person's holding of money is held for one motive or another; it is better if total money holdings are regarded as depending on the combined influences of these motives. If one motive gets stronger and the others remain the same, a person will try to satisfy the former at the expense of the others.

Summary

Because money is the only perfectly liquid asset, there is a demand for money to hold. Keynes considers that people will hold (1) active balances, M_1 according to the level of money income, (2) idle balances, M_2, according to the rate of interest.

Since money is perfectly substitutable between M_1 and M_2, the division is a purely expositional device; at high rates of

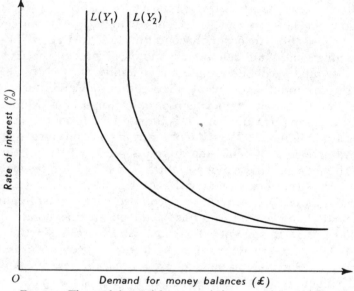

FIG. 44.—The total demand for money balances, active and idle.

interest, people may economise on M_1 in order to gave liquid reserves for speculation, M_2. To overcome this difficulty, we can say simply that there are two main motives for holding money, income and the rate of interest, and combine the two demands in an overall demand for money (L). That is, $L = L_1(Y) + L_2(i)$. Thus the curves $L_1(Y_1)$ and $L_1(Y_2)$ shown in

Fig. 42(*b*) can be combined with the curve L_2 in Fig. 43 to show the total demand for money at two levels of national income. (Fig. 44). Here the difference in the two income levels is indicated by the horizontal difference between the two curves; in practice, there will be an infinite 'family' of curves for all possible levels of income.

SUGGESTED READING

F. S. Brooman, *Macroeconomics*, 4th ed. (Allen & Unwin, 1970) ch. 11.

T. F. Dernburg and D. M. McDougall, *Macro-economics*, 3rd ed. (McGraw-Hill, 1968) ch. 8.

M. Fleming, *Introduction to Economic Analysis* (Allen & Unwin, 1969) ch. 28.

A. H. Hansen, *A Guide to Keynes* (McGraw-Hill, 1953) ch. 6.

J. M. Keynes, *The General Theory of Employment, Interest and Money* (Macmillan, 1936) chs 13, 15, 17.

G. L. S. Shackle (ed.), *A New Prospect of Economics* (Liverpool U.P., 1958) ch. 12.

CHAPTER 9

THE SUPPLY OF MONEY

MONEY, as we have seen, is anything which is immediately and unquestionably accepted in payment of a debt. Applying this definition, the supply of money consists of: (*a*) coin; (*b*) notes; (*c*) bank deposits. The first two are now regarded as the 'small change' of the monetary system; sufficient is always made available for the practical convenience of the public. Thus at Christmas and holiday-time, the supply of notes is increased.

It follows, therefore, that any variation in the supply of money from the point of view of controlling the economy must involve a change in bank deposits. Our discussion will therefore concentrate on the supply of bank deposits in the context of current practice in the U.K.

I. THE CREATION OF BANK DEPOSITS

The cheque as a substitute for cash

Joint-stock banks are companies which exist to make profits for their shareholders. They do this by borrowing money from 'depositors' and using these sums as a base for lending at a higher rate of interest to other persons. Borrowers are private persons, companies, public corporations, the money market and the government. The more a bank can lend, the greater will be its profits.

Banks are able to lend because people who deposit cash with them seldom want to withdraw more than a small fraction of their cash at any one time. Instead they settle debts by writing a cheque transferring their deposits to the creditor. Cheques are, for practical purposes, generally acceptable; thus the bank deposits act as money.

It should be noted that no cash need actually change hands. All the bank does is to make book entries debiting the account of the debtor and crediting the account of the creditor. The fact that no cash changes hands enables the bank: (a) to lend deposits; (b) to create deposits in order to extend its lending activities. A simple example will show how both are possible.

Suppose that I have paid £100 into my banking account. Imagine, too, that my builder banks at the same branch and that I owe him £50. I simply write him a cheque for that amount, and he pays this into the bank. To complete the transaction, my account is debited by £50, and his account is credited by that amount. No actual cash changes hands. A mere book entry in both accounts has completed the transaction.

Perhaps my builder will, towards the end of the week, withdraw some cash to pay his workers' wages. But it is likely that most of his payments, e.g. for building materials, petrol, and lorry servicing, will be by cheque. Similarly, while from the £50 still standing to my account I may withdraw some cash to cover everyday housekeeping expenses, the probability is that many of my bills, e.g. club subscription, half-yearly rates, hire-purchase instalments on the car, mortgage repayments, will be settled by cheque or by a credit transfer directly from my account. Furthermore, even where cash is withdrawn, it is often replaced by cash being paid in.

Since the development of the cheque system, the proportion of cash which is required for transactions has decreased. As a result, banks have discovered that in practice only about 10 per cent of their total deposits need be retained in cash to cover all demands for cash withdrawals. In short, only £10 of my original deposit of £100 is needed to form an adequate cash reserve.

The creation of credit

It is obvious, therefore, that £90 of my original cash deposit of £100 could be lent by the bank to a third party without me· or anybody else being the wiser. What is not so obvious is that the bank can go much further than this – and does!

Let us assume that there is only one bank and that all lending is in the form of advances to the public. When a person is granted a loan by his bank manager, his account is credited with the amount of the loan or, alternatively, he is authorised to overdraw his account up to the stipulated limit. In other words, a deposit is created in the name of the borrower by the bank.

When he spends the loan, the borrower will probably do so by cheque, in which case there is no immediate demand for cash. There is no reason, therefore, why the whole of my cash deposit of £100 should not act as the safe cash reserve for deposits of a much larger sum created by the bank's lending activities. But the bank must not overdo this credit creation. To simplify, let us assume that, to be safe, cash must always form one-tenth (in practice, it is 8 per cent) of total deposits. This means that the bank can grant a loan of up to £900. Because it is the only bank, there is no need to fear that cheques drawn on it will be paid into another bank and eventually presented for cash.

The process of credit creation is illustrated in Fig. 45. X pays £100 in cash into the bank. This allows the bank to make a loan of £900 to B. B now settles his debts to C and D of £400 and £500 respectively by sending them cheques. These cheques

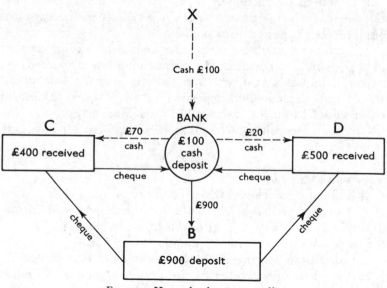

FIG. 45.—How a bank creates credit.

are paid into the bank. *C* withdraws cash rather heavily, £70; but this is compensated for by *D* who only withdraws £20 in cash. This leaves £10 cash – enough to cover the average withdrawal which *X* is likely to make. At the same time as these cash withdrawals are being made, other cash is being paid in, thereby maintaining the 10 per cent ratio.

In practice there are many banks, but for the purpose of credit creation they are virtually one bank, because they are able to eliminate a large demand for cash from each other by their clearing arrangements through the London Clearing House. Moreover, banks keep in line with one another as regards their credit creation. Were one bank to adopt, say, a 6 per cent cash ratio, it would find that because its customers were making such a large volume of payments to persons who banked elsewhere, it would be continually called upon to settle a debit with the other banks in cash at the end of the day's clearing. Its cash reserve at the Bank of England would therefore fall so low that it would have to modify its lending policy. (In fact, this form of competition is ruled out because all the U.K. banks are required by the authorities to maintain a minimum 8 per cent cash ratio.)

The effect of lending on the bank's balance-sheet

Suppose that the receipt of the £100 in cash and the loan to *B* are the sole activities of the bank so far. We ignore shareholders' capital. Its balance-sheet will then be as follows:

Liabilities	£	Assets	£
Deposits:			
Deposit account	100	Cash in till	100
Current account	900	Advances	900
	1,000		1,000

The advance to *B* is an asset; it is an outstanding debt. On the other hand, his account has been credited with a deposit of £900 – just as though he has paid it in. It can be seen, therefore, that *every loan creates a deposit*.

II. CONSIDERATIONS DETERMINING A BANK'S LENDING POLICY

In practice the structure of the bank's assets is more varied than that above. This can be explained as follows.

Creating deposits in order to lend at a profit entails certain risks. In the first place, the loan may not be repaid. Secondly, and more important, there may be a run on the bank for cash, the original depositor wishing to withdraw his £100, or B, C and D requiring between them an abnormally large amount of cash. Any suggestion that the bank could not meet these demands would lead to such a loss of confidence that other depositors would ask for cash, and the bank would have to close its doors.

The bank, therefore, is limited in its lending policy both quantitively and qualitatively. Not only must loans be limited to $11\frac{1}{2}$ times the cash reserve, but they must afford adequate *security, liquidity and profitability*.

As regards security, the bank endeavours not to lend if there is any risk of inability to repay. While it usually requires collateral, e.g. an insurance policy, the deeds of a house, or share certificates, this is chiefly to strengthen its demand for repayment against an evasive borrower rather than to serve as a safeguard against default.

Liquidity and profitability pull in opposite directions – the shorter the period of the loan, the greater the bank's liquidity, but the less it will earn by way of interest. The difficulty is resolved by a compromise: (1) loans are divided among different types of borrower and for different periods of time; (2) the different types of loan are kept fairly close to carefully worked-out proportions. In short, the bank maintains a 'portfolio' of assets (Fig. 46).

It must be emphasised that, apart from cash and bank buildings, these assets are covered only by credit created by the bank. For example, Treasury bills and government securities are paid for by cheques which will increase the accounts of the sellers. If they are new issues, there is an addition to the government account at the Bank of England; if they are old issues, the bank is merely taking over from somebody else a loan already made to the government. In writing these cheques,

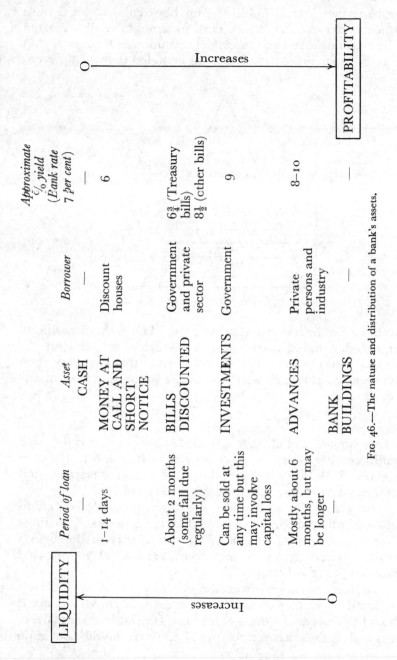

Period of loan	Asset	Borrower	Approximate % yield (Bank rate 7 per cent)
—	CASH	—	—
1–14 days	MONEY AT CALL AND SHORT NOTICE	Discount houses	6
About 2 months (some fall due regularly)	BILLS DISCOUNTED	Government and private sector	6¾ (Treasury bills) 8½ (other bills)
Can be sold at any time but this may involve capital loss	INVESTMENTS	Government	9
Mostly about 6 months, but may be longer	ADVANCES	Private persons and industry	8–10
—	BANK BUILDINGS	—	—

LIQUIDITY ← Increases   Increases → PROFITABILITY

FIG. 46.—The nature and distribution of a bank's assets.

the bank increases its liabilities, for book-entry deposits have to be created to cover them. This 'pyramid of credit', created to buy earning assets and to make loans upon an 8 per cent cash basis, is shown in Fig. 47. It should be noted that the different

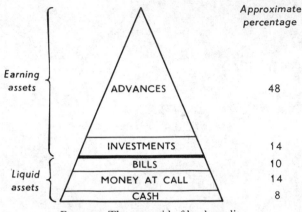

FIG. 47.—The pyramid of bank credit.

assets are not held in equal proportions. The authorities simply require that liquid assets do not fall below 28 per cent. In point of fact, the banks could safely reduce their liquidity ratio (to about 25 per cent) and add to the proportion lent on advances.

Modification of the cash-ratio approach

Our explanation of how a bank creates credit has followed traditional lines – credit bears a fixed relationship to the cash reserves. This approach is the easiest to understand and conforms closely to what happens in most countries.

However, while in Britain the basic principles of credit creation still hold true, some modification is necessary to allow for modern banking practice. The peculiarity of the British banks' position stems largely from the special nature and importance of the Treasury bill.

The Treasury bill is, from the banks' point of view, almost as liquid as cash, for cash can be easily secured against it should the necessity arise. While the convention of an 8 per cent cash ratio still remains, the 28 per cent liquid-asset ratio

(covering cash, money at call, and bills discounted) has become
the more important figure This is because: (1) the monetary
authorities now regard cash simply as the small change of the
monetary system, and vary it according to the needs of trade;
(2) banks are more concerned with their general liquidity
position rather than the one item, cash, when deciding upon
their lending policy. In particular, they watch their holding of
Treasury bills.

This means that the banks, instead of creating credit up to
$11\frac{1}{2}$ times their holding of cash, can only create credit up to
roughly $2\frac{1}{3}$ times their holding of liquid assets.

External limitations on a bank's lending

So far we have merely looked at the internal decisions of
the bank. It seeks to achieve the best possible compromise
between liquidity and profitability. Given that there are
sufficient credit-worthy borrowers to take up all the loans
available, it will create credit up to $2\frac{1}{3}$ times its holding of
liquid assets.

But the size of the liquid assets held by the commercial banks
as a whole will be determined by external factors. While the
amount of cash held by the public for its own needs outside the
banking system and the quantity of bills of exchange held by
institutions other than the banks will have some influence, the
determining factor will be the policy of the Bank of England
operating in conjunction with the Treasury. It is the central
monetary authorities which determine the overall supply of
cash and Treasury bills, thereby putting a limit on how much
credit can be created. How this is achieved will now be examined.

III. CONTROL OF THE MONEY SUPPLY

The Bank of England is the 'central bank' of the U.K.; that is,
it is the institution which, on behalf of the government,
exercises the ultimate control over the policies of the commercial banks and other financial institutions. In the words of
the Radcliffe Report, 'The Bank of England stands as the
market operator between the public sector (to which it belongs)
and the private sector.' For the sake of simplicity, therefore,

we can take the 'central monetary authorities' as being synonymous with the Bank of England.

As the central bank, the Bank of England carries out a wide variety of functions on behalf of the government. Thus it issues notes, keeps the central government accounts, manages the Exchange Equalisation Account and administers exchange control, represents the government in international financial transactions, and administers the national debt. As we shall see, all these functions have a bearing on its main function of managing the monetary system in accordance with government policy. Here we concentrate on its method of varying the supply of money.

(1) *Open-market operations*

Since only the Bank of England can issue notes, it is the ultimate source of cash. Over and above this, however, it can control how this cash is distributed between its own holding and that left with the private sector by open-market operations. Any decrease in the cash reserves held in the private sector will be reflected mainly in less cash being held by the commercial banks. This will, as we have seen, reduce their ability to create credit.

The easiest way to obtain cash from a person is to sell him something he wants. This is the policy adopted by the Bank of England when it wishes to decrease the supply of money. Provided the price is sufficiently attractive, banks and their customers are always prepared to buy Treasury bills and government securities. Hence whenever the Bank of England wishes to reduce the cash reserves, it can offer more Treasury bills at the weekly tender or sell securities on the Stock Exchange. These are known as its 'open-market operations'. Bills and securities are purchased by the banks and their customers, and are paid for by cheques payable to the Bank of England. As a result, the cash reserves of the banks (held in accounts at the Bank of England) are decreased. The reverse applies when the Bank restricts its weekly sale of bills or buys securities.

(2) *Funding*

Until the Radcliffe Report (1959), the major method of monetary control consisted of open-market operations aimed at the cash base. Cash is the only completely liquid asset, and so it was assumed that banks created credit almost entirely upon the basis of their holdings of cash. The supply of credit could be adjusted, therefore, by simply operating on the banks' cash reserves.

But, as we have seen, banks now base their credit-creation policy more on their holding of liquid assets than on their holding of one item only – cash. And, of these liquid assets, Treasury bills have a special importance, both as regards their quality and, in recent years, as regards their quantity.

As regards their quality, Treasury bills are, to the banks, almost as good as cash. This is because the Bank of England has, by work and deed, let it be known that cash is always immediately available against Treasury bills, although its terms may differ. The reasons why the Bank of England takes this line are:

(a) It is the 'lender of last resort'. Hence, in order to avoid financial panics by runs on the banks, it provides indirect help through the discount houses.

(b) It is responsible for influencing economic activity through monetary policy. Frequent changes in the rate of interest might have unwanted effects on expectations of entrepreneurs, etc. Thus to prevent interest rates rising when banks are short of cash for reasons other than deliberate government policy, the Bank will give direct help (the 'open back-door') to the banks through its Special Buyer who buys bills and short-term government stock at the current rate of interest.

(c) The Bank of England is responsible for managing government debt. Here it is cheaper to borrow short-term through Treasury bills, and increasing the liquidity of such bills enables them to be sold on more favourable terms.

The significance of this aspect of Treasury bills is that the authorities cannot carry out a policy of restraint by open-market operations in Treasury bills – the loss of cash is simply made good by another asset which is regarded as being almost as liquid. Thus neither total deposits in general nor advances in particular are reduced. The authorities have to concentrate, not on the cash ratio, but on the liquidity ratio. It is the latter, fixed since 1963 at 28 per cent, which is the significant figure from the point of view of credit creation. Of the liquid assets, Treasury bills tend to be the most important, and the quantity held by the banks must be the main object of the authorities' attention.

The Bank of England can keep the banks short of Treasury bills in two ways. First, without reducing the overall supply of Treasury bills, it can try to confine them to institutions outside the commercial banks. If it then carries out open-market operations by selling Treasury bills, it will draw in cash from the banks (as the banks' customers pay for the bills), but the banks will not receive any liquid asset in return. (This was more or less what happened before 1914 when commercial bills formed the bulk of bills of exchange. Not only were banks deprived of cash as a result of open-market operations, but the higher short-term rate of interest caused merchants to discount their bills abroad at relatively cheaper rates, thereby reducing the short-term assets available in London and thus the liquidity of the commercial banks.)

Now while industrial and commercial companies, insurance companies, non-bank financial intermediaries (e.g. discount houses), government departments, Commonwealth and foreign banks do purchase Treasury bills as a means of holding short-term balances, much of this holding (e.g. by the discount houses) is of a temporary nature. Thus with the present scale of government borrowing, the banks' holding of Treasury bills must form a considerable proportion. Indeed this predominance of the banks in the holding of Treasury bills has been reinforced by a fairly recent development. Brokers have emerged in short-term local authority loans, and the outside short-term lenders have used this new outlet for their funds. This has meant that the banks have been left to take up the supply of Treasury bills.

The result is that the Bank of England has to follow the second method – reducing the overall supply of Treasury bills offered at the weekly tender. But the government still needs funds. Thus reducing the supply of Treasury bills necessitates offering medium- and long-term bonds instead of issuing Treasury bills. This is known as 'funding'.

Funding, however, presents three main difficulties: (a) it adds to the cost of government borrowing; (b) it raises the long-term rate of interest, with all the disadvantages this entails (see

Chapter 13); (c) if the commercial banks hold liquid assets well above the required minimum, funding will have to occur on a large scale, and this will have a violent effect on interest rates. It is only since the late 1960s, therefore, when the government allowed the long-term rate of interest to rise, that there has been any considerable funding of the short-term debt.

(3) 'Special deposits': an alternative to varying the liquidity ratio

Instead, to get over the difficulty of the considerable quantity of Treasury bills in the hands of the banks, the Bank of England in 1960 made use of a new device, 'special deposits'. This requires the banks to deposit with the Bank of England a given percentage of their total deposits. In effect, this means that the Bank requires a higher liquidity ratio, for although special deposits earn interest at the current Treasury bill rate, they do not count as part of the banks' liquid assets. A 1 per cent call results in approximately an £80 million reduction in total deposits.

In theory, a call for special deposits should ensure that funding operations exert pressure on the liquid-asset position more quickly with the result that they do not have to be so drastic. In practice, however, the device has come up against a major difficulty.

If the banks create credit on the basis of their liquid-asset ratio, it follows that the main 'cushion' in times of stringency is 'investments'. If these are large, and any capital loss on their sale is outweighed by the return that can be obtained on 'advances', special deposits can be raised, not by squeezing advances, but by selling investments.

This was the position in 1960. Investments were 20 per cent of total deposits and the banks parted with them when the demand for special deposits was made. The banks' task was made easier by the government which, rather than let the rate of interest rise, bought bonds as they were put on the market. Consequently, advances were not reduced, and spending was not curbed.

Therefore, in 1961 when further special deposits were called for, the Bank of England told the banks that the adjustment had to be made along specified lines – by reducing advances and not by selling investments. In practice, this means that it is now 'moral suasion' (as requests are frequently termed) which is the really effective weapon. The call for special deposits, like bank rate, is merely a 'warning shot'. The reasons for moral suasion must, however, be postponed to Chapter 13. For our present purposes, we can leave monetary policy at the point where the supply of bank deposits is controlled by varying the quantity of cash and Treasury bills held by the commercial banks, or by changes in the 'special deposits' required – the equivalent of varying the liquidity ratio as practised in many other countries.

IV. 'NEAR' MONEY

So far we have conducted our analysis in terms of the only *completely* liquid asset – money, consisting of cash and bank deposits. But does this mean that we have now covered all the factors governing the supply of money? In terms of 'true' money, yes; in terms of liquidity as a whole (and this is what we are really interested in), no. Such liquidity is afforded by assets other than money. Moreover, it is constantly changing.

In practice, liquidity is a matter of degree. Strictly speaking, sums in my deposit account at a bank are not completely 'money'; they are subject to seven days' notice of withdrawal, so that I cannot write a cheque on them. Nevertheless, a phone call to my bank manager is usually sufficient to have such deposits transferred right away to my current account, subject only to loss of interest. Such an arrangement means that I have to keep less 'true' money in my current account to cover my liquidity requirements for the three motives described in Chapter 8.

But now that we have started to enlarge our concept of money, why stop at deposit accounts? If I hold local authority bonds, shares in a public company, or even an insurance policy, there are means of turning them into cash. Indeed, a house. that is partly paid for provides some liquidity, for money can be raised on the security of it. In short, all assets afford some degree of liquidity to their owners, and some are so liquid that they can be regarded as 'near' money. Their existence means that the demand for 'true' money can be correspondingly less, and we shall assume that this has been allowed for in our demand curves, which therefore depict the demand for 'true' money.

Furthermore, liquidity in the economy is constantly changing. First, new intermediaries come into being to provide a market in certain assets, thereby increasing the liquidity of those assets. Thus, in recent years, traders have become more liquid through the development of factor houses to which trade debts can be sold immediately for cash, certain brokers specialise in buying and selling local authority bonds, finance companies now provide finance for house purchase, and second-mortgage brokers have become active in providing funds against the security of a house. Secondly, the attitude of institutions other than banks to what is a safe margin of liquidity can influence the provision of funds and the amount of 'near' money in existence. For example, suppose a person deposits £500 in a building society. This means that the society has more funds to lend. If it maintains a safe liquid ratio of 20 per cent, £400 is lent and, when this is spent on purchasing a house, it enters into the income flow. If the recipients as a whole save a quarter of this income and deposit it with the building society, the society's deposits will again increase by £100 and, of this, £80 will be re-lent. As the process continues, the original deposit of £500 leads to total credit creation (and secondary investments) of £625. Were the building society to adopt a safe liquidity ratio of 10 per cent, the multiple credit creation would amount to £645.

SUGGESTED READING

W. M. Dacey, *Money under Review* (Hutchinson, 1960) chs 1–3.
Radcliffe Report, *Report on the Working of the Monetary System*, Cmnd 827 (H.M.S.O., 1959) chs 4 5.
R. S. Sayers, *Modern Banking*, 7th ed. (Oxford U.P., 1967) chs 1–5, 7, 8.
B. Tew, *Monetary Theory* (Routledge & Kegan Paul, 1969) chs 1–2.

CHAPTER 10

THE DETERMINATION OF THE RATE OF INTEREST IN THE COMPLETE KEYNESIAN SYSTEM

I. THE CLASSICAL ECONOMISTS' EXPLANATION OF THE RATE OF INTEREST

WE commence by summarising the classical economists' explanation of the rate of interest.

To the classical school, that rate of interest was the price of savings, and like any other price, it was determined by demand and supply.

Demand for savings originated in the productivity of capital assets. An investment demand curve for savings at different rates of interest could be drawn. The lower the rate of interest, the greater the demand for investment; the explanation followed very closely our explanation in Chapter 6 of the MEI curve.

The supply of savings depended upon 'thrift'. To most people 'a bird in the hand is worth two in the bush'. This preference for present as opposed to future consumption was referred to as 'time preference', and a reward – interest – had to be paid to overcome it.

Now as savings increase, present income declines relative to future income, and time preference increases. It followed, therefore, that in order to expand savings, a higher rate of interest had to be offered. This gave a supply curve of savings, savings expanding as the rate of interest rose (Fig. 14).

The equilibrium rate of interest (determined by the intersection of the demand and supply curves) was the rate at which the marginal productivity of capital equalled the time preference of income-spenders.

Criticisms of the classical theory

(1) The volume of saving was assumed to be a function of the rate of interest. The influence of the level of income on saving was ignored, although this is likely to be far more important.

(2) It assumed that investment is interest-elastic.

(3) It implied that the MEI curve is fairly stable; but in fact the curve changes its position frequently through changes in expectations.

(4) It ignored short-term institutional influences on the rate of interest. But:

(a) joint-stock banks keep to fairly stable rates, discriminating in their choice of borrowers;

(b) the government influences the rate of interest, e.g. by bank rate and open-market operations.

(5) It assumed that the whole of income saved is actually lent to entrepreneurs. But besides being reluctant to save, people are reluctant to lend – they prefer to be liquid in certain circumstances. Thus lending involves two decisions. First, whether to consume or not to consume (that is, to save). Second, how to hold one's assets – in money or loans. Interest is paid, not just for abstinence, but for the inconvenience of parting with a perfectly liquid asset. This is the starting-point of Keynes's theory.

II. KEYNES'S 'STOCK' APPROACH TO THE RATE OF INTEREST

Introduction

The classical economists treated money solely as a passive medium of exchange – a 'numéraire'. Money was wanted simply to effect transactions. Full employment was implicitly assumed and so any increase in the quantity of money meant that more money would be offered against a given volume of transactions. The result was a rise in the general price level. This is the basis of the Quantity Theory of Money which we shall study in more detail in Chapter 15.

Keynes disagreed with this theory in two main ways. First, he did not accept full employment and thus the volume of transactions as given. Second, he argued that money does not fulfil merely a passive role as a numéraire; it is a form of asset, different from other assets in that it is perfectly liquid. Consequently, people have a demand for 'idle' balances of money, their demand varying according to their estimate of the future price of bonds. As a result, money plays an active role in the capital market, and in doing so determines the pure rate of interest – the 'bench-mark' around which rates of interest for all types of securities range.

It should be emphasised that Keynes was concerned solely with short-term fluctuations in the level of activity produced by the trade cycle. He was not concerned with long-term secular growth. Such short-term fluctuations are produced by relatively short-term changes in investment which, in their turn, can be brought about partly by changes in the long-term rate of interest. Thus Keynes sought to explain the causes of short-run changes in the long-term rate of interest.

The explanation can be couched either in terms of the price of bonds or in terms of the rate of interest – for both are simply different sides of the same coin (*see* p. 120).

The determination of the price of bonds

Since liquidity is a desirable attribute in an asset, money can be regarded as an acceptable way of holding wealth, differing from others only in that, being perfectly liquid, it does not earn a return. A person, therefore, has to arrange his portfolio of assets according to the emphasis he puts on liquidity as

MONEY	Time deposits	Building society deposits	Local authority bonds and Treasury bills	Debentures	Shares in companies	Land and real assets

FIG. 48.—Alternative ways of holding wealth.

opposed to yield. If he wants complete liquidity, he holds money; if he prefers some degree of return, he holds other assets. There is a whole spectrum over which he can exercise his choice, as illustrated in Fig. 48.

To concentrate on the role of money and to eliminate complications arising because loans may involve different periods and risk, we shall assume that all assets are undated government stock, which we shall term 'bonds'. Thus we have a model in which there are only two ways of holding wealth – bonds or money (Fig. 49). The price of bonds will also give us the rate of interest on riskless, undated securities (*see* p. 120).

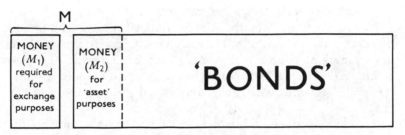

FIG. 49.—The alternative of holding wealth as money or 'bonds'.

On the capital market there will be bonds offered for sale. Some will come out of the existing stock held by people; others will be new bonds arising from current government borrowing. But their price will be determined by demand and supply, just as the price of rubber, tin, wool, cotton and any other commodity is in their respective markets.

How much money people have will depend upon the total supply of money in the economy and how much they want to hold for the transactions and precautionary motives. In our earlier terminology, M_2 (the amount of money available for speculation) $= M$ (the total money supply) $- M_1$ (the amount of money held for active balances), though, as we have already indicated, there is no hard-and-fast line dividing the two (Fig. 49).

People holding money bid on the capital market for the bonds offered. If they hold on to their money, they are not bidding for bonds; if they bid for bonds, they do not want to hold money.

At the end of a day's dealing, all bonds may have changed hands. But this need not be so. If the price of bonds is low, some would-be sellers may prefer to hold on to them. On the other hand, if the price of bonds is high, some would-be purchasers may prefer to retain their money. But a price will have been found at which people have finished dealing – nobody will wish to exchange more bonds against money, and nobody will wish to exchange more money against bonds. There is equilibrium at this price. This price is the inverse of the current 'pure' rate of interest – the bench-mark referred to earlier.

The justification of the Keynesian stock approach

It can be seen from the above analysis that a change in the demand for money relative to bonds, given the stock of money and of bonds, will bring about a change in the rate of interest. Thus, if it becomes less attractive to hold money, the price of bonds will rise – that is, the rate of interest will fall.

But changes in the relative quantities of money and bonds, that is, in the sizes of the stocks of each, will also produce variations in the rate of interest. If, for instance, the quantity of money increases and the demand for money and the stock of bonds remain unchanged, more money will be offered against bonds, with the result that bond prices will rise. Looked at in an alternative way, the owners of wealth cannot, at the given rate of interest, be induced to hold the whole stock of money. Thus there will have to be a reduction in the inducement *not* to hold money, that is, in the rate of interest. Similarly, if the quantity of bonds increases, the demand for bonds and the supply of money remaining unchanged, the price of bonds will fall. Looked at in an alternative way, at the given rate of interest owners of wealth cannot be induced to hold the whole stock of bonds. Hence the inducement to hold bonds, that is, the rate of interest, will have to rise.

In practice, stocks, both of money and of bonds, are not subject to great variations except over fairly considerable periods of time. The supply of money is controlled by the government (see Chapter 9). The supply of bonds coming on to the market comes chiefly from existing stocks of old bonds.

In comparison, the flow of new bonds (issued by the government as it borrows) is small. Current government borrowing will therefore have little impact on the rate of interest. It is thus the supply from the existing stock of bonds, together with demand, which determine the price of bonds at any one time – *and the price of any new issues follows this price.* Keynes's stock theory can therefore be contrasted sharply with the classical theory, where the rate of interest is determined by current *flows* of supply and demand.

We can illustrate by reference to the stock market in 1968. The corporation tax had made it cheaper to raise capital by debentures rather than by the issue of shares, and new share issues dried up. A subsequent all-round increase in the demand for equities, however, produced a rise in the price of old shares, and this meant that any new shares could command a high price on the market. This, together with the high rate of interest on debentures, made it profitable once more to raise capital through the issue of shares.

The significance of the demand for money

Keynes considers, therefore, that it is much more realistic to analyse the rate of interest from the point of view of the variable which is most likely to change over the short period – the demand for money. And here he stresses the role of speculation.

In the market for bonds there will be many persons whose main interest will be in their future price. Indeed, as we have seen, Keynes thinks the speculative element dominates all other considerations. If so, then the demand for bonds is largely the result of the present price of bonds. Or, the demand for money is primarily a function of the current rate of interest.

Instead of approaching the rate of interest through the demand for and supply of bonds, therefore, it is possible to approach it through the demand for and supply of money, the alternative asset.

The demands for active and idle balances can be combined in a single curve (Fig. 44, repeated in Fig. 50). The demand for money for active balances is indicated by the distance of the vertical sections of the demand curve from the y-axis. Thus, if income increases from Y_1 to Y_2, the increase in the demand for active balances is equal to the horizontal difference between the two. To this demand for active balances must be added the demand for idle balances – the sloping portion of the curve.

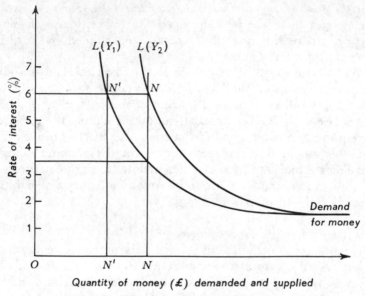

Fig. 50.—The determination of the interest rate.

The supply of money is fixed by the government and the banking authorities (*see* Chapter 9). Suppose it is equal to ON (Fig. 50). If the level of income is low, Y_1, the rate of interest is $3\frac{1}{2}$ per cent. With a higher level of income, Y_2, more money is demanded for active balances. This leaves less for idle balances and the rate of interest rises to 6 per cent, and so on.

A smaller supply of money, ON', would produce a rate of interest of 6 per cent with Y_1.

The structure of interest rates

It merely remains to remove our earlier simplification that the only type of asset in existence apart from money is bonds.

In practice people can put their money into a range of assets each varying in the degree of liquidity and lender's risk involved. These assets can, however, be regarded as fairly close substitutes for one another, and there will be a rate of return on each depending on the relevant demand and supply schedules. These rates will be interrelated because, since they are close substitutes, the demand for one type of asset will be affected by the rate of return on the asset most similar to it. For instance, a rise in the rate of return on short-dated government stock will cause a movement of funds to it from its immediate close substitutes, such as Treasury bills. This sets up a ripple running through the whole structure of interest rates until eventually equilibrium has been restored. Of course, this ripple could easily start by a change in the demand for or supply of money. It is likely to have its first effect on short-term (three-month) securities, and eventually the long-term rate is brought into line, though this may occur only over a considerable period of time.

III. AN APPRAISAL OF KEYNES'S THEORY OF THE RATE OF INTEREST

The classical economists held that:
(1) the rate of interest was determined by the interaction of saving and investment;
(2) since there was no speculative demand for money, the supply of money had a direct impact on prices.

Keynes disagreed. His view was that the relationship of saving and investment determined the level of income. The rate of interest was a monetary phenomenon depending upon the demand for and the supply of money. He emphasised changes in the demand for money – a factor largely ignored by the classical economists who failed to appreciate fully the role of money as a liquid store of wealth. Moreover, he held that any change in the supply of money would have only an indirect impact on the level of activity or prices – through the change which would result in the rate of interest and therefore in investment spending. Finally, Keynes held, the price of new issues on the stock market was determined by the price at which old stock was currently selling.

In fact both schools of thought have a measure of right and wrong. Three major questions have to be answered:

(1) Can saving and investment influence the rate of interest even under the Keynesian model?

(2) Can an increase in the supply of money have a direct effect on consumption and investment, and thus on the level of activity?

(3) May not, in practice, changes in the flow of different assets on to the market have a greater effect on their price than Keynes indicated? We will deal with each question in turn.

IV. THE INFLUENCE OF SAVING AND INVESTMENT UNDER THE KEYNESIAN MODEL

The truth is that Keynes left his argument concerning the rate of interest more or less where we ended section II of this chapter. The rate of interest was determined as shown by Fig. 50.

But this does not give us a determinate rate of interest. It simply says that, if we know the level of income, the demand for and the supply of money will tell us the rate of interest. But it overlooks the fact that we cannot tell the level of income until we know when the rate of interest is, for the rate of interest affects investment spending (and perhaps consumption spending too). Our equilibrium rate of interest must satisfy simultaneously the real forces of investment and saving (the flow approach), and the monetary forces of liquidity preference and the supply of money (the stock approach).

The full equilibrium position can be depicted by linking Fig. 30, 21, 41 and 43 around a single origin (Fig. 51).

Fig. 51 is interpreted as follows:

I. Investment is shown as a function of the rate of interest and marginal efficiency of investment. With a rate of interest equal to i and expectations, etc., fixing the MEI curve, we have a level of investment equal to OI.

II. In equilibrium, investment = saving. The $S(Y)$ curve shows the propensity to save at different levels of income. For saving to equal investment OI, the level of income must be OY.

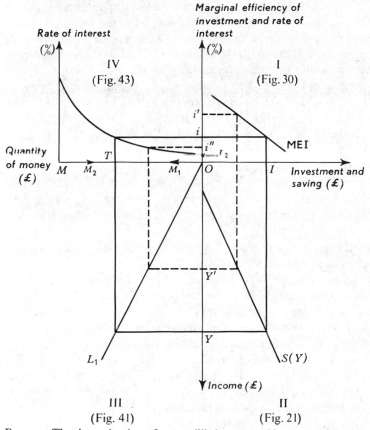

FIG. 51.—The determination of an equilibrium rate of interest and income level.

III. At different levels of income, the demand for M_1 is given by the L_1 curve. Thus at an income level of OY, the demand for M_1 equals OT.

IV. The total supply of money, fixed by the authorities at OM, is measured from the origin. From M we measure the demand for M_2 as a function of the rate of interest; this is shown by the curve L_2. An increase in the demand for M_1 means that less money is available to satisfy M_2. The rate of interest therefore rises. With a demand for

M_1 equal to OT, the rate of interest will be Oi. This means that the real forces of saving and investment (which largely determine Y) and the monetary forces (which largely determine i) are in harmony.

We can now see how changes in investment or in saving can, through their influence or the level of income, affect the rate of interest, other functions remaining unaltered.

Suppose entrepreneurs become more pessimistic as regards profits. The MEI curve moves to the left. This will produce a lower level of investment and, given the same desire to save, will cause the level of income to fall There is thus less demand for M_1, and more money is left over for M_2. As a result the rate of interest falls – as the classical economists predicted, but via a different mechanism. (This fall in the rate of interest will produce some increase in investment, and so on, but a new equilibrium will eventually be reached at a level of income less than OY.)

An increase in saving will produce a similar result, for the $S(Y)$ curve will move to the right.

As an exercise, you should work out the effect of:

(a) an economising in active balances M_1;

(b) an increase in the quantity of money by the authorities;

(c) a decrease in liquidity preference for M_2 balances.

Indeed, this diagram is useful for indicating the effects on the system of any given change in a variable. It should be noted, however, that it depicts *simultaneous* changes, not *sequential* changes; that is, it is a static equilibrium model, not one which depicts accurately the path of change.

This can be seen immediately if we transform the quadrant diagram (Fig. 51) into the more usual *IS/LM* diagram (Figs. 52–54). In quadrants I and II we see the real flows determining the level of income and thereby having an influence on the rate of interest; in quadrants III and IV we have the monetary forces, the demand for and supply of money, which influence the level of income through their effect on the rate of interest. We can combine (a) the real forces in a single diagram, and (b) the monetary forces in a similar diagram.

(a) If we are given the MEI and saving curves, we can, from quadrants I and II, read off the level of income which results from any rate of interest. Thus if the rate of interest is Oi, the level of income which will result is OY (Fig. 51). If the rate of interest rises to Oi', a new level of income OY' results. By continuing this process we can derive the curve IS (Fig. 52) – the locus of all combinations of i and y for which, given the investment and saving schedules, investment equals saving.

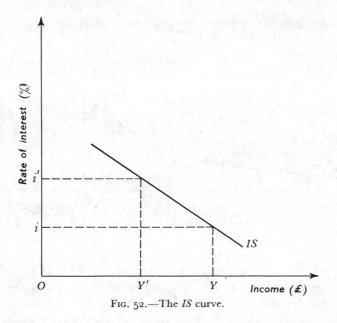

FIG. 52.—The IS curve.

(*b*) We can carry out a similar procedure for the monetary forces – the demand for and supply of money as given in quadrants III and IV. Since the quantity of money is fixed by the authorities, and we know the $L(Y)$ and $L(i)$ curves, we can read off the rates of interest which will result from any level of income (Fig. 51). Thus, when the level of income is OY, the rate of interest which must result from the monetary side is Oi. In Fig. 53, if the level of income is OY', the rate of interest which must result from the monetary side is Oi'', and so on. Thus we derive a curve, called an LM curve because it is the product of the liquidity curves and the supply of money.

It is the locus of all combinations of income and the
rate of interest for which the demand for money equals
the supply.

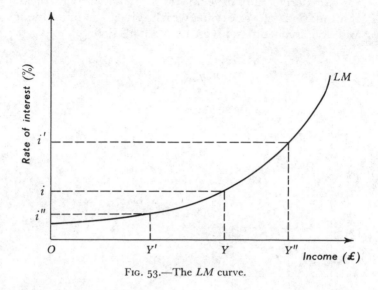

FIG. 53.—The *LM* curve.

In equilibrium, the rate of interest and the level of income
which result must satisfy simultaneously the investment,
saving and demand for money schedules, and the given supply
of money. There is only one point at which this can occur –
where the *IS* and *LM* curves cut one another when they are
combined on the same diagram (Fig. 54). Hence the rate of
interest is Oi and the level of income OY.

We conclude, therefore, that saving and investment do have
an influence on the rate of interest – but not directly as the
classical economists thought. It is an indirect influence via
the level of income and the consequent change in the demand
for money which leaves more or less to satisfy the demand for
liquid balances. (As an exercise you should trace out the effects
on the *IS/LM* diagram of: (*a*) an improvement in entrepreneurs'
expectations; (*b*) a decrease in the propensity to save; (*c*) the
payment of wages monthly instead of weekly; (*d*) an increase in
liquidity preference – for 'idle' balances.)

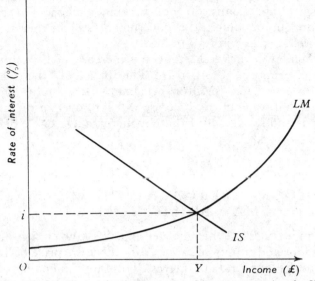

Fig. 54.—The equilibrium level of income and interest rate using the *IS–LM* approach.

V. THE POSSIBILITY OF A DIRECT EFFECT OF AN INCREASE IN THE MONEY SUPPLY ON CONSUMPTION AND INVESTMENT

So far we have followed the Keynesian view that any change in the supply of money will only influence AD indirectly – through its effect on the rate of interest, and thus on the level of investment spending. But it is possible for an increase in the supply of money to have a direct effect:

(1) People may feel that the increase in the supply of money will have inflationary consequences. As a result, the demand for idle balances falls; the L_2 curve moves to the left as people now spend some of their idle balances on real goods.

(2) Under present-day institutional arrangements, it is not the rate of interest but rather rationing by the banks and government controls over credit facilities which limit consumption and investment spending. Any increase in the supply

of money thus directly provides the *means* for an increase in such spending. Loans do not become cheaper but simply easier to obtain, unless the government still further tightens its controls, e.g. over hire-purchase.

(3) While Keynes held that any increase in the supply of money is simply absorbed in idle balances, the Chicago school of economists (Milton Friedman, H. G. Johnson, etc.) consider that some of the increase will spill over to the marker for goods and services and thereby increase aggregate demand directly (*see* p. 227).

VI. THE WEAKNESS OF THE KEYNESIAN 'STOCK' APPROACH – WHEN 'FLOWS' MAY BE SIGNIFICANT

The simple model of this chapter explains how changes in the demand for and supply of money can affect the price of 'bonds' and thus the 'pure' rate of interest. This rate can be regarded as the 'bench-mark' around which other rates take up a position according to the relative risk and liquidity of the particular asset concerned. In short, from the model depicted in Fig. 49, we move to the more realistic situation of many types of asset shown in Fig. 48.

Equilibrium exists in the 'asset market' because the prices of the different assets are such that nobody wishes to hold more of one or less of another. Furthermore, this equilibrium can be achieved because any change in the demand for or supply of one particular asset (including money) will send ripples throughout the whole structure until once more equilibrium is restored. In practice, flows of newly-created assets will not in the short run be large enough to have any significant effect on the price of the asset, for their impact will be diffused throughout the whole of the asset market where 'old' assets are the dominant source of supply.

Now the assumption which lies behind this model is that the market in assets is perfect – people have complete knowledge of prices ruling in every part of the market, act solely on the basis of price, and can switch easily between different types of asset whether they are asset-holders (lenders) or liability-holders (borrowers). Equilibrium results throughout the whole of the market (which can be regarded as a single market) because people are able to distribute their assets and liabilities according to relative prices and their preferences.

In practice, however, such perfection does not exist. Asset-holders may not switch their holdings in response to a price change elsewhere because of lack of knowledge, inertia, or the cost of switching. Borrowers are often hampered by institutional factors in switching liabilities, and frequently loans are allocated not on the basis of price but by the ability to negotiate.

Take, for instance, debentures, the rate of interest on which Keynes would regard as significant to the level of investment. An increase in the issue of debentures will increase the *flow* on to the market. This will tend to depress their price, and the rate of interest will rise. However, in our model ripples will pass through the *whole* of the asset market, and the impact on debentures will be damped down.

But what if barriers exist round the *debenture* market so that the effects of the increased flow cannot extend to other assets? Now the full impact is felt in one particular part of the market only (alternatively the debenture market can be regarded as a separate market); as a result, the price of debentures may fall considerably. In practice, such imperfections do occur. Private companies, for instance, may find it difficult to borrow through debentures because they do not have sufficient sup-porting assets as security, or because profits fluctuate so much that they cannot afford to be highly geared. They may also find it difficult to sell equities, because too little is known by outsiders about the company and its prospects, or because the directors do not wish to relinquish control by extending voting shares. Such barriers exist round other types of market, some more so than others, e.g. real property.

We conclude, therefore:

(1) The Keynesian 'stock' approach provides a simple model showing how equilibrium can be reached in the asset market *generally*. It emphasises the demand for money, stressing the part this plays in determining the equilibrium rate of interest.

(2) In practice, the *different types of asset* markets may be hedged round with barriers. When this happens, any change of demand or supply in a market will have a greater effect than

if there were complete freedom of movement between all the different asset markets, giving virtually one market.

(3) Because of such barriers, a change in the demand for or the supply of money may not, in the short run, especially have such a significant effect on certain asset prices (e.g. debentures) as Keynes imagined. Any effect on the level of investment will therefore be correspondingly less, and policy to regulate investment through altering the supply of money may come up against difficulties.

SUGGESTED READING

*G. Ackley, *Macroeconomic Theory* (Macmillan, New York, 1961) ch. 14.

F. S. Brooman, *Macroeconomics*, 4th ed. (Allen & Unwin, 1970) ch. 12.

A. H. Hansen, *A Guide to Keynes* (McGraw-Hill, 1953) ch. 7.

R. F. Harrod, *Money* (Macmillan, 1969) ch. 7.

M. G. Mueller (ed.), *Readings in Macroeconomics*, No. 12 by L. S. Ritter (Holt, Rinehart & Winston, 1969).

R. S. Sayers, *Modern Banking*, 7th ed. (Oxford U.P., 1967) ch. 10.

A. W. Stonier and D. C. Hague, *A Textbook of Economic Theory*, 3rd ed. (Longmans, 1964) ch. 23.

B. Tew, *Monetary Theory* (Routledge & Kegan Paul, 1969) chs 3-4.

CHAPTER 11

GOVERNMENT FINANCE AND THE LEVEL OF INCOME

It is now time to return to our discussion of the determination of the equilibrium level of income. Let us restate the condition of equilibrium under our simplifying assumptions. A given income level can be maintained only if there is sufficient investment to match saving out of that income. If investment is insufficient, income will be reduced until intended saving and investment are once more equal. Put mathematically, income is at an equilibrium level when:

$$C(Y) + \bar{I} = C(Y) + S(Y),$$

where $\bar{I}$ denotes a given level of planned investment, and $C(Y)$ and $S(Y)$ the functional relationships determined by the propensities to consume and save.

We now relax our assumption of no government activity. But we still assume: (a) no undistributed profits, (b) a closed economy.

The government can: (i) collect tax revenue, termed T; (ii) spend on goods and services, termed G. Transfer payments are regarded as negative taxes. Thus T is the net tax flow, that is, total taxes minus transfers. We shall now extend our national income analysis to show the effects of T and G on the level of income, and what happens when either is changed. Our investigation will provide the theoretical basis for fiscal policy, discussed in Chapter 14.

I. THE EFFECT OF GOVERNMENT REVENUE AND SPENDING ON THE CIRCULAR FLOW OF INCOME

The conditions of equilibrium

Government taxation, whether direct or indirect, represents, like saving, a 'leak' from the circular flow of income. On the other hand, spending by the government adds to aggregate demand; like investment, it is an 'injection'. These additional flows are shown in Fig. 55, where I, G and Y are assumed to be independent of income.

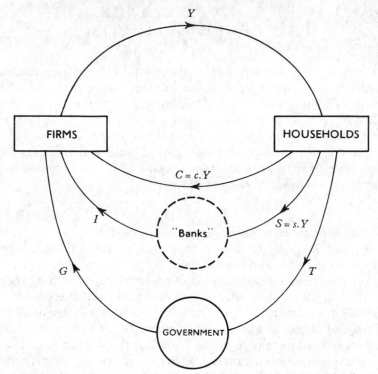

Fig. 55.—The circular flow of income including government expenditure and taxation.

An equilibrium level of income is reached when total injections equal total leaks. Hence, from the diagram, the condition is:

$$I + G = S + T.$$

Thus if:

(1) intended saving = investment, G must also equal T;

(2) intended saving is greater than investment, there is an equal excess of G over T, that is, a budget deficit;

(3) investment is greater than intended saving, there is an equal excess of T over G, that is, a budget surplus.

It follows that, where G and T are appreciable proportions of national income, the government has potentially powerful weapons with which to counteract changes in the level of activity. An expansion of income (e.g. when there is less than full employment) or a contraction (e.g. when there is inflationary excess demand) can be achieved by adjusting G or T or both together. If an expansion (reduction) of income is desired but consumption or private investment cannot be altered, the government can increase (decrease) G. Similar changes in income can be achieved by appropriate adjustments of T provided that private consumption responds to the new level of disposable income (*see* p. 213).

Complications

In practice, government policy is not so simple as merely estimating the deficiency (or excess) of spending in the private sector and adjusting government spending or taxation by an equivalent amount. The following complications have to be taken into account:

(1) *Changes in government spending may influence the consumption and investment functions.* If, for instance, any change in G acts as a substitute for private spending (e.g. education), or gives rise to a fear of inflation, it will affect the shape and position of the consumption curve.

(2) *Changes in the pattern of taxation may influence both the consumption and investment functions.* If, for instance, progressive taxes are decreased, people with high incomes will benefit most, and thus consumption will increase proportionately more at high income levels. Thus, in Fig. 56, the consumption function moves from C to C_1. On the other hand, a decrease in indirect taxes (especially those which are specific) will give proportionately more benefit at lower incomes, so that the consumption function changes from C to C_2.

Similarly, if the government lowers corporation tax or increases depreciation allowances, private investment may be stimulated.

(3) *Changes in government spending or taxation are subject to the multiplier.*

(4) *The whole of any change in taxation is unlikely to fall entirely on consumption.*

(5) *Taxation is not a constant but is likely itself to be related to income and expenditure.* Thus, as income rises, taxation is likely to yield more both through income taxes and expenditure taxes.

(6) *Changes in government spending may influence:* (a) the yield from taxation (through the resulting change in income); (b) other forms of government spending (e.g. the unemployed find work as income expands).

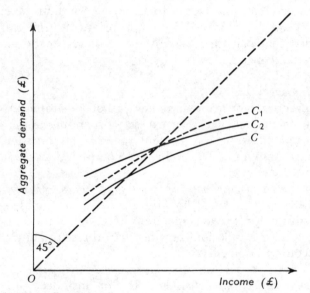

FIG. 56.—The effects of different tax cuts on the consumption function.

Assumptions

Because of the above complications, we must proceed with our analysis in stages. The following assumptions will apply throughout:

   (a) consumption is a constant proportion of disposable income;

(b) changes in government spending or taxation do not affect the propensity to consume or private investment;

(c) all post-tax net profits are distributed to shareholders, and therefore add to disposable income.

Further assumptions, and later relaxations of them, will be made as the analysis proceeds. The analysis will take the form of answers to a series of questions.

II. AUTONOMOUS CHANGES IN GOVERN- MENT SPENDING AND TAXATION

(1) *What will be the effect on income of autonomous changes in government spending?*

Assume:

(a) no taxation;

(b) no government transfer payments;

(c) an autonomous change in government spending on goods and services of ΔG.

Let us take as an example our original model in Chapter 7. Originally Y is in equilibrium at 10,000. The marginal and average propensities to consume $= 0.6Y$ at all levels of Y. Thus $C = 6,000$, $S = 4,000$ and $I = 4,000$. The government now starts spending at a rate of 2,000; thus $\Delta G = 2,000$.

Y therefore increases to 12,000 in period 2. As a result, $C = 7,200$ and $S = 4,800$. This gives a new level of Y in period 3 of 13,200, and so on (Fig. 57). Equilibrium is achieved when $Y = 15,000$.

It can be seen that an increase in government spending (ΔG) has exactly the same effect as an increase in investment or an increase in autonomous consumption:

$$\Delta Y = \Delta G \times \text{the multiplier.}$$

The model can also be illustrated on a 45° diagram. Thus in Fig. 37, if, instead of the increase in I, the increase in AD took the form of $G = 2,000$, the $C + I$ line would become $C + I + G$ at the higher position of $C + I'$, and the new level of Y would still be 15,000.

In the above example, equilibrium is brought about by the leakage of income into saving. If there were also a tax 'leak', the increase in Y would be smaller.

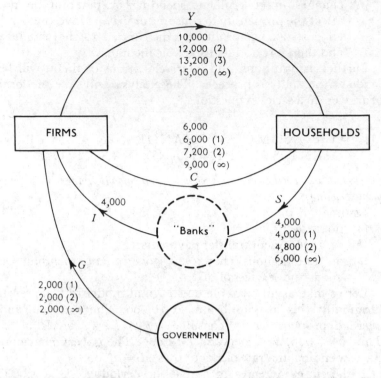

FIG. 57.—The effect of government expenditure (without taxation) on the circular flow of income.

(2) *What will be the effect on income of a lump-sum tax?*
    Assume:
    (*a*) no government spending;
    (*b*) no government transfer payments;
    (*c*) a lump-sum tax ΔT is levied (as opposed to a change in the rate of, say, income tax).

We assumed that people's consumption depends upon their disposable income. We therefore have: $C = f(Y_d)$ and $Y_d = Y - T$. On the usual assumption of $c < 1$, the result of the lump-sum tax will be less consumption *and* less saving. In our example, initially:

$$Y = 0.6 Yd + 4,000$$

$$\therefore Y = 10,000.$$

Assume a lump-sum tax of 200 is imposed. We therefore have:

$$Y_1 = 0{\cdot}6\,(Y_1 - 200) + 4{,}000$$
$$\therefore 0{\cdot}4\,Y_1 = 4{,}000 - 120$$
$$\therefore Y_1 = 9{,}700.$$

Thus consumption falls from 6,000 to 5,700, and saving from 4,000 to 3,800. What this means is that not all the lump-sum tax will fall on consumption; a part will come from an existing leak, saving. The initial reduction in spending through the tax is $0{\cdot}6\,\varDelta T$. This initial reduction is subject to the multiplier.

In general terms, there is a reduction in Y equal to

$$\frac{c\varDelta T}{1 - c}.$$

Certain corollaries follow from the above analysis:

(i) The effect on income of an increase in tax will be more pronounced the greater the marginal propensity to consume. When $c = 1$, the whole of the increase falls on consumption; the change in income is then explosive towards zero.

(ii) Taxes which fall more heavily on consumption (perhaps indirect taxes) compared with taxes which fall on income (perhaps direct taxes) will produce a larger fall in income for a given yield.

(iii) Suppose the government, starting from a position where the budget is balanced, has to expand income in order to achieve full employment. It wishes to keep its budget deficit as small as possible. Should it expand income by increasing G or reducing T?

The answer is that, since a part of the decrease in T will leak into saving, a larger reduction in T will be necessary for a given income increase than if G were increased. A reduction in T would therefore, unless the marginal propensity to consume equals 1, require a larger budget deficit.

III. WHAT WILL BE THE EFFECT OF AN INCREASE IN INVESTMENT OR IN GOVERNMENT SPENDING IF TAXATION IS RELATED TO INCOME?

Our analysis so far has been based on the assumption that,

when I or G increase and income expands as a result, the amount raised by taxation does not change; the increase in income results in an identical increase in disposable income.

To be more realistic, we must assume that, as income expands, a higher proportion of income leaks, not only into saving, but also into taxation, for higher income means higher direct tax yields.

Assume:

(a) taxation $= tY$, where t is the proportion of income going to taxation and is constant at all levels of income;

(b) investment and government spending are independent of the level of Y;

(c) there are simultaneous increases in investment $(\varDelta I)$ and government spending $(\varDelta G)$.

We therefore have:

$$Y = c(Y - T) + I + G$$
$$= c(Y - tY) + I + G$$
$$\therefore Y = c\varDelta Y - t\varDelta Y + \varDelta I + \varDelta G$$
$$= \frac{\varDelta I + \varDelta G}{1 - c + ct}.$$

Certain corollaries follow from the above analysis:

(i) The effect of the income tax is to introduce a leak additional to saving which reduces the size of the multiplier from $\dfrac{1}{1-c}$ to $\dfrac{1}{1-c+ct}$. For example, if $c = 0{\cdot}6$ and $t = 0{\cdot}5$, the multiplier changes from $2{\cdot}5$ to $\dfrac{1}{1 - 0{\cdot}6 + 0{\cdot}3} = \dfrac{1}{0{\cdot}7} = 1{\cdot}4$ approximately.

(ii) Where taxes fall more heavily on consumption (through indirect taxes) than on income as a whole (direct taxes), a given increase in I or G will lead to a smaller increase in income.

IV. WHAT MODIFICATIONS MUST BE MADE FOR CERTAIN TRANSFER PAYMENTS?

With some government transfer payments, e.g. unemployment

benefits, we have to allow for the fact that, as income (and therefore employment) increases, less will be paid in benefits.

Assume:

(a) taxation $= tY$;

(b) the only government transfer payments are to the unemployed $= A$;

(c) the whole of the payments to the unemployed are tax-free;

(d) there is unemployment;

(e) as income expands, payments to the unemployed decrease at the rate of aY.

How will assumption (e) affect the change in income when investment or government spending increase?

The reduction in unemployment benefits will increase T by ΔA, since T represents total taxes less transfers.

We have, therefore,

$$Y = \quad C \qquad\qquad\quad + I + G$$

$$\Delta Y = \Delta C \qquad\qquad\quad + \Delta I + \Delta G$$

$$= c[\Delta Y - (\Delta T + \Delta A)] + \Delta I + \Delta G$$

$$= c\Delta Y - ct\Delta Y - ca\Delta Y + I + \Delta G$$

$$= \frac{\Delta I + \Delta G}{1 - c + ct + ca}.$$

Thus, as income expands, there is a further leak – the reduced spending on unemployment benefits as men find employment. This again reduces the size of the multiplier.

V. WHAT WILL BE THE EFFECT ON INCOME IF THE GOVERNMENT DECIDES TO INCREASE ITS EXPENDITURE BUT TO BALANCE ITS BUDGET?

Assume:

(a) income is in equilibrium with a balanced budget;

(b) there is less than full employment;

(c) investment is autonomous, remaining the same as income expands;

(d) the government increases its spending by ΔG, but at the same time it raises taxation by ΔT $(=\Delta G)$ in order to retain a balanced budget.

We have:

$$\Delta Y = c(\Delta Y - \Delta T) + \Delta G.$$

But since $\Delta T = \Delta G$, we can write:

$$\Delta Y = c(\Delta Y - \Delta G) + \Delta G$$

$$\therefore \Delta Y(1 - c) = \Delta G(1 - c)$$

$$\therefore \Delta Y = \Delta G.$$

Thus, even when the budget remains balanced, there is a net increase in income equal to the initial increase in government spending. The reason is that, in spite of the balanced budget, there is a small net increase in original spending because part of the tax receipts come from saving, since $c < 1$. This net original increase equals $\Delta G - c\Delta T$, which can be written $\Delta G - c\Delta G$ or $\Delta G(1 - c)$. Like any other original increase, this is subject to the multiplier, $1/1 - c$, giving a total increase in income, when income is once more in equilibrium, of ΔG.

Certain corollaries follow from the above analysis:

(i) Even if a rise in government spending, ΔG, is exactly offset by taxation, income will expand by ΔG. This is often known as the 'balanced budget theorem'.

(ii) Unemployment can be reduced, even with a balanced budget, by raising government spending.

(iii) At full employment, any increase in government spending, e.g. on defence or welfare, will be inflationary unless taxation is increased by *more* than the increase in government spending. In other words, the government must budget for a surplus.

(iv) With full employment and a balanced budget, any reduction in government spending will cause unemployment unless taxation is decreased *more* than the decrease in government spending. That is, the government must budget for a deficit.

(v) If there is large-scale unemployment, as in the 1930s, the government will be wise to resort to 'deficit finance', that is, an unbalanced budget, because:

(*a*) the increased expenditure will raise income much more quickly if taxes are not raised at the same time, for, with zero taxes, $\Delta Y = \Delta G/(1-c)$, whereas with a balanced budget, $\Delta Y = \Delta G$;

(*b*) the high taxes necessary to balance the budget will be politically unpopular, and may also have adverse effects on effort.

APPENDIX:
MATHEMATICAL PROOFS

(*a*) *An increase in government expenditure (no taxation)*

$$Y = C + I + G. \qquad (11.1)$$

Here there is no ΔI; therefore:

$$Y + \Delta Y = C + \Delta C + I + G + \Delta G. \qquad (11.2)$$

Taking (11.1) from (11.2),

$$\Delta Y = \Delta C + \Delta G$$
$$= c\Delta Y + \Delta G$$
$$\therefore \Delta Y = \frac{\Delta G}{1-c}$$
$$= \Delta G \times k, \text{where } k \text{ is the multiplier.}$$

(*b*) *An increase of a lump-sum tax from T to $(T + \Delta T)$*

$$Y = \quad C \quad + I + G$$
$$Y = c(Y - T) + I + G. \qquad (11.3)$$

Here there is no ΔI or ΔG.

$$\therefore Y + \Delta Y = c(Y + \Delta Y - T - \Delta T) + I + G$$
$$\therefore Y + \Delta Y = cY + c\Delta Y - cT - c\Delta T + I + G. \qquad (11.4)$$

Taking (11.3) from (11.4),

$$\Delta Y = c\Delta Y - c\Delta T$$
$$\therefore \Delta Y = \frac{-c\Delta T}{1-c}.$$

SUGGESTED READING

F. S. Brooman, *Macroeconomics*, 4th ed. (Allen & Unwin, 1970) ch. 9.
T. F. Dernburg and D. M. McDougall, *Macro-economics*, 3rd ed. (McGraw-Hill, 1968) ch. 6.
G. C. Harcourt, P. H. Karmel, R. H. Wallace, *Economic Activity* (Cambridge U.P., 1967) ch. 11.
G. L. S. Shackle (ed.), *A New Prospect of Economics* (Liverpool U.P., 1958) ch. 15.
A. Williams, *Public Finance and Budgetary Policy* (Allen & Unwin, 1963) ch. 13.

CHAPTER 12

FLUCTUATIONS IN THE LEVEL OF INCOME AND THE ROLE OF THE GOVERNMENT

I. CYCLICAL FLUCTUATIONS

Growth and cyclical fluctuations

CHANGES in the level of income are broadly of two kinds. First, there is the long-term secular trend, usually showing a 'growth' rate of 2–4 per cent per annum. In Chapter 18 we consider some of the theories of economic growth. Second, there are the short-term or cyclical fluctuations superimposed upon the long-term growth path. It is these fluctuations which we study in this chapter.

The difference between the two is illustrated in Fig. 58. The line *AB* represents the secular growth path; in (*a*) there is no growth, whereas in (*b*) there is an upward trend. *AC*

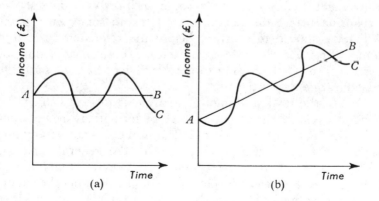

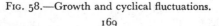

FIG. 58.—Growth and cyclical fluctuations.

represents the cyclical fluctuations around the long-term growth trend.

The nature of cyclical fluctuations

In the predominantly private enterprise economies, fluctuations in economic activity have, over the last century, tended to occur fairly regularly. Up to 1914, the phenomenon followed a pattern in which the average period of the cycle (from peak to peak or trough to trough) was five to eight years and the average fluctuation in the level of output from 5 to 10 per cent. Between the two world wars the same pattern could be discerned, although the fluctuations took place in unusually depressed conditions. Since 1945, however, fluctuations have been much less marked, mainly because the government has used counter-cyclical policies to 'smooth out' the cycle.

Although when we look back on economic events it is fairly easy to pick out a general cyclical path over which the economy has passed, it is important to note that this 'overall cycle' is in fact composed of innumerable cycles in particular sectors of economic activity. Not all these cycles move in harmony; some will 'lead' the overall picture, some will 'lag' behind it. As Stanley Bober has put it: 'In one sense, a business cycle is not a "real" phenomenon, but a way of describing the net effect on the economy of short-run cyclical movements in individual activity.' Thus, if we say that there was a trough in U.K. activity in 1931 and a peak in 1937, these are really just convenient 'reference dates'; some sectors will have shown expansion before the reference trough and some after; some will have started to contract before the reference peak, and some after. At the reference date, overall contraction or expansion is just beginning to mass sufficient force to push the economy one way or the other.

One of the tasks of economic analysis is to look behind the general cycle at the large number of individual cycles comprising it. For example, it is useful to find out whether any one activity has cycles which coincide with the general cycle, or which lead or lag. A discovery that a particular activity always tends to lead the general cycle will help us to predict the course of overall activity. Thus in the U.K., a typical leading series is sales of consumer durable goods.

The process is shown diagrammatically in Fig. 59, where *P* and *T* indicate the reference dates of the cycle. At any point *T*, we can imagine the expansionary forces equally balanced with the contracting forces; beyond *T*, more and more series

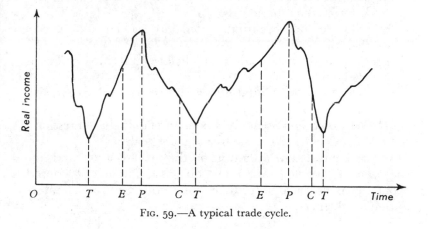

FIG. 59.—A typical trade cycle.

join the expansionary forces. We can picture the expansionary forces reaching their highest proportion of the total at, say, *E*. After *E*, more and more contracting forces develop, until at the peak, *P*, the forces are once again equally balanced. The contracting forces will reach their highest proportion of the total at, say, *C*, after which expansionary forces accumulate again, and so on.

It follows from the above that although an analysis of business cycles will provide us with clues for predicting the future course of events, no cycle is likely to be identical with its predecessors; the forces leading to expansion in one cyclical phase may be quite differently proportioned from the forces which led to expansion in a preceding phase. A single comprehensive theory of cyclical activity is therefore really unattainable; all we can do is to develop sets of theories which can help in predicting the outcome of particular assortments of changes. What follows must be regarded simply as a generalised explanation of short-term fluctuations in the overall level of activity.

The questions to be answered

Any explanation of cyclical fluctuations must answer the following questions:

(a) Why do the upswings and downswings occur?

(b) Why are they cumulative?

(c) Why do they eventually come to an end and reverse their direction?

(d) Why may the boom break before full employment is reached?

(e) Why are the capital-goods industries and export industries more severely hit?

(f) Why do prices rise in the boom and fall in the depression?

(g) Why does the cycle last five to eight years?

We concentrate our attention on the private sector and, for the sake of completeness, relax our assumption of a closed economy in order to introduce some consideration of international influences.

The upswing

Let us consider the point *C* (Fig. 59). Until now there has been a cumulative downswing, the forces of decline growing relatively to the forces of expansion. But from *C* onwards the forces of decline are shrinking and the forces of expansion growing. *T* is the point of balance, and from then until *P* is reached the economy starts to expand. What we have to ask, therefore, is why the balance of forces shifts in this way between *C* and *E*.

In our model, income can increase because (a) investment, but not saving, increases; (b) saving, but not investment, decreases. Both become more likely the lower income falls.

Investment may revive for a variety of reasons. Stocks may have run low and, as new orders begin to be placed, firms feel the upturn is drawing near and seek to restore their normal stock ratios. Fixed equipment wears out and replacement can only be postponed for something like three to four years. Additional fields of profitable investment arise as, with time, new techniques or even new industries are developed.

Saving decreases because the marginal propensity to consume increases as income falls. People may even spend past savings in order to maintain their standard of living.

It is possible that business saving will increase as profits rise, for companies are hardly likely to pass the whole of the increase on to shareholders as distributed profits. But even here there may be some 'feedback': the increased resources may induce investment, for firms are more likely to expand when this can be achieved from internal resources instead of having to go to the market.

But this is not all. When investment increases, the initial effect on AD is magnified by the multiplier. Moreover, a revival in one part of the economy is likely to make entrepreneurs more optimistic elsewhere. They also begin to reinvest. Expansion may gather momentum, too, because as plants operate nearer to their optima, costs fall and profitability increases. The upswing is cumulative.

Added impetus is provided by the accelerator. Until now, entrepreneurs have been reluctant to replace their machinery. Thus the increase in demand for consumer goods finds them short of productive capacity. The acceleration principle shows the marked effect that this has on the capital-goods industries. The climb back to greater prosperity gathers momentum as the revival spreads. The factors responsible can sustain it for three to five years.

The break in the boom

Why should the boom break? Why, at E, should the forces of expansion begin to lose ground relative to the forces of decline? The reason is that the increase in AD begins to level off. This happens because both the proportion of income consumed and investment eventually fall.

As income increases, the marginal propensity to consume falls. Not only do people spend a smaller proportion of their income as income rises, but it is likely that more of that income is going to profit-recipients who are likely to spend a smaller proportion of it than wage-earners. In addition, with progressive taxation, the marginal rate of taxation will increase. Added to this, as employment rises, government spending on unemployment payments falls. The result is that, unless increased investment or other government spending is sufficient

to match increased saving and taxation and smaller unemployment payments as income expands, the expansion in income
will come to an end.

Will investment increase sufficiently to maintain income?
Certain considerations make it seem unlikely.

(1) New fields of investment, e.g. through the invention of
new techniques or the development of new industries, are not
likely to be forthcoming at a quick enough rate to make good
the exhaustion of existing opportunities.

(2) Rising costs as output expands may exert pressure on
profit margins:

(a) As higher levels of employment are reached, less and
less efficient resources will be employed. For example,
with regard to hiring labour, we can expect profit-
maximising entrepreneurs to hire the most productive
workers first, and the least efficient last. Hence labour
costs will tend to rise as the cycle proceeds. Firms will
have been built with a certain capacity output rate in
mind; as the expansion proceeds, this output should be
reached by more and more firms. Beyond this output,
costs will start to rise because the proportion of fixed to
variable factors is less than that in the optimum position.

(b) Bottlenecks will tend to develop. There may be shortages
of particular kinds of labour, e.g. skilled workers, or component factories may be working to capacity; stocks of raw
materials may run low and, especially where these have to
be imported, may be difficult to restore to normal levels.

(c) As prices begin to rise, wage rates may rise as workers
obtain increases to compensate for the rising cost of living.

(d) As expansion proceeds, funds for investment will become
harder to obtain; interest rates will tend to rise, and banks
will begin to be more selective in granting credit. While
this may have little direct effect on large firms – they can
bear the extra cost or expand out of their liquid reserves –
they are bound to wonder how it will affect the purchasers
of their products. Any pressure on profit margins will
cause firms to revise their current output plans, and also
their plans for future expansion. As they cut current costs
to restore their profit margins, they will reduce overtime
working and then work a shorter week, 'hoarding' labour

as much as possible in case the cycle turns upwards again quickly. (We should therefore expect an overtime series to 'lead' the general employment series.)

(3) All types of investment may fall simply because entrepreneurs become less optimistic. For one thing, more profitable-looking investment schemes will have been undertaken first so that as costs begin to rise and profit expectations dwindle, entrepreneurs will begin to be more pessimistic. For another, capital may prove to be less profitable than expected because it has been invested by different entrepreneurs in competing products so that, in relationship to the total demand, there is over-investment. When investment is running at a high rate, the confidence of entrepreneurs is vulnerable to even minor set-backs. This is particularly so when, as in the inter-war period, cyclical fluctuations in the level of activity appear to be inevitable. Then entrepreneurs' expectations were always more vulnerable to changes in direction than they are today when the government has been successful in maintaining full employment since the Second World War.

Probably the most important reason for the downturn in the expectations of entrepreneurs, however, is provided in the theory of the accelerator, as follows.

(4) As the accelerator shows, not only must investment increase to cover the increasing propensity to save, but it must be sufficient maintain the *rate of increase* in AD. Towards full employment, this is unlikely; at full employment, it becomes impossible. Towards full employment, bottlenecks develop in finding the skilled labour to operate machines. Therefore, even if capital can be 'widened' by adding to existing machines, there would be little point in building them. But, at full employment, new machines cannot be built for physical reasons. Thus the accelerator cannot operate. As we have seen, once investment is not sufficient to maintain the rate of increase of AD, the accelerator commences to operate in reverse. Then the level of investment falls back to where it is just sufficient for re-placement purposes only, no additional capacity being required.

Finally, if we allow for international trade, a contraction of income can occur through imports increasing in value more than exports (see Chapter 16) At some stage in the boom, this is likely to happen.

(a) As incomes expand, not only are more imports demanded, but goods which might have been exported are diverted to the home market.
(b) The nearer a country approaches full employment, the greater is the tendency for costs and prices to rise. Her exports, therefore, become less competitive.
(c) Important buyers of exports may suffer a depression before the home country. As a result, their demand falls. This is particularly serious for a country so dependent on international trade as the U.K. When this happens, AD falls – a slump has been 'imported'. It could happen, too, that the government, rather than alter the rate of exchange, takes deflationary measures to remedy a chronic balance of payments disequilibrium.

Thus we see that both the depression and the boom contain the seeds of their own destruction.

The downswing

The break in the boom is followed by a downswing which gathers momentum. Falling expenditure in one part of the economy leads to reduced expenditure elsewhere: the multiplier is working in reverse. Pessimistic expectations of entrepreneurs are therefore justified, and the drop to the bottom of the depression is a sharp one. Nor will interest policy prove effective. While a rise in the rate of interest may break a boom, a decrease is unlikely to halt a depression. As expectations of entrepreneurs grow more pessimistic, so the marginal efficiency of investment curve falls to the left, and this outweighs any reduction of the rate of interest aimed at restoring investment (see Chapter 6).

Eventually, however, for the reasons already given, the bottom is reached, and the cycle starts all over again. The cycle varies both in the time taken and in its severity.

II GOVERNMENT RESPONSIBILITY FOR THE LEVEL OF ACTIVITY

Automatic stabilising influences

As income expands or contracts, there are various automatic or 'natural' stabilising forces which come into play. Indeed, it is because of these that we have the cyclical nature of the trade cycle. The most important are:

(1) *Monetary*
   (a) As income expands, more money is demanded for the transactions and precautionary motives so that there is a tendency for the rate of interest to rise.
   (b) As prices rise, the Pigou effect comes into play, for the real value of people's cash holdings falls, and so consumption is reduced to restore cash holdings to their former level in real terms.

(2) *Consumption*
   (a) The overall distribution of income may be so altered in boom and depression that the propensity to consume alters in the desired direction If in a boom, for example, incomes move from wage-earners to profit-earners, then it is likely that the propensity to consume falls as a larger proportion of incomes is being saved. The opposite would apply if the level of activity fell.
   (b) There may be a time-lag in adjusting consumption to changes in income because, in the short term, consumers maintain *previous* living standards – Duesenberry's argument (*see* p. 70).
   (c) Companies tend to follow dividend equalisation policies irrespective of the level of profits and thus business saving increases. (This may be counteracted by investment being positively related to the level of undistributed profits.)
   (d) There is a diminishing marginal propensity to consume, so that income expansion or contraction comes to an end.

(3) *Investment*
   (a) The accelerator, which is a destabiliser, eventually goes into reverse because the rate of increase in consumption is not maintained (see 2(d) above).
   (b) The growth in the public sector of the economy, where investment is not so volatile as in the private sector, has had a stabilising effect, limiting bull/bear expectations.

(4) *International trade*

    (*a*) As incomes expand (*see* Chapter 16) exports decrease, and imports increase owing to: (i) the income effect, (ii) price effects.

    (*b*) If exports increase/decrease or imports decrease/increase, the income effects in (*a*) come into play to stabilise exports or imports.

(5) *Fiscal*

Progressive taxation, unemployment insurance benefits, etc. act as stabilisers (*see* Chapter 14).

But while these 'natural' automatic stabilisers may exert a moderating effect, they are insufficient to prevent changes in the level of activity. More positive action is required if income is to be maintained at the full employment level.

The role of the government

Such action involves maintaining an adequate level of AD. For the following reasons, this must be the responsibility of the government.

First, only the government can assume and exercise powers of coercion, particularly with regard to the collection of statistics and information which are necessary for adequate planning. Indeed its powers of coercion may go further, direct economic controls being exercised by orders and regulations.

Secondly, the government has power to levy taxes, pay out subsidies or vary the supply of money.

Thirdly, apart from its extraordinary powers, the government can act like any other consumer or producer in the economy. The main difference is that it is much larger, its spending on consumer and investment goods being about 40 per cent of national expenditure. Like any private firm it can borrow and buy inputs to make a commercial profit. Or, if it chooses, it may use them for non-commercial purposes.

Fourthly, the knowledge that the government is committed to a full employment policy will eliminate much of the uncertainty from which cyclical fluctuations begin.

Difficulties of a full employment policy

But the difficulties of the government's task must not be underestimated.

First, it has to decide on its criterion of full employment. Does it mean that the number of vacancies equals the number of unemployed seeking work? Or, following Lord Beveridge, does it mean that the number of vacancies should always exceed the number of unemployed persons? Furthermore, must the opportunities open to the unemployed be comparable with their previous jobs?

Secondly, the government has to reconcile its aim of full employment with its other economic objectives. These include price stability, a healthy balance of payments position, an adequate rate of growth, a balanced regional development, and a more equal distribution of income. Certain of these objectives are complementary to one another. Thus while a full employment policy is chiefly concerned with maintaining an adequate level of AD, attention has to be paid to the distribution of that demand to see that it corresponds to the unemployed resources available. Consequently, measures to promote the development of special regions may form part of a full employment policy. Similarly, a strengthening of the gold and foreign currency reserves may be a prerequisite of economic growth, for such reserves provide a cushion against the balance of payments deficits which are likely to arise for a time when the level of activity is high.

On the other hand, certain objectives may be competitive. For instance, as the level of unemployment falls, prices rise more quickly. Thus the government must choose between a range of possibilities – for example, 5 per cent unemployment but little rise in the price level, or 2 per cent unemployment with something like a 5 per cent rise in the price level. To what extent shall full employment take priority over price stability? When objectives conflict, the government has to decide where the balance of advantage lies.

Thirdly, statistics upon which action can be based may be inaccurate or unavailable. The types of question which have to be answered are: How will consumption respond to a change in income? What will be the effect of tax allowances on the level of investment? Answers to such questions are necessary if the right degree of adjustment to AD is to be made. It must be remembered too that statistics take time to collect. This makes the timing of changes by the authorities more difficult. Thus decisions as to whether the brakes should be put on or taken off have to be based on prediction.

Here the fact that different sectors of the economy expand and contract at different times can be made use of. Studies of how these various sectors move may provide us with clues as to the future course of activity. This is achieved by: (a) identifying leading, lagging and average series; (b) accumulating experience of 'false' leads; (c) correlating the amplitudes of particular cycles with their causal forces where this is possible The authorities are thus provided with warnings of expected upturns or downturns, and of the expected severity of any change. It is clearly important for the authorities to obtain knowledge as far in advance as possible. Otherwise they may take deflationary action to check a boom when the forces of contraction have already begun to gather force, or inflationary action to pull the

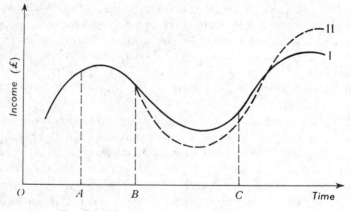

Fig. 60.—Unsuccessful counter-cyclical policies.

economy out of a trough when it has already begun to turn up of its own accord. In such cases, 'counter-cyclical' policy could accentuate the peaks and troughs instead of smoothing them out!

In Figure 60, curve I shows the path which would be

followed by the trade cycle without government interference.
Curve II shows the path if the government interferes, and its
timing is incorrect. Thus, to smooth the boom, the government
should, say, increase taxes and hire-purchase controls at time
A, but in fact it does not do so until time *B*, when the peak has
been passed. It therefore pushes the economy into a worse
slump than necessary. It reduces taxes, etc., at time *C* (too late
again – the trough has been passed) so that the economy runs
into a boom greater than it would have done. The true aims of
counter-cyclical policy are achieved in Fig. 61.

Finally, it must be remembered that, although most of our
analysis of the factors determining the level of activity has been
conducted in terms of moving from one static position to another,
the government is faced with the more difficult task of a dynamic economy. How will the expectations of entrepreneurs
change as a result of government policy? How will consumption
change as the level of income rises? How will the extra income
be distributed and will this distribution affect consumption?
How long will it take for output to be adjusted to a rise in
AD? To what extent will the trade unions exploit their bargaining power as unemployment declines? The government has to
attempt to answer these difficult questions.

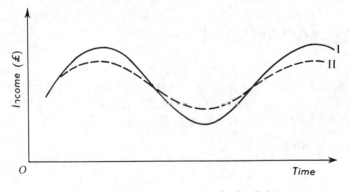

FIG. 61.—Successful counter-cyclical policies.

The nature of government policy

The role of the government in controlling the economy can
be likened to that of the driver of a car going to work in the city.

At no time can the car run on its own without some direction, and the man at the wheel has to make the necessary adjustments continuously. From time to time, too, he is concerned with more definite alterations, varying his pressure on the accelerator and changing gear. He may even modify his route, making detours to avoid traffic congestion.

But in all these manoeuvres, different drivers act differently. Some use the gear lever rather than the accelerator in changing speed. Others estimate that the traffic congestion will not be so bad as to warrant a detour. Nor does the same man do exactly the same things each day. He knows many different routes to work and, being flexible, makes use of them as he thinks fit.

So it is with the government. Like the driver guessing the traffic congestion along the route, the government has to work from incomplete information in estimating what change in AD is necessary to produce the desired result and the extent to which the measures it adopts will produce that change. But it usually has to combine measures in different ways. Not only does one reinforce the other, but a different emphasis has to be placed on each at different times in order to meet the needs of the prevailing situation. Where a quick change in the direction or tempo of the economy is required, more weight must be given to those which begin to work immediately. Should it be desired, for instance, to increase consumption, it can be achieved much more quickly by reducing taxes than by lowering the rate of interest (to discourage saving).

APPENDIX:
A SIMPLE DYNAMIC MODEL OF THE TRADE CYCLE USING THE ACCELERATOR, MULTIPLIER AND A CONSUMPTION LAG

Let us assume:

(1) Income is in equilibrium at 1,000, with $C = 500$, $I = 500$. This is the base period = year 0.

(2) The marginal propensity of consume remains at 0·5 at all levels of income. The multiplier is thus 2.

(3) There are unemployed resources, so that output can increase proportionately to an increase in aggregate demand.

(4) Consumption is based on the *previous* period's income, i.e.

$$C_t = \tfrac{1}{2} Y_{t-1}.$$

(5) Up to an income of 1,000, all investment is autonomous and equal to 500. From 1,000 onwards, any increase in income induces further investment. This induced investment is equal to twice the *increase* in consumption spending in the same period, i.e. the coefficient of capital (the accelerator) equals 2.

$$I_{(\text{Induced})} = 2\Delta C.$$

What happens now when the equilibrium position is upset by an autonomous change in spending, e.g. in investment or in government spending?

The initial increase in income has two repercussions:

(a) Because of the lagged response of consumption to income, consumption spending will increase in each period as the multiplier works itself out, until equilibrium is reached.

(b) The *increase* in consumption induces further investment. This is the 'accelerator' effect. It is important to note that the induced investment is dependent on the *increase* in consumption. It is this which produces the cyclical fluctuations in income. (Such fluctuations would not occur if induced investment were directly proportionate to the level of income, i.e. if $I = b + iY$.)

In Table 6 below, we shall simplify the figures by showing only the change in income from 1,000. This change is initiated by an increase in autonomous investment from 500 to 600. From this point onwards we have to consider not only the effect of autonomous investment on income, but the induced investment which results (assumption (6)).

Conclusions

(1) When there is induced investment based on a change in consumption, income need not go on expanding from one period to another as it moves towards a new equilibrium, but will proceed in cyclical movements and even produce a lower income (thus more unemployment) than in the base year.

(2) This absolute decline occurs when the negative effect of *induced* investment exceeds induced consumption + *autonomous* investment.

TABLE 6

CYCLICAL FLUCTUATIONS DUE TO THE ACCELERATOR AND A LAGGED
CONSUMPTION FUNCTION

(1) Period	(2) Autonomous investment	(3) Induced consumption ($= \frac{1}{2}C$ of previous period)	(4) Induced investment ($= 2\Delta C$ of current period) that is $2 \times C_t - C_{t-1}$)	(5) Total change in income ($=$ the sum of changes in I_{aut}, C, and I_{ind}, $= (2) + (3) + (4)$ $= b + \frac{1}{2}Y_{t-1} + 2\Delta C$)
Base 0	500	—	—	—

From this base, we measure only deviations from the base period income

1	100	0	0	100
2	100	50	100	250
3	100	125	150	375
4	100	187·5	125	412·5
5	100	206·25	37·5	343·75
6	100	171·875	− 68·75	203·125
7	100	101·5625	− 140·625	60·9375
8	100	30·46875	− 142·1875	− 11·71875
9	100	− 5·859375	− 72·65625	21·284375
10	etc.	etc.	etc.	etc.

We must recognise, however, that the above model is only a very simple indication of the way in which cyclical fluctuations may be caused. For one thing, the acceleration principle is subject to numerous criticisms (*see* pp. 95–6). For another, we have ignored the difficulty which is posed by 'negative induced investment'. It is unrealistic to suggest that firms would deliberately destroy capital equipment (although gluts in particular commodities have sometimes led to the destruction of stocks, e.g. Brazilian coffee in the inter-war period). To some extent, negative induced investment can be accounted for by less of other types of investment. When investment as a whole is zero, there is no net investment in fixed capital (depreciation is just covered) or stocks. Minus investment can therefore be explained by: (*a*) depreciation, replacement not covering the wearing-out of fixed capital; (*b*) the running down of stocks. The first is limited by technical considerations, for the upper limit is determined by the rate at which machines wear out. The second is possible only up to the limit of stocks held.

SUGGESTED READING

*S. Bober, *The Economics of Cycles and Growth* (Wiley, 1968) chs 2–3.

F. S. Brooman, *Macroeconomics*, 4th ed. (Allen & Unwin, 1970) ch. 14.

T. F. Dernburg and D. M. McDougall, *Macro-economics*, 3rd ed. (McGraw-Hill, 1968) chs 18–21.

G. C. Harcourt, P. H. Karmel, R. H. Wallace, *Economic Activity* (Cambridge U.P., 1967) ch. 15.

*J. M. Keynes, *The General Theory of Employment, Interest and Money* (Macmillan, 1936) ch. 22.

R. C. O. Matthews, *The Trade Cycle* (Nisbet Cambridge U.P., 1959) chs 1–2.

*M. G. Mueller (ed.), *Readings in Macroeconomics*, No. 18 by P. Samuelson (Holt, Rinehart & Winston, 1969).

D. C. Rowan, *Output, Inflation and Growth* (Macmillan, 1968) ch. 20.

*E. Schneider, *Money, Income and Employment* (Allen & Unwin, 1962) pp. 172–85.

CHAPTER 13

MONETARY POLICY

THE rate of interest, as we have seen, is determined by the demand for and supply of money. By altering the supply of money, the monetary authorities can, therefore, alter the rate of interest. In Chapter 10 we saw how changes in the supply of money can be effected.

Monetary policy, it would seem, simply entails altering the supply of money in order to vary the rate of interest. In practice, it is not so simple. Questions which still remain to be answered are:

(1) Can interest policy always be relied upon as an effective weapon in controlling the level of activity?

(2) Even if changes in the rate of interest are effective, are there circumstances in which they are undesirable?

(3) Should interest policy be undesirable, has the government any alternative means of influencing how much is borrowed for consumption and investment spending?

(4) What practical difficulties do the monetary authorities run up against in restricting the availability of credit?

These and other questions will be considered in the following discussion of monetary policy.

We define monetary policy in terms of modern practice – measures which seek to influence the level of total spending by varying:

(1) the rate of interest – the cost of credit;

(2) liquidity – the availability of credit.

I. INTEREST POLICY

The logic of interest policy stems from the fact that interest is the price of credit. A rise in the rate of interest, therefore, should contract the demand for credit, and thus reduce AD. The authorities can influence both the short-term and the long-term rates of interest.

Changes in the short-term rate of interest

Changes in the short-term rate of interest are effected by: (i) changing the bank rate; (ii) buying or selling Treasury bills. By both methods, fine adjustments can take place at frequent intervals – at least weekly.

By convention, changes in bank rate directly affect the rate of interest charged on bank advances and influence other short-term rates, e.g. money at call, bills discounted, local authority loans, hire-purchase finance. But it is doubtful whether such changes have much effect on investment or consumption spending. As we have seen, small firms may have to reduce their holding of stocks, and consumers may be precluded by the higher repayments from negotiating personal loans with banks or from entering into hire-purchase commitments. But this is unlikely. The interest charge represents only a part of the cost of carrying stocks or of the total instalment repayment on a loan. Nor, since most personal saving is now contractual, are higher interest rates likely to encourage personal saving.

But while short-term interest policy may do little to discourage spending, at its lowest evalution it does *nothing* to *encourage* it. Thus it might improve an inflationary situation – were it not for certain practical defects.

First, it adds to balance of payments difficulties on current account by increasing the cost of short-term borrowing from abroad. Second, it adds to the cost of servicing the national debt. Third, the sale of Treasury bills, by which bank-rate policy is reinforced, does little to change the overall liquidity position of the banks, for it merely replaces cash by another liquid asset. Fourth, the rise in the short-term rate may pull up the long-term rate – and this may conflict with other aims of government policy (see later). Since short-term loans are substitutes for long-term loans, there is bound to be a tendency for the rates of interest on each to move in the same direction. But the extent to which the long-term rate does move in response to a change in the short-term rate depends upon people's expectations of the future long-term rate. As regards the latter, the Radcliffe Committee (reporting in 1959) considered that people had come to expect a 'normal' rate (then about 5 per cent). Their view was that if the long-term rate appeared on the low side, say 3 per cent, people would consider that, when short-term rates rose, there was room for an upward adjustment in the long-term rate, and start to move out of long-term securities (since they would fear a price fall). On the other hand, if the long-term rate was already high (say 7 per cent) it would probably be thought that, in spite of higher short-term rates, the future long-term rate would still be in a downward direction. A major switch, therefore, from long-term bonds (whose price is expected to rise) would be unlikely and so the rise in the short-term rate would have little effect on the long-term rate of interest. We have to conclude, therefore, that a change in the short-term rate may or may not affect the long-term rate. If it does, it may not be in harmony with government policy; on the other hand, by influencing the long-term rate, it may affect the level of AD. It is the latter relationship we must now examine.

Changes in the long-term rate of interest

When we turn to an examination of changes in the long-term rate of interest as a means of influencing the level of AD, we find again that there are major difficulties:

(1) In a depression, it may be impossible to lower the rate of interest.

(2) In certain circumstances, changes in the long-term rate may have little effect on the level of AD.

(3) A high long-term rate may be inimical to government policy generally.

(4) A high long-term rate may be incompatible with the Bank of England's function of managing government debt.

We shall consider each difficulty in turn.

(1) The 'liquidity trap' floor to the rate of interest

The long-term rate of interest can be lowered by decreasing the demand for money or by increasing the supply of money (through government buying of long-term securities on the open market).

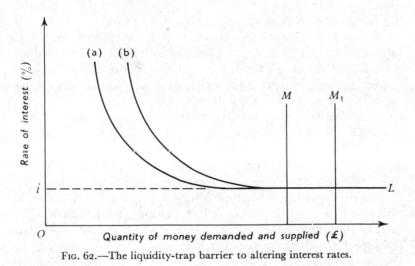

Fig. 62.—The liquidity-trap barrier to altering interest rates.

The demand for money will decrease, that is, the liquidity preference curve moves from (*b*) to (*a*) (Fig. 62), if there is an appropriate change in attitudes to either active or speculative balances, though neither is independent of the other. Thus the demand for active balances will fall if the government pursues a deflationary policy, if incomes are paid at shorter intervals, if the liquidity of other assets is increased, or if people are willing to suffer the inconvenience of making do with smaller balances. The demand for speculative balances depends upon what people regard as the 'normal' rate of interest. If their idea of what is the 'normal' rate is revised downwards, their demand for speculative balances will decrease.

But changing the long-term rate of interest by causing people to shift their demand for liquidity is not practicable. The desired change can be brought about more quickly and effectively by altering the supply of money. Indeed, in so far as the rate of interest is lowered, other assets become more liquid for there is less risk of having to sell them at a capital loss. That is, an increase in the supply of money not only lowers the rate of interest directly (since more money is left over for speculative balances), but also lowers it indirectly by a movement of the liquidity preference curve to the left (since there is less demand for true money as other assets become more liquid).

But what happens in a depression if the rate of interest is already very low, e.g. 2 per cent? Here the capital loss which would result from only a fractional rise in the rate of interest outweighs the small return offered. Thus the demand for money is infinitely elastic (*see* Chapter 8). Any increase in money by the authorities is absorbed by adding to liquid hoards; it goes into the 'liquidity trap'. In other words, when bonds rise to a certain price, people are so convinced that the next move will be downwards that the supply of bonds offered to the government is infinite at this price because people just want liquidity.

There is thus a level below which the rate of interest cannot fall unless a penalty is imposed in holding idle balances. This means that the authorities are powerless to force down the rate of interest further in order to increase investment (that is, below Oi (Fig. 62)). The only means by which income can be expanded is by moving the investment curve to the right by improving entrepreneurs' expectations or by increasing the propensity to consume.

In terms of the LM/IS diagram (Fig. 63), we have a current level of income OY, whereas we require a full employment level of OY_f. If the rate of interest could be lowered to Oi_l, this

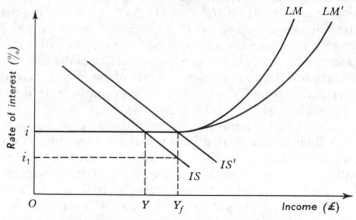

Fig. 63.—Monetary and fiscal policy and the liquidity trap.

full employment level of income could, with given investment
and saving, be achieved. But increasing the supply of money
simply moves the *LM* curve to *LM'* and has no effect on that
part of the curve between Y and Y_f. Because everybody prefers
money to bonds, the government cannot force down the rate of
interest below Oi. Thus the only way in which income can be
expanded is by moving the *IS* curve to the right (*IS'*) by
increasing investment or by lowering saving.

(2) *The inability of changes in the rate of interest to affect the level of*
income
   Even if the rate of interest can be altered, it may have little
effect on the level of AD. There are two main cases:

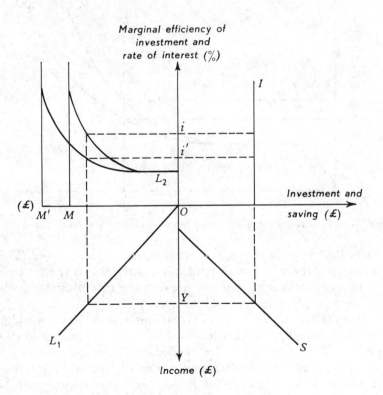

FIG. 64.—The effect of a perfectly inelastic investment demand curve.

(a) *Investment may be interest-inelastic.* As we have seen (Chapter 6), there is a strong possibility that investment may be unresponsive to changes in the rate of interest. If so, interest policy can do little *directly* to influence the level of investment spending.

The extreme case is shown in Fig. 64. An increase in the money suplpy from OM to OM' lowers the rate of interest from Oi to Oi'. But it has no effect on the amount of investment and the level of income does not change.

In terms of the LM/IS diagram (Fig. 65), the interest-inelastic curve produces an IS curve which is vertical. As a result, even if the rate of interest can be lowered, it is ineffective in expanding Y. We simply have the same level of income with a lower rate of interest.

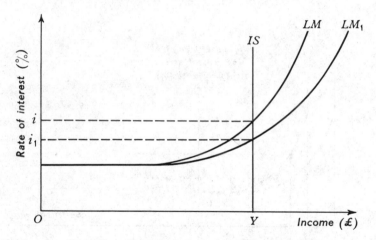

Fig. 65.—The effect of a perfectly inelastic investment demand curve.

(b) *The marginal propensity to consume may be relatively low.* This means that there is a small multiplier, and hence any change in investment resulting from a change in the rate of interest will not greatly affect the level of income.

The above analysis shows that interest policy, working through the effects which follow *directly* from a change in the price of borrowing, will be ineffective where investment is interest-inelastic or the marginal propensity to consume is low. If either of these conditions holds, the main effort must be directed to shifting the position of the IS curve by playing on the expectations of entrepreneurs or by varying the propensity to consume.

Such a change in the expectations of entrepreneurs may result *indirectly* from interest policy. Thus, by lowering the rate of interest, the government may convince entrepreneurs that it is set on an expansionary policy. Consequently the *MEI* curve (and therefore the *IS* curve) move to the right.

Is this likely to happen? The answer is that the chances are greater in the mid-way stage between boom and slump. When the boom is gathering momentum, a high rate of interest may not deter investment. Similarly, in a depression when entrepreneurs are pessimistic, a low rate of interest may be ineffective in promoting a recovery.

(3) *High long-term rates of interest and overall government policy*

Not only may interest policy be ineffective (except in so far as it affects expectations) but, for the following reasons, it may be undesirable:

(*a*) A small change in the long-term rate of interest may result in a much larger change in short-term rates, thus producing complications in the short-term market. This is because, with a short-term security, early repayment of the full nominal value is guaranteed; any fall in its price, therefore, can really only come about because there has been a general rise in interest rates, and thus the yield to maturity of this particular security has correspondingly declined.

Take, for example, a £100 4 per cent bond due to mature in a year's time. If the current rate of interest is 4 per cent, its price in the market will stand at £100. Should the current rate of interest now rise to 5 per cent, the bond will only yield £1 less in the course of the year than a one-year bond bought now. Thus its price will only fall to £99. Similarly, if the rate of interest rises to 7 per cent, its price will only fall to about £97.

But what is the situation with a similar security, but undated? Here a rise in the rate of interest to 5 per cent will result in a fall in its price to £80; if the rate rises to 7 per cent, its price will be £57. Such a rise in the long-term rate is also likely to produce a switch from short- into long-term bonds, for the feeling is that the next change in the price of long-term bonds must be upwards. Thus the price of short-term bonds falls –

and, as we have seen above, this represents an almost equivalent rise in the short-term rate of interest. Should the price of our one-year 4 per cent short-term bond fall to £95 for instance, the short-term rate will be 9 per cent.

To avoid changes in the long-term rate of interest having such magnified effects on the short-term rate, the authorities must convince people that the change in the long-term rate is permanent. In other words, people have to revise their idea of what the 'normal' rate is. In this case, changes in the short-term rate need be less violent, for there will be less pressure to switch from short-dated into long-dated bonds.

It should be noted that, when interest rates fall, there is a limit to the rise in the price of the short-term bond in our example. When the price of long-term bonds rises, people move into short-term bonds. But, at a price of £200 for the undated bonds, the rate of interest will have fallen to 2 per cent, which, as we have seen, is about the lowest level possible. This means that the price of the one-year bond will be £102. If it rises to £103, the short-term rate of interest will have fallen to 1 per cent. This is probably its lowest limit, for any smaller return will hardly compensate for the cost of switching or loss of liquidity. The result will be a switch into money rather than into short-term bonds.

(b) A higher rate of interest increases the cost of borrowing from abroad, especially where there has been a considerable impact on the short-term market. This increases invisible payments on the current account of the balance of payments.

(c) A higher rate of interest increases the cost of internal borrowing, thereby adding to the taxation burden of servicing the national debt.

(d) Interest policy does not discriminate between: (i) firms which export a high proportion of their output and firms which do not; (ii) projects of high and low social value, e.g. a slum-clearance scheme and a gaming club. (This disadvantage arises from a basic defect of the price system – it has to work within the existing unequal distribution of income.)

On the other hand, it cannot be held that interest policy discriminates against investment, inhibiting future growth. The fact is that investment in real terms can be achieved only if there is real saving, setting resources free from producing consumer goods. If, when the interest rate is raised, the desire to invest still exceeds saving in real terms, the effect of a rise in the rate of interest is to cut investment nearer to the saving available. If more investment is required, then increased real saving must be encouraged, e.g. by reducing taxes which impinge on saving.

(e) Interest policy may increase instability. Unlike fiscal policy where there is an element of automatic stabilisation (see Chapter 14), a change in the rate of interest (except for the influence which an increase in income may have on the demand for active balances) requires a deliberate decision of the authorities. Such a decision may occur at the wrong time, for there is a large measure of uncertainty as regards the speed at which an interest change will work or the exact effect on the expectations of entrepreneurs. An error in timing may increase instability, e.g. if a rise in the rate of interest coincides with the downturn in business activity (see p. 180).

(4) *A high long-term rate and the management of government debt*

As we have seen (Chapter 10), government borrowing by Treasury bills has had to be reduced because it was putting too large a supply of liquid assets in the hands of the banks. On the other hand, a switch to long-term borrowing implies an addition to the supply of long-term bonds and thus a fall in their price – a rise in the long-term rate of interest. Can the authorities permit such a rise? Until 1969 they seemed to set their face against it for the following reason.

The major holders of long-term government debt have, through inflation, tended to lose confidence in holding it, for they have seen its capital value eroded over the last twenty years. Only if it possesses a high degree of liquidity that is, it can be sold without capital loss – will they be induced to hold such debt. This means that holders must be convinced that its price is not likely to fall; that is, that the authorities will not let the long-term rate rise, at least in the near future. Any weakening here would result in a considerable rise in the cost of government borrowing, for people would be unwilling to take up bonds except at an initial high rate of interest.

In practice, however, this puts the authorities on the horns of a dilemma. If there are more sellers of bonds than buyers, the government has to instruct its broker to buy the surplus in the market in order to support the existing price (the situation in early 1969). But this means that the Bank of England is carrying out open-market operations in the wrong direction – instead of squeezing credit it is putting extra cash in the hands of the public and increasing the liquidity of the commercial banks. The latter can be handled by instructing the banks to restrict lending. The former presents few difficulties provided people simply add to their liquid balances in the bond market. But suppose this Keynesian view does not prevail, and that, as the Chicago school suggests (*see* p. 227), there is an overflow of the extra money directly on to the markets for goods and services? Then the authorities' task of managing the government debt as economically as possible comes into direct conflict with the aim of controlling inflation.

Summary of conclusions regarding interest-rate policy

Interest-rate policy may be both limited in its effectiveness and undesirable in that it clashes with other government objectives. But few experts would discard it altogether as a weapon for regulating the level of activity.

In the first place, the authorities must increase the supply of money as activity revives or else there will come a point when all the money supply will be required for active balances. Here, any further increase in investment would not expand the level of income but simply cause the rate of interest to rise (Fig. 66).

Secondly, although the rate of interest may be ineffective at the top of the boom or at the bottom of the depression, between these two extremes it may fulfil a useful role both as regards its impact on costs (particularly for long-term projects) and its psychological effects.

Thirdly, changes in the rate of interest can be applied quickly and to a fine degree. It may be that the effects, except in so far as they revise expectations, take time to be felt, but this difficulty can be largely offset by making the necessary changes in good time.

Fourthly, in order to offset the rate of interest's failure to discriminate between different types of borrower, selective credit controls may be introduced.

Thus while it is now recognised that the economy cannot be

regulated by interest policy alone, it is still used as one of a number of measures which, since they reinforce one another,

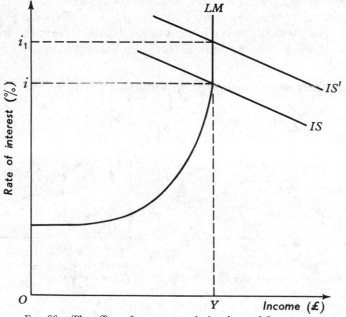

FIG. 66. The effect of a zero speculative demand for money.

are put together in a 'portfolio' and varied according to the needs of the prevailing situation. And, because at times it is felt desirable to hold down the rate of interest, resort has to be made to restricting the availability of credit.

II. THE AVAILABILITY OF CREDIT

The reason for credit controls

Because of the disadvantages of a high long-term rate of interest, the monetary authorities since the Second World War have, as far as possible, fixed the rate of interest and carried out measures to maintain that rate.

In practice, this has meant keeping the long-term rate below the rate which would be determined in the market by the demand for and supply of funds. In short, we have a controlled price below the market price, and the inevitable result follows –

demand exceeds supply. Consequently, almost continuously since 1945 and especially during the cheap-money period immediately after the war, advances have not been allocated by interest rates; instead some kind of non-price 'rationing' has always had to be imposed by the banks, usually on requests from the authorities. The situation is shown in Fig. 67(a).

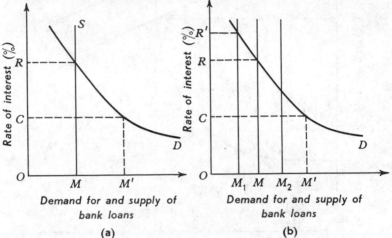

FIG. 67.—The effect of maintaining the rate of interest below the market equilibrium.

The controlled rate of interest OC is below the 'market 'rate, OR. This means that given the supply of money OM, demand exceeds supply by MM'.

'Varying the availability of credit', therefore, simply means that the authorities are changing the stringency of their 'rationing' terms. The policy takes three main forms:

(1) changing the amount of liquidity in the economy;
(2) direct controls over both the amount and type of credit;
(3) hire-purchase controls.

(1) Liquidity

Liquidity in the economy is varied chiefly by influencing the liquidity of the banks. If the supply of money in the economy is allowed to increase, someone (institutions, firms or persons) is becoming more 'liquid' and thus in a better position to spend or to lend to someone else who wishes to spend.

As we have just shown, the rate of interest is 'controlled' below the market rate. The demand for bank loans exceeds their supply. Thus curbing the supply of money, e.g. by a movement from M to M_1 (Fig. 67(b)), does not cause the rate of interest to rise to OR', as it would in a free market; it simply means that bank loans are reduced from OM to OM_1, the excess demand for credit increasing from MM' to M_1M'. Similarly, if the authorities increase the supply of money from OM to OM_2, advances can increase. But rationing is still necessary; it is simply less stringent, OM_2 funds now being available for demand OM' instead of only OM.

(2) *Direct controls*

'Rationing' of funds has had two main effects.

First, the Bank of England has indicated the lines upon which the banks shall operate their 'rationing' policy. This is the weapon often referred to as 'moral suasion'. Banks are asked to discriminate between different types of borrower, continuing to grant loans to exporters, for instance, but restricting credit to property developers. While the instructions of the Bank of England are faithfully carried out, most banks would prefer to work on their own estimate of the credit-worthiness of borrowers. They do not like being placed in the awkward position where they have to grant a loan to one customer but refuse it to another of equal financial standing.

Second, non-banking financial intermediaries have had to be brought within the scope of the Bank of England's requests. While banks are the main source of liquid funds and the level of their deposits will have a big effect on the flow of money income, they are not the only source. In a market for goods, control by rationing does nothing to eliminate excess demand – it merely spills over to other goods or on to a black market. And so with credit: the limitations imposed on the banks have merely led to the development of other sources of credit – 'near' money.

As we have seen, liquidity is only a matter of degree and it can be combined with yield. There is no essential reason why a person must hold his funds in a *bank*. If other institutions can offer almost equivalent liquidity and a higher yield, people will be tempted to lend to them. And this is what has happened; these other institutions have competed successfully, with the banks for funds. Insurance companies, building societies, merchant banks, firms prepared to grant trade credit and, above all, finance companies have had funds available for lending. Moreover, institutions, such as factors who 'buy' trade credit, have sprung up to increase the liquidity of such debts.

Thus, as bank lending has become tighter, borrowers have turned to these 'spillover' sources. While many of these sources, e.g. building societies, originated as and remain specialist lenders, others, such as insurance companies and particularly finance companies, have extended their activities. For instance, they now compete with banks in giving credit for the purchase of durable consumer goods and for company development.

This extension of liquidity has compelled the authorities to bring these intermediaries within the scope of the weapons being used. This was achieved by the Bank of England extending its 'requests' to limit credit to such non-bank financial institutions.

Here the Bank of England could have been thwarted. Requests to the banks are backed by the statutory sanction of 'directions'. But this sanction does not cover other financial institutions. Nevertheless they did respond, chiefly because, Professor Sayers thinks, they are in close proximity to the banks in the City of London and thus all feel they are part and parcel of monetary policy. Consequently statutory authority has not had to be sought, and moral suasion still operates on the basis of a gentleman's agreement with the 'Old Lady of Thread-needle Street'. This gives greater flexibility to policy, allowing the authorities to decide according to convenience who shall be subject to requests and the nature of those requests. Thus in the credit squeeze of 1965-7, the government relaxed restrictions on lending by building societies in the interests of its housing policy.

The above discussion indicates that in the past the view of liquidity has been too narrow. As a result the traditional weapons of open-market operations, bank rate and varying liquidity ratios are not as effective in controlling the economy as was imagined. While they are still used as part of a 'package', they have to be supplemented chiefly by 'moral suasion' which can be more extensive and discriminating in its operation.

At times, control has been further strengthened either by

licensing building over a certain value or, as during the Second World War, by vetting all investment spending above a given figure through a Capital Issues Committee.

(3) Hire-purchase controls

Consumption spending (and some short-term investment spending, e.g. on machinery) is regulated by varying the conditions (the percentage deposit and time of repayment) upon which hire-purchase credit can be obtained.

The merits of direct monetary controls

(a) *They can be introduced or changed quickly.* Measures to curb credit (e.g. open-market operations and, particularly, direct controls, such as special deposits, requests to banks and hire-purchase regulations) can be taken quickly and at any time. Moreover, adjustments can, if necessary, be made by fine degrees, the Bank of England varying its pressure on the financial intermediaries, chiefly the banks, by the extent of its requests and selling of securities.

(b) *The effects of changes are quickly felt.* This arises because direct controls are invariably negative – they stop somebody doing something he would otherwise do. If it wished, a government with sufficient power could reduce fixed investment to zero almost overnight. Similarly, with consumption, stiffer hire-purchase terms can be made to bite immediately.

(c) *Direct controls can be discriminatory.* Because controls are negative, a discriminatory element can be introduced into the type of credit which will be granted, e.g. for exports, or the kind of activity which will be allowed, e.g. building. Interest policy, on the other hand, merely works on the price mechanism, while fiscal policy still allows people to choose how they shall spend the disposable income left to them. Even so, it must be recognised that fiscal policy can have some discriminatory intentions, e.g. by burdening some social classes and industries more than others with particular direct and indirect taxes.

The disadvantages of direct monetary controls

In spite of the above advantages, difficulties arise when controls are imposed for a considerable period of time.

(a) *Activity tends to be frozen into existing channels.* Controls over investment tend to prevent efficient firms from expanding and to inhibit innovation, e.g. in new techniques. Licences and credit are granted on past performance, for the bureaucrat finds it easier to decide on this basis.

(b) *A cumbersome administrative organisation is required to work them.*

(c) *The extent to which discretionary powers can be used is limited politically.* A large body of opinion is opposed to extending the powers of politicians and civil servants to make subjective decisions, particularly in individual cases. Investment decisions, for instance, may be determined, it is claimed, by political considerations (e.g. capital for the nationalised industries) rather than on economic merit.

(d) *Controls are effective only in limiting expansion.* When it is necessary to expand the level of activity, the removal of controls may not help. Investment optimism may have been damaged by the very imposition of controls, while if people no longer wish to spend, the mere removal of restrictions will not make them do so.

(e) *Certain controls tend to discriminate against the small firm.* The institutions which feel most severely the restrictions on credit are the banks – a major source of capital to the small firm. When the banks have to ration loans, they tend to favour the large firms, whose credit-worthiness is better. This is particularly hard on the small firm which has not the alternative sources of the large firm, e.g. internal reserves, the open market, a merger with another company having large liquid assets, etc.

(f) *Controls over consumption give rise to particular difficulties.* Hire purchase-restrictions tend to fall exclusively on a narrow range of industries, chiefly cars and consumer durables. Not only is this unfair, but it tends to disrupt the flow of demand and output. Thus spending on durable items tends to be bunched (producing what can be described as a 'hire-purchase cycle') and firms find it more difficult to plan for future expansion. Many of these industries are 'growth' industries, and export a large part of their output. Moreover, as they tend to work under conditions of decreasing cost, restriction of output can lead to higher prices, both for the home and export markets.

(g) *Controls increase the strain in other parts of the economy.* Controls do nothing to mop up excess liquidity. Price control, rationing or hire-purchase restrictions thus mean that, in time, excess demand forces prices to rise elsewhere. With investment controls, however, this danger is less. If, for instance, a firm is forbidden to build a factory, it is not likely to turn to building a hotel instead. On the other hand, controls over investmen, cannot be continued indefinitely if a satisfactory rate of future growth is required. The long-term solution must be to encourage real saving.

(h) *In time, controls are circumvented.* Applications are drafted to meet the requirements of a Capital Issues Committee, ways are found to overcome hire-purchase restrictions, and sources of finance outside the commercial banks come into existence. Thus while borrowers do not find a perfect market (in that they can obtain all the funds they require at going market rates), they do find other sources when the usual sources (e.g. banks, insurance companies, etc.) are stopped up. It means that they are put to the extra trouble of 'negotiating' a loan.

Conclusions

Controls over the availability of credit may be useful in the short run and have the advantage that they can be discriminatory. Thus they are useful as emergency measures designed to supplement and strengthen other weapons, particularly if the latter take time to become fully effective.

But they cannot be regarded as an *alternative* to such measures in the way that governments since the Second World War have tended to use them to keep down the rate of interest and lower the cost of servicing the national debt. The reason is that, in the long run, controls are not effective in limiting the total flow of consumption and investment spending. When borrowers cannot obtain funds from the banks, they often manage to obtain them from outside the banking system by offering higher rates of interest. And the fact is that, while the government persists in borrowing through Treasury bills, it virtually ensures that the private sector of the economy possesses sufficient liquid assets to provide such credit if the rates of interest offered are high enough. If the government borrows through Treasury bills, these provide the liquid assets. In short, the government, as a borrower, cannot isolate itself from market forces. No control of bank advances is likely to succeed for long in reducing spending unless it is accompanied by a general restriction of liquidity and a general rise in interest rates.

Furthermore, the borrowers who are denied advances and bid up rates as they seek money elsewhere are those who require funds so urgently, e.g. to finance short-term investment or to complete investment programmes already under way, that they are not discouraged by higher rates. This suggests that the main effect of interest policy is likely to be exerted on long-term investment plans – and consequently may take some time to take effect. Thus the attack on inflation must be broader-based, not relying on monetary policy alone, but extending to fiscal policy.

But even fiscal policy, to be successful, must be supported by an effective monetary policy. This means that the government must break out of the strait-jacket imposed by the size of the government debt and the need to service it as cheaply as possible. It is significant that at the present time (1970) firms can borrow more cheaply than the government by coupling their offer of stock with future rights to convert into shares. The government, too, must offer some inflation hedge if it is to keep down its cost of borrowing, e.g. by linking the capital sum which is repaid on maturity to a price index. This might enable it to reduce the supply of money without putting up the cost of borrowing – but only if it succeeds eventually in halting the rise in prices. The two are inter-linked.

SUGGESTED READING

F. S. Brooman, *Macroeconomics*, 4th ed. (Allen & Unwin, 1970) ch. 10.

R. E. Caves, *Britain's Economic Prospects* (Allen & Unwin, 1968) ch. 2.

W. M. Dacey, *Money under Review* (Hutchinson, 1960) Prologue, chs 4–9.

R. F. Harrod, *Money* (Macmillan, 1969) ch. 10.

Radcliffe Report, *Report on the Working of the Monetary System*, Cmnd 827 (H.M.S.O., 1959) chs 2, 5, 6, and 7.

D. C. Rowan, *Output, Inflation and Growth* (Macmillan, 1968) ch. 24.

R.S. Sayers, *Modern Banking*, 7th ed. (Oxford U.P., 1967) ch. 9.

CHAPTER 14

FISCAL POLICY

By fiscal policy is meant changes in government expenditure and taxation designed to influence the pattern and level of activity. In this chapter we confine our attention to the level of activity, largely ignoring the pattern.

Changes are broadly of two types:

(1) those which operate automatically;
(2) those which are discretionary, being specifically initiated by the government to increase the speed or intensity of operation of the automatic or built-in stabilisers.

I. AUTOMATIC STABILISERS

As we have already seen, one of the difficulties of anti-cyclical policy is knowing when, and by how much, expenditure needs to be varied. It is obvious that there would be great advantages in a system where forces automatically came into play to correct any movements away from the full employment level of AD. More specifically, if AD was expanding to the point where it was becoming excessive, these forces would reduce private and government spending. If AD was contracting to the point where there was less than full employment, they would operate in the opposite direction, expanding private and government spending. The government would be freed from the task of making specific decisions to counteract cyclical fluctuations.

To some extent, this does occur. As income expands or contracts, monetary and real forces come into play which, by influencing consumption, investment and international trade, act as dampers (*see* Chapter 12).

This also happens in the public sector. Indeed, the increase in the importance of government activity in the modern State has meant the government income and expenditure operate as major stabilisers.

(1) *Taxation*

As incomes increase, so does the yield from taxation. In this respect, taxes on income are the more effective for they are mostly progressive. Thus, as the level of activity expands, a higher proportion of income is taken in taxation.

The effect of indirect taxes is less pronounced. Many indirect taxes are specific, and only if demand is income-elastic, e.g. motoring and consumer durables, will they have a great stabilising effect. Purchase tax is the best indirect tax as a stabiliser because it is basically an *ad valorem* tax, and it is progressive in the sense that these goods which have a high income elasticity of demand tend to be taxed at the highest rate.

One important point must be made. If the stabilising effects of taxation are to work, the government must not increase its own expenditure as tax receipts rise, or reduce it when receipts fall.

(2) *Unemployment insurance benefits*

As the level of activity expands from a position of unemployment, government payments to the unemployed fall, while receipts from contributions rise. The opposite applies if the level of activity contracts. The higher the benefits and contributions paid, the greater will be the stabilising effects.

It must be noted, however, that these do not operate when aggregate monetary demand has passed the full employment level. Then there can be no change in unemployment, and so this automatic stabiliser no longer comes into play.

(3) *Agricultural price supports*

Agricultural price supports limit the extent to which the government will allow farm prices to fall; they thus maintain farmers' incomes. In other words, they prevent the multiplier from having its full effect in this sector of the economy. However, only if this sector is relatively important will there be a great stabilising effect.

Weaknesses of built-in stabilisers

Built-in stabilisers are advantageous in that they work auto-matically and do not require the government to exercise frequent discretionary powers to adjust the economy. But they cannot be relied upon entirely for the following reasons:

(1) *It is necessary to take corrective measures before changes in AD actually occur.*

Fluctuations are largely the result of changes in expectations. Such expectations are contagious and gather momentum. Towards the peak, therefore, some check is usually required before the fall in AD would occur automatically; similarly a boost is required in the downswing before inflationary stabi-lisers produce their full effects. The timing of these measures is extremely difficult, as the U.K. has discovered in the post-war period.

(2) *The delayed action of stabilisers can accentuate fluctuations*

For example, it may be that a company is paying large sums in corporation tax for the previous year when the level of activity was high although at the present time the level of activity has fallen and some reflation is desirable.

(3) *The tax leakage reduces, but does not eliminate, the multiplier*

The multiplier equals $1/(1 - c + ct)$. Thus the effect on income of any autonomous change in investment or government spend-ing will be multiplied but not by as much as if there were no leak to taxation. The higher the rates of progressive taxation, the greater will be the stabilising effect, for the rate of tax will increase as income expands, and decrease as income contracts. Nevertheless, high tax rates are not feasible politically, and in any case may have an adverse effect on effort, initiative, etc.

It also follows from the above multiplier formula that changes in taxation as a means of varying the level of activity are only effective to the extent that consumption responds. Thus if the effects of the tax changes fall entirely on saving, consumption is unaltered.

(4) *The amount of government expenditure that varies with the level of income is relatively small*

Most government spending is dictated by policy (e.g. hospitals, education, defence) or is contractual (e.g. national debt interest). It cannot therefore be varied to the level of income.

(5) *Operating stabilisers according to a formula to make them more effective comes up against practical difficulties*

Because built-in stabilisers are so desirable, some people have recommended reducing taxation automatically according to an agreed formula, e.g. the overall unemployment percentage, the average rate of unemployment over three months in those industries particularly sensitive to booms and slumps. The difficulty is that actual situations vary in cause and intensity, and a formula which might be right at one time could be unsuitable at another. There must be room for government discretion, not a mere slavish application of rules. Such discretion can be used to reinforce or modify the built-in stabilisers.

II. DISCRETIONARY CHANGES INITIATED BY THE GOVERNMENT

Because automatic stabilisers cannot be relied upon to control the level of activity sufficiently, the government has to reinforce them by *ad hoc* measures according to its assessment of current needs. These measures take three main forms:

(1) Changes in the form or structure of taxation in order to influence consumption and investment indirectly.

(2) Changes in the level of government spending.

(3) Changes in the level of taxation in order to leave more or less disposable income with consumers.

(1) *Changes in the structure of taxation*

We shall assume that the government wishes to raise the same amount of revenue, maintain its expenditure at the current level, but at the same time adjust the level of private consumption and investment.

To some extent this can be achieved by changing the tax

structure. Consumption can be raised by transferring the tax burden from spenders to savers. Relief from direct taxes can be given at the lower income levels (e.g. by larger allowances) and the loss in revenue recouped by making the tax more progressive at higher income levels. A similar effect would follow if the burden of taxation was transferred from indirect taxes (which are on balance regressive) to direct taxes (which are progressive). It should be noted, however, that the opposite of these measures (to increase saving) might be unpopular politically and thus more difficult to implement. But personal saving might respond to income-tax reliefs (such as those given on National Savings and Trustee Savings interest, pension and insurance contributions, etc.), and corporate saving by tax measures which encouraged the retention of profits rather than their distribution (e.g. the corporation tax).

Private investment spending can be stimulated by generous depreciation allowances when assessing tax liability.

The above changes have serious practical limitations. Thus higher rates of direct tax may adversely affect effort and initiative. In practice, therefore, the government has to rely mainly on adjusting the balance between government spending and revenue.

(2) Changes in the level of government spending

In the last quarter of a century, government spending (including transfer payments) has increased to such an extent that today it accounts for over 40 per cent of national expenditure – through the central government, local authorities and the nationalised industries. This has added to the government's ability to vary AD directly by adjusting its own spending.

Furthermore, as we saw in Chapter 11, any change in government spending will have a multiplier effect (provided it does not reduce spending in the private sector by an equivalent amount). The more its spending is concentrated on the poorer sections of the community, where the propensity to consume is higher, the greater will be the multiplier.

Higher welfare payments have an immediate effect on spending (though a limit to any increase in such payments is set by the incentive requirement that they should not exceed the incomes which people in work receive). Subsidies or interest-free loans to private enterprise may be used to induce greater investment spending in the private sector.

The weakness of varying the amount of transfers is that its expansionary effect is confined to *induced* spending only. This limitation does not apply when the government spends directly on goods and services, for this exerts both direct and induced effects. Over its own investment, e.g. on roads, hospitals, schools, public buildings, etc., the government has direct control, and it can exercise a decisive influence over the capital spending of the nationalised industries and local authorities. Such investment spending may be changed in an upward or downward direction.

When there is unemployment, the government can increase its own investment spending. Naturally worth-while projects will be preferred, for these will provide higher living standards in the future. But, since any additional expenditure will have a multiplier effect and thus lead to extra employment in the private sector, it is better, as Keynes pointed out, for the government to employ some men to dig holes and others to fill them up again rather than leave them standing idle.

Thus, in contrast to a reduction in taxation where there is no certainty that the increase in disposable income will actually be spent, public investment achieves actual spending. But attention must be drawn to certain snags:

(a) Certain government spending, e.g. on education and health services, may simply relieve private spending. To this extent, therefore, there is no net increase in spending.

(b) Whilst the government can increase its spending by stepping up its demand for equipment of various kinds, e.g. for defence, schools and hospitals, any large increase in spending would have to take in major public works. Here there are certain drawbacks:

(i) Government investment projects have to be planned well ahead. It is essential that as little time as possible is wasted in stimulating demand at the beginning of a recession. Some delay, however, is inevitable. Plans have to be prepared and approved, land acquired (possibly being delayed by objections to compulsory purchase), existing buildings razed, and contractors chosen by tender. It is possible that local authority expenditure does not encounter these difficulties as much as a national public works programme, e.g. a motorway. Hence more use might be made of local government investment in anti-cyclical policies.

(ii) Many government projects, e.g. roads, hospitals, universities, schools, and investment by nationalised industries, cannot be kept on the shelf until there is a deficiency in private investment. Basic government long-term policy, not simply short-term marginal adjustments according to the level of activity, must decide the extent to which such projects are given priority over private investment.

(3) *Changes in the level of disposable income via taxation*

Because of the above disadvantages, public spending programmes are unlikely to be sufficiently flexible as the complete answer to anti-cyclical policy. Fortunately, the government has another weapon, often referred to as 'budgetary policy'.

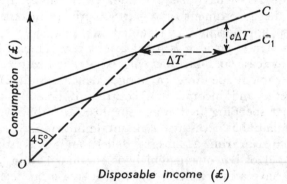

FIG. 68. The effect of an increase in direct taxes.

Briefly, it can influence private consumption by varying the amount of personal disposable income it leaves with people. The latter is achieved by changes in the level of taxation, usually at the time of the annual budget. This is shown diagrammatically in Fig. 68. We simplify by assuming an increase in a direct, lump-sum tax of T. This reduces disposable income by ΔT. As a result, consumption is immediately reduced (according to the marginal propensity to consume) by $c\Delta T$, and via the multiplier produces a reduction in Y equal to

$$\frac{c\Delta T}{1-c}.$$

The budget is thus no longer regarded as the means by which revenue is raised to meet the estimated expenditure for the year, but rather as the weapon whereby taxation is adjusted in order to vary private spending. Leaving more income with private persons by reducing taxation will, unless the whole of that income is saved, increase private spending – and this will increase income according to the multiplier. In terms of Fig. 68 the curve C_1 will rise to C. Thus, if government spending remains unchanged, the curve $C+I+G$ will rise, resulting in an increase in national income.

Attention must be paid to the phrase 'if government spending remains unchanged'. Budgetary policy is essentially one of adjusting the relationship between government taxation and expenditure. As we have seen, taxation represents an appropriation by the government of a part of private incomes. The amount so appropriated is retained in the circular flow of income only in so far as it is spent by the government. Hence, AD will increase and income will expand if taxation is less than government spending (a budget deficit). Similarly, AD will decrease and income will contract if taxation exceeds government spending (a budget surplus). In other words, if AD is less than that necessary to maintain full employment, the government can run a budget deficit and thus stimulate spending out of borrowing which, if continued from year to year, will have a multiplier effect and increase the size of the national income flow. Conversely, in an inflationary situation, by increasing taxation while holding its expenditure constant, or by reducing its expenditure while holding taxation constant, or by some combination of both, the government can accumulate a budget surplus and thus increase public saving to balance the deficiency in private saving.

The *main advantage* of adjusting AD on the revenue side is that it enables the national product to be divided between private and communal uses according to their relative priorities. There are certain tasks which can be undertaken better by the State than by private enterprise, e.g. defence, justice, social welfare, roads and health, and the government must decide on the proportion of the national product which should be devoted to them. How much is spent by the government would therefore have its due priority and not be varied according to changes in the level of private spending in order to maintain AD at the full employment level. Thus taxation policy can also be regarded as a means by which private demand is adjusted so that sufficient resources are released for the needs of the public sector. If there is full employment, and private demand is leaving insufficient resources to meet the needs of the public sector, taxation must be increased. If, on the other hand, the outlay left to private demand after the government has finished spending is inadequate to employ fully that part of production left to it, then more purchasing power must be left with private consumers by reducing taxation. In this way, full employment can be achieved without complete direction of resources. Once the essential claims of the public sector on the economy have been met, the rest of the national product can be produced and distributed according to the private enterprise system. Thus the main advantages of that system – the efficiency which springs from the profit motive, individual choice, the accurate measurement of consumer's wants, and the provision for those wants – are retained.

Such a policy, however, is not without its difficulties:

(a) The *convention of annual budgets* means that major adjustments to taxation can be made only at infrequent intervals. While there are advantages of an annual budget, some flexibility is required, such as the 'regulator' which since 1961 has allowed the Chancellor of the Exchequer to vary indirect tax rates by 10 per cent.

(b) The policy only works if spending changes directly with changes in disposable income. If there is unemployment, for example, and the government reduces taxation, AD will only expand if people spend at least some of their increase in disposable income. Such spending is more likely to occur if the tax reliefs are concentrated on the lower income groups. Similarly, an increase in taxation will only influence AD in so far as people reduce consumption. If, as in 1968, they respond by reducing saving, there is no change in AD. In contrast to tax adjustments, changes in government spending have a direct effect on AD.

(c) For administrative reasons, changes in many taxes, e.g. P.A.Y.E., take time to operate. Thus adjustments may often have to be concentrated on items which are likely to adjust the consumer's purchasing power quickly, e.g. indirect taxes, National Insurance contributions, the rate of release of deferred tax credits (such as post-war income-tax credits).

(d) As with monetary policy, timing, although difficult, is all-important. Time-lags, if not allowed for, may accentuate fluctuations in AD.

(e) Using taxation to adjust AD may conflict with other policies. For example, raising income tax to achieve a budget surplus may affect incentives and the rate of growth of the economy.

(f) Overall budgetary policy makes it difficult to direct demand into particular channels. Thus, where there is a deficiency of demand, it is better if the major part of any additional spending is concentrated on those districts and industries where unemployment is highest. Such a consideration underlines the necessity of having a variety of measures – not budgetary policy alone – which can be applied according to the needs of the particular situation.

(g) The policy may require continuous deficit spending with a consequent increase in the national debt. This is a problem to which we must now turn.

III. THE PROBLEM OF THE NATIONAL DEBT

Deficit finance, that is, a budget deficit, means that the government is obtaining funds by borrowing rather than by taxation. It has been suggested that this policy could have undesirable repercussions on the private sector of the economy. Entrepreneurs, steeped in the principles of orthodox finance, will be alarmed when the government does not balance its budget. As a result, private investment will fall, thereby undoing much of what has been achieved by budgetary policy.

Such fears today are probably groundless. The theory behind

government budget policy is now part of the training of most of the entrepreneurs who make the major investment decisions. In fact the knowledge that the government is committed to maintaining a high level of activity will itself encourage entrepreneurs to go ahead with their own investment plans.

But there is a more real problem. If the government has to supplement AD continually by deficit spending, will it not lead to an unwelcome increase in the national debt? In short, will the policy not hang a heavy burden round the necks of future generations?

The latter question reveals a misconception of the nature of the national debt. Suppose a country is fighting a war. To do this, it needs guns, shells, ships, aircraft, tanks and so on. These have to be produced at the time – by factors of production which would otherwise be producing consumer goods. Thus the cost of the war has to be met currently – the real cost is the consumer goods which would otherwise have been produced. What then does the government achieve by borrowing? Simply this – it exhorts people to save and to lend its savings to the nation. But it is the act of saving that is important. By not spending in consumer goods, savers are releasing the real resources which are necessary for the production of armaments. Since there is now less expenditure on the reduced amount of consumer goods, there is thus less pressure towards rising prices. As an alternative to borrowing, the government could merely print more notes. This would cause prices to rise until people could no longer afford to buy as many goods as previously. Entrepreneurs would thus be forced to reduce their production of consumer goods, thereby releasing resources for the armaments industries. The government would thus have achieved its aim by 'forced saving' – through higher prices.

In principle, therefore, the national debt entails no real cost to the nation as a whole. It merely represents what some citizens owe to those other citizens who orginally postponed their consumption. With a few possible exceptions, its existence makes the nation as a whole no better or worse off. It is just as though a son borrowed £1 from his father; it would make no difference to the wealth or income of the *family*.

Nor does the government need to worry about paying off the original capital, for this makes no call on the country's real resources. If a person asks for repayment when his loan matures, all the government has to do is to sell stock of an equal amount to somebody else. The debt can therefore go on for ever – provided the government raises sufficient money to pay the interest.

The above principles must now be modified to allow for the few exceptions referred to earlier. The qualifications are of two main kinds. The first arises because part of the debt may be owned by foreign residents abroad. The second occurs because a large debt can produce undesirable internal repercussions.

Where a part of the debt is owned by residents abroad, there is a claim on the nation's resources. As residents abroad receive interest or capital repayments on the debt in sterling, so a claim on goods produced in the U.K. is established. In other words, this claim can only be met by exports. There are thus fewer goods to be enjoyed at home. But even here, it must be noted, such a debt may not be disadvantageous. If the loan has been used for capital construction, the extra return may be more than sufficient to cover the interest charges and amortisation.

Internally, a large national debt may be undesirable for the following reasons:

(1) *It may have a harmful effect on the size of the national product*
A large national debt creates heavy prior interest charges on the budget. In so far as these have to be met out of progressive taxation, they may have a disincentive effect on effort and initiative, with a consequent overall reduction in the size of the national income.

(2) *It may have deflationary effects*
This is important when the government is seeking to expand the economy, for an increase in the national debt tends to lower both consumption and investment. Interest charges tend to redistribute income in favour of those who save at the expense of those who spend, especially if they are met by regressive taxation. In addition, increased government borrowing is likely to raise the rate of interest with consequent harmful effects on investment.

(3) *It may clash with other objectives of fiscal policy*

Where progressive taxation is already high, it is likely that interest payments will have to be met by increasing regressive taxes. This increases the inequality of incomes.

Furthermore, inasmuch as the national debt is owned by older persons, it redistributes income in their favour as against the young. As a result, capital may be channelled into safe rather than the risky, though possibly more rewarding, projects.

(4) *It may prevent resources being distributed in the best possible way between the public and private sectors*

Rather than face the undesirable effects of increasing taxes in order to raise revenue for interest payments, the government may cut its own expenditures. As a result, desirable projects, e.g. roads, schools, etc., are not proceeded with, while less important projects in the private sector, e.g. bingo-halls, go ahead.

(5) *It may make it less easy for a government to use monetary policy as a weapon for controlling the economy*

This applies only in an inflationary situation. As we have seen (Chapter 13), raising the rate of interest increases government interest charges and thus government spending. This in itself works against a deflationary policy, especially if the national debt is large. In addition, a large debt creates problems of meeting maturities and more important of the structure of the debt itself. While borrowing through Treasury bills is cheaper, it increases liquidity in the economy.

(6) *It may make the government less determined to control an inflationary situation*

Inflation benefits debtors. The government, as the largest debtor, may be tempted to let prices rise as a means of reducing the burden of the national debt in terms of real resources.

The above drawbacks must be viewed in their true perspective. As compared with the disadvantages of leaving resources idle, they pale into insignificance. In any case, we must remember that the national product is growing at about 3 per cent per annum. If the debt does not increase as fast as this, then interest charges will form a diminishing proportion of the national income. In fact, this is what has happened over the last 150 years. Whereas at the beginning of the nineteenth century interest charges formed about 8 per cent of the national income, today (1970) they form only 4 per cent. This tendency has been helped over the last twenty-five years by the creeping inflation which has taken place.

SUGGESTED READING

F. S. Brooman, *Macroeconomics*, 4th ed. (Allen & Unwin, 1970) ch. 9.

R. E. Caves, *Britain's Economic Prospects* (Allen & Unwin, 1968) ch. 1.

T. F. Dernburg and D. M. McDougall, *Macro-economics*, 3rd ed. (McGraw-Hill, 1968) ch. 6.

D. Dillard, *The Economics of John Maynard Keynes* (Crosby Lockwood, 1958) ch. 6.

R. L. Heilbroner, *Understanding Macroeconomics* (Prentice-Hall, 1965) ch. 8.

J. M. Keynes, *The General Theory of Employment, Interest and Money* (Macmillan, 1936) ch. 24.

M. G. Mueller (ed.), *Readings in Macroeconomics*, No. 25 by M. A. P. Lerner (Holt, Rinehart, & Winston, 1969).

A. Williams, *Public Finance and Budgetary Policy* (Allen & Unwin, 1963) ch. 15.

CHAPTER 15

THE GENERAL LEVEL OF PRICES
I. INTRODUCTION

The price level

EMPLOYMENT depends upon output. Output can be measured in real terms – so many tons of coal, so many cars, etc. but it is simpler to measure it in money terms.

The money value of national output is the product of the quantity of actual goods and services produced and the price level at which they sell. In order to concentrate on *real* output while still measuring it in money terms, we have so far assumed that no changes occurred in the price level.

It is now time to remove this assumption and to consider the general price level. While micro-economics can, as we saw in Chapter 1, explain the structure of *relative* prices and movements of prices relative to one another, it cannot explain why the prices of *all* goods and services sometimes rise or fall together. The latter is a macro problem for it is concerned with the only thing which is common to all prices – money, in terms of which they are expressed. A rise in the general level of prices means that any given unit of money will purchase less; thus a rise in the price level is synonymous with a fall in the value of money, and a fall in the price level with a rise in the value of money.

We shall not consider how changes in the price level can be measured. Usually an index number series is constructed, e.g. the Index of Retail Prices compiled by the Department of Employment. We shall simply assume that there is a generally recognised measure and concentrate on the theoretical explanation of changes in that measure.

Money as a stock and flow

As a preliminary to an examination of the price level, it is useful to clarify certain relationships.

(1) *The stock of money*

At any given time, the monetary authorities and the banking system have supplied a certain stock of money, M. As we saw in Chapter 9, all this stock must, for various motives, be held by somebody – individuals, firms, banks, etc. Thus money stock supplied must be identical to money stock demanded; that is, $M_s = M_d = $ active balances + idle balances.

(2) *Money flows*

When we consider a *period* of time, e.g. a month, as opposed to a *moment* of time, it is necessary to incorporate the idea of money flows. Let us simplify by assuming that the stock M remains unchanged throughout the month.

Now the sum total of all money receipts must equal the sum total of all money expenditures. (If I buy a book for £2, my expenditure is exactly equal to the receipts of the bookshop.) For the economy as a whole, if transactions T occur in a month at an average price of P, then total receipts = total expenditures $= PT$.

Clearly, all these transactions T must have been financed by the given stock of money M. Two relationships may be traced here. First, for any individual, the stock of money which he has at the end of the month will differ from that which he had at the beginning by the difference between his flows of receipts and expenditures. Thus if he starts with a cash balance of £20, receives £100 during the month and spends £90, his balance will rise to £30. But, since the stock of money in the economy as a whole is fixed at M, other people's balances must have fallen by £10. Second, because the given stock of money M has financed a total value of transactions equal to PT, each unit of money must, over the month, have changed hands *on average* PT/M times. Thus, if PT is £12 million, and the stock of money is £3 million, $PT/M = 4$. This *rate*, PT/M, at which money is turning over is referred to as the transactions *velocity of circulation of money*, V.

Aggregate monetary demand and the price level

Aggregate demand is the flow of money being offered against the flow of goods for the same period. During any period, the price of goods in general depends upon: (*a*) the supply of goods available for sale; (*b*) the amount of money (*AMD*) being offered against that supply. If the supply of goods decreases and *AMD* remains the same, prices in general will rise during the period. Similarly, if the supply of goods remains fixed and *AMD* increases, prices will rise.

This is merely a statement of fact, not of cause. But it does emphasise what any theory of the price level must take account of: (*a*) the supply of goods and services available for sale; (*b*) aggregate demand *in money*.

Since *AMD* is in money terms, our analysis of the price level is concerned with two major problems:

(1) *The connection between money as a stock and money as a flow of spending power*

In other words, what is the relationship between the supply of money and the level of *AMD*? The answer to this involves further questions: Can the velocity of circulation vary, and, if so, within what limits? What determines the relative proportion of the money supply held in active or idle balances? Is there any *direct* relationship between changes in the stock of money and *AMD*?

(2) *The relationship between AMD and the price level*

Here we are chiefly concerned with the question of whether the price level changes differently at different levels of *AMD*.

We deal with the first problem by discussing the views of the classical economists and, briefly, those of the modern Chicago school. Consideration of the second problem follows from this, dealing with Keynes's views and their development in the light of recent experience. In the main, our analysis will be in terms of rising prices, the situation which has confronted most economies since the Second World War.

II. THE QUANTITY THEORY OF MONEY

Introduction

On many occasions in the past, a rise in the general level of prices has been associated with an increase in the supply of money. This occurred in Britain in the sixteenth century when the coinage was debased, and again in the nineteenth century when the discovery and exploitation of goldfields increased the supplies of metallic money. Similarly, when governments have printed money because of their financial difficulties, prices have often soared.

From this simple relationship between the supply of money and the level of prices, the Quantity Theory of the value of money was derived. The theory attempts to explain changes in the general level of prices by reference to changes in the stock of money.

In its simplest form the theory merely states that the general level of prices, P, will depend upon the stock of money in circulation. An increase will raise prices, a decrease will lower them. Usually, however, it goes further, asserting that P varies positively and proportionately with the stock of money in circulation. Thus, if the stock of money is doubled, the general level of prices will double.

The Fisher Equation

But the crude version of the theory fails to see that the volume of goods and services, T, exchanged against money can alter and that, over a given period, the same amount of money may be used many times to finance different transactions; that is, the velocity of circulation, V, can alter.

To meet these criticisms, Professor Irving Fisher expressed the theory in a more precise form: provided T or V are constant, an increase or decrease in the quantity of money will result in a proportionate increase or decrease respectively in the general level of prices. More usually, the theory is expressed in the 'Fisher Equation': $P = MV/T$.

Criticisms of the Fisher Equation

If we are just concerned with the Fisher Equation as a statement of fact, there is nothing to quarrel with, for it is merely a tautology. If we rewrite the equation as $MV = PT$, the two sides are equal *by definition* for, as we saw earlier, they merely represent total expenditure and total receipts.

The tautology is useful in that it separates and concentrates attention on the three variables which are important in determining the price level. But when it is put in the form of a

theory to *explain* changes in the price level, it is open to fundamental criticism. As Fisher pointed out, P is proportionately
related to M only if V and T are assumed to be constant.
Can we make this assumption? If not, the theory has no
validity.

If we are concerned with movements over a fairly long period
– twentyfive years or so – we usually find a fairly steady average
V and a steady gentle upward rise in T. Given this relative
constancy, therefore, changes in M can explain the historical
movements in the price level.

In the short period, however, the assumption does not hold:
in different phases of the trade cycle, V and T may both vary
considerably.

In a slump, for example, the authorities attempt to encourage spending by open-market purchases reinforced by a
cut in bank rate; that is, they increase M. But only if businessmen are sufficiently optimistic will this result in increased
investment spending. A depression may mean that they are
unwilling to borrow at *any* rate of interest; here the creation of
additional bank liquidity is of no avail – it merely lies idle.
In terms of the Quantity Theory, the quantity of money has
been increased but its average velocity of circulation has
fallen because more is being held idle. Thus MV remains
unchanged, and so there is no increase in P!

But, ignoring this difficulty, let us assume that businessmen
do increase their borrowing when the banks offer more and
cheaper credit. Now the increase in M has led to more spending,
but will it affect P? So long as there are unemployed resources,
the increased spending is more likely to stimulate output than
prices. In terms of the Quantity Theory, as MV increases, T
increases. Thus P remains unchanged. Only as the economy
moves closer to full employment is P likely to rise. Thus a close
relationship between increases in M and increases in P is only
likely to hold at full employment.

Even then a further complication can arise: we cannot
assume that V remains constant as M increases. Once full
employment has been reached, an increase in M which produces a rise in P may so increase V (through expectations) that
further rises in P result, and an inflationary *process* begins, with
the rise in prices outstripping the increase in M.

To sum up, although the Quantity Theory affords one possible explanation (among others) of historical changes in the price level, it is inadequate as regards the short period. In seeking to show a direct causal connection between the quantity of money and the level of prices, it oversimplifies. First, by concentrating on the supply of money, it fails to analyse the demand for it. As a result, it fails to ask: 'Can V be accepted as a constant?' Secondly, by paying insufficient attention to the level of activity, it fails to allow for increased production when increased demand gives work to idle resources. In short, the theory falls down because it is essentially a classical theory implicitly assuming full employment. Finally, from the aspect of policy it is misleading. The theory suggests that an anti-inflationary policy need consist of little more than tight control of the money supply. Now there are dangers in the government's increasing the money supply – and the theory draws attention to them. But it fails to point out that the amount of money being offered against goods over a given period – in other words, aggregate monetary demand – is of much greater significance than the actual stock of money.

The Keynesian approach allows for this; changes in the price level are corollaries of changes in the level of activity. Thus they can be explained indirectly by analysing the causes of changes in the level of output. As we have seen, the relationship between intended saving and investment is of crucial importance here. Before examining these views in more detail, however, we shall digress to consider a development of the Quantity Theory.

III. THE CAMBRIDGE EQUATION

The Cambridge Equation, developed in the 1920s, is a refinement of the Quantity Theory. It relates the holding of money to the level of income.

In the Fisher Equation, T referred to the volume of transactions. This covered all transactions – in raw materials, labour, intermediate goods, stocks and shares, and finished goods. Hence P did not really refer to the general level of prices (usually confined to the Index of Retail Prices) as we understand it today, but rather to a vague, average value at which all transactions are being carried out, impossible to measure by an index number.

The Cambridge Equation remedies this. It covers only transactions in new final goods (both consumer and capital goods) in a given period. These we can call O. P' refers to the prices of these goods and V' to the speed with which money is offered against them. Hence $MV' = P'O$.

But $P'O$ is really, by definition, money national income; Y. And V' is the speed at which money is turning over in the purchase of final goods; that is, it is the income velocity of circulation of money. Now if money is turning over say five times a year to purchase such goods, the average holding of money over the year is one-fifth of income. Thus the equation becomes $M = kY$, where k is the fraction of money income held in cash balances. By comparing the equations, we see that $k = 1/V$, but the emphasis has now moved from the velocity of circulation to the holding of cash.

Suppose people want to hold one-fifth of their incomes in the form of cash, as above. Then in equilibrium, Y must be such that $1/5 Y = M$, for all the money in existence must be held somewhere. To achieve this, money must move on average five times per year in income-creating transactions.

What happens if, from an equilibrium position, M is increased? People now have more cash than they want to hold. So they spend it. As a result, money national income grows, the process continuing until M once more represents the fraction of income which people want to hold as cash. Like the Quantity Theory, the Cambridge Equation assumes that an increase in M leads directly to an increase in aggregate monetary demand.

Criticisms of the Cambridge Equation

Whichever way the Cambridge Equation is written, $MV' = P'O$ or $M = kY$, it is just as much a tautology as the Fisher Equation. But it does have advantages.

First, in emphasising the holding of cash rather than the supply, it leads to the Keynesian analysis of the motives for holding money and so to the modern theory of the rate of interest. Secondly, by introducing Y, it points out that changes in the level of money income can come about through changes in the price level, through changes in real output (the level of activity), or through both at once.

Nevertheless, when put forward as a *theory*, the Cambridge Equation is still inadequate:

(1) Like the earlier version, it predicts the effect on the price level of an increase in M by assuming that V' (that is, k) and O are constant. But k will be constant only if we regard money as a medium of exchange, not a liquid asset. The assumption ignores the speculative demand for money – if the increase in money is absorbed in 'idle' balances, there is no change in the price level. In terms of the equation, V' has decreased (k has increased). There is thus a break in the connection between the supply of money and the flow of aggregate monetary demand. On the other hand, expectations regarding the future price level may have the opposite effect, inducing an increase in V'.

Similarly with O; we can only assume output is constant if there is full employment.

(2) In so far as it tries to explain the level of income in terms of the quantity of money, the Cambridge Equation is misleading. For example, an increase in the propensity to consume or an improvement of entrepreneurs' expectations can increase the level of income although the quantity of money remains unchanged. The fixed quantity of money only affects expansion indirectly, the rise in Y leading to a larger demand for cash for transactions purposes and so to a higher rate of interest, which has a restrictive effect on investment and the level of income (see Fig. 50).

IV. THE CHICAGO SCHOOL'S VIEW OF THE EFFECT ON THE PRICE LEVEL OF AN INCREASE IN THE SUPPLY OF MONEY

Both the Quantity Theory and the Cambridge Equation view money as a medium of exchange – it is wanted only for spending. Thus any increase in the supply of money simply adds to aggregate monetary demand and, with full employment, drives up prices.

Keynes, on the other hand, introduces a new reason for holding money – speculation. An increase in the money supply has no *direct* effect on the level of aggregate monetary demand; the addition goes into idle balances where its impact is on the rate of interest. Only indirectly, through the effect of a lower rate of interest on investment, will it affect the level of income.

In recent years, Milton Friedman and Harry Johnson have challenged the pure Keynesian view by arguing that an addition to the money supply will not be fully absorbed in idle balances. Instead, it may spill over into the markets for goods and services, and thus have an immediate impact on the price level. Not only does their approach represent a part-resuscitation of the Quantity Theory, but it has policy implications – one condition for halting a rise in the price level is checking the rate at which money is being pumped into the economy.

The theory of the Chicago school is still the subject of empirical testing. It seems probable that there is something in both views, the Chicago school role of money operating more in the very short run or in times of rapidly rising prices, and the Keynesian view in the longer term when any addition to the money supply has worked right through the economy. The dispute really hinges on the question as to whether people automatically adjust the velocity of circulation of money to any changes in its supply. So far we have been inclined to accept that they do; Friedman, etc., are beginning to undermine this view.

V. THE RELATIONSHIP OF AGGREGATE DEMAND, THE LEVEL OF ACTIVITY AND THE PRICE LEVEL

The Keynesian approach to the price level

The Classical economists, by implicitly assuming full employment, were concerned mainly with micro-economic problems and had a separate theory, the Quantity Theory of Money, to explain the *general* level of prices.

Keynes, on the other hand, is able to deal with the price level as part of his general theory; the price level and the level of activity are jointly determined. At different stages in the level of activity, the price level moves differently. The role of the stock of money is confined to determining, with liquidity preference, the rate of interest.

To examine Keynes's theory of the price level, we shall start from and position where AMD is at such at low level that there is a high rate of unemployment. Here some prices have fallen: the supply of primary products (foodstuffs and raw materials) is typically inelastic; the unit cost of manufactured goods falls as production is concentrated on the more efficient factors; money wages fall with decreased bargaining power and raw materials cost less. Even so, many firms may just be covering variable costs.

As AMD expands, these influences will be reversed, and prices may rise to their pre-depression level. But the general

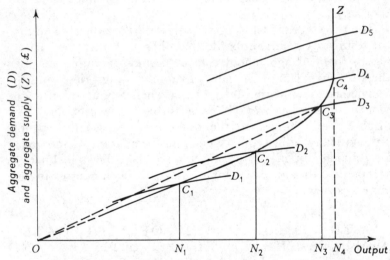

FIG. 69. The effect of changes in aggregate demand on the price level.

picture is one of increased spending being matched by increased output as unemployed resources come into production. The price level, therefore, tends to remain steady until a fairly high level of employment is reached.

We can illustrate the process by the aggregate demand (D) and aggregate supply (Z) curves introduced in Chapter 2. The Z curve (Fig. 69) shows the receipts which are necessary if entrepreneurs are to produce any particular level of output. These are the costs of producing that particular level of output. At output ON_1, the average price level is therefore equal to:

$$\frac{\text{Total costs}}{\text{Output}} = \frac{C_1N_1.}{ON_1}$$

The increase in the price level as output increases from ON_1 to ON_3 is shown by the increased slope of the line OC_3 over OC_1.

An increase in AMD from D_1 to D_2 will increase output but not the price level, as average costs are constant over this range of output.

Beyond an output of ON_2, however, costs start to rise. Thus an increase in AMD to D_3 produces both an increase in output *and* a rise in the price level – shown by the increased slope of the OC_3 line. Costs rise as bottlenecks develop through the immobility of resources. Diminishing returns set in, and less efficient labour and capital are employed. Output increases at a slower rate than a given increase in AMD, and this leads to higher prices.

The effect of the immobility of labour can be seen in the 'regional' problem. When income expands, spending is directed towards consumer goods having a high income elasticity of demand (e.g. cars, consumer durables) and certain capital goods (e.g. vehicles, machine-tools, computers). In these industries (and therefore in the regions where they are located) full employment is achieved fairly quickly, whereas in others a high level of unemployment persists. The reason is that labour does not move from the latter to the former. If the government seeks to achieve low overall unemployment (e.g. 2 per cent) by an overall increase in AMD, there is bound to be excess demand in certain sectors.

As full employment is approached, bottlenecks increase. Furthermore, rising prices lead to increased demand, especially for stocks. Thus prices rise at an increasing rate.

At some stage (e.g. 2 per cent unemployment), full employment (as defined in Chapter 1) will be attained. Those who are still out of work are structurally unemployed, or changing jobs, or unemployable. Any increase in AMD beyond full employment, ON_4, means that more money is being offered against an absolutely fixed supply of goods. Excess demand now applies to the economy as a whole, not just to certain sectors, and finds its outlet solely in higher prices. Thus when AMD increases from D_4 to D_5, the price level rises but output remains unchanged at ON_4.

In practice, the rise in prices may be suppressed by the government or delayed (repressed) by firms. The government may attempt to control prices, and institute rationing. If it is successful, people will be compelled to save any increase in AMD. But the inflationary pressure is still present and, for administrative reasons, it is unlikely that the government will be able to control *all* prices. Similarly, even if the government allows shortages to be met by increased imports, it can only be a short-term solution, for eventually imports must be covered by increased exports.

Firms, too, may delay price rises by drawing on stocks or lengthening order books. In time, however, stocks run out or firms discover that more goodwill is lost through delayed deliveries than by price increases. Eventually, therefore, prices rise.

Limitations to the above approach

The analysis so far shows that, as AMD increases, we should expect the price level to rise at an increasing rate as full employment is approached. Moreover, any increase in AMD *after* full employment is reached will find its outlet in a rising price level since, by definition, output cannot be increased.

This approach has the virtue of emphasising that the objectives of full employment and price stability may be inherently irreconcilable. As a result, an economy may have to choose between: (*a*) a *moderate* rate of price increase with the economy running at, say, 98 per cent capacity; (*b*) a *slow* rate of price increase with the economy running, say, at only 95 per cent capacity; (*c*) full employment with a comparatively *high* rate of price increase.

On the other hand, it has two main defects. First, it singles out demand as the cause of inflation whereas, in practice, inflation may start from the cost side. Suppose some major trade unions in the economy obtain wage increases not matched by a corresponding increase in productivity. This will tend to raise the costs of any given output; the aggregate supply curve moves from Z to Z' in Fig. 70. Provided other changes, chiefly further wage rises based on the rising cost of living, do not

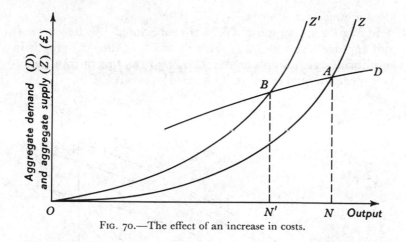

FIG. 70.—The effect of an increase in costs.

occur (see section VI), this will reduce equilibrium output from ON to ON' and *raise* the price level from AN/ON to BN'/ON'. A rise in import prices (e.g. through inflation abroad or by devaluation of the importing country) will result in a similar upward shift of the Z curve.

Secondly, the analysis implies that, when AMD increases, the price level rises just enough to absorb the excess demand, and that is that. Policy would largely consist, therefore, simply of raising the level of AMD to D_4 (Fig. 69) where there would be full employment at a given price level. This ignores the possibility, however, that price rises may generate further increases in AMD, and thus further price rises. If they do, inflation is not a simple static condition of excess demand, or even a series of isolated events. Rather it is a *process* which starts *before* full employment is reached.

VI. THE INFLATIONARY PROCESS

When we look at inflation as a process sustained over a period of time (perhaps indefinitely), it is again necessary to distinguish between changes on the demand side and the supply side.

(1) *A demand-induced process*

In Figure 71, suppose *AMD* is represented by the curve *D* and aggregate supply by Z. This means that the economy is in equilibrium at full employment, *ON*, for at this output necessary receipts equal receipts. The price level is *AN/ON*.

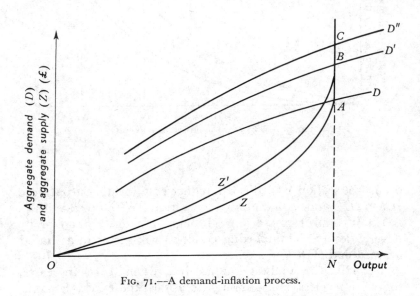

Fig. 71.—A demand-inflation process.

Now suppose *AMD* increases to *D'* because, for example, investment or the propensity to consume increase. Our previous analysis indicates that the price level will rise to *BN/ON*. But the process only ends there if the price rise does not induce other changes.

In practice, while higher prices benefit some people, e.g. profit-sharers, many lose. Their attempts to maintain their standard of living can be achieved in two main ways.

First, they can maintain real expenditure by saving less out of current income, by drawing on past savings, or (particularly in the case of the government) by borrowing. But output is fixed – and profit-sharers are already enjoying a larger share of it because of their higher incomes. Thus extra spending merely causes prices to rise still further.

Secondly, and more important, workers are likely to seek higher wage-rates to compensate them for the rise in the cost of living. Since, in full employment, trade unions are in a strong position, such wage rises are likely. In both ways, therefore, AMD is likely to rise still further, say to D'', pushing the price level to CN/ON.

But this is not all. If wage rates rise, costs of production rise and the curve shifts upwards, say to Z'. Thus we have the inflationary spiral, higher demand increasing costs, increased costs leading to higher demand.

Is there any reason why this process should peter out, or will it go on indefinitely? From Fig. 71, it can be seen that if the D curve shifts up less than the Z curve each time wage-rates are increased, the process will be a diminishing one. Eventually, the D and Z curves will cut at the full employment output, but at a much higher price level. In other words, AMD now equals aggregate supply (expected receipts equal necessary receipts) and here there is equilibrium.

Such a possibility is likely for the following reasons:

(a) *Some income groups cannot secure increases in income when prices rise.* Suppose that there is some inflationary 'shock' to the economy, initially in equilibrium at full employment. As prices rise, workers and entrepreneurs can increase their money incomes, whereas rentiers' money incomes are fixed. In such a situation, the process of inflation can continue until workers and entrepreneurs have regained their original level of real incomes. On the other hand, rentiers, because of the increased price level, suffer a fall in real income. In other words, equilibrium is brought about by a redistribution of income. The time taken to reach a new equilibrium, and the way in which redistribution occurs, will depend largely on institutional factors, e.g. the strength of organised labour, and the proportion which rentiers' income bears to total income. The larger the proportion, the smaller will be the price rise necessary to bring the inflation to an end.

(b) *Certain income groups may be able to secure only a part increase in income as prices rise.* Rentiers' income need not be fixed absolutely in terms of money. Inflation will eventually work itself out if one group does not try, or is not strong enough, to maintain fully its real income by increases in money income. Thus the 'money illusion' may mean that labour does not seek full increases to maintain real wages, while salary-earners may not be able to press their claims. Eventually such groups will have lagged so far behind in increases in money wages that the stronger groups will have maintained their real income at the expense of the weaker.

(c) *Expected price rises are less than actual price rises.* This again will damp down the amount by which the D curve rises, allowing the Z curve to catch up.

(d) *Import prices do not rise as incomes and AD increase.* In this case, there is no need for incomes to increase in the same proportion as the prices of *home*-produced goods in order to maintain real income, but only in proportion to the general price level including imports.

(e) *The propensity to consume may fall as prices rise.* This may occur through:

   (i) A redistribuiton of real income (e.g. from wage-earners to profit-earners).

   (ii) *A time-lag in increasing real consumption.* Where increased real incomes go to profits, companies may be slow to increase dividend distribution. Although such profits are usually retained for future investment, a period of time may elapse before this actually takes place, e.g. through bottlenecks in the capital-goods industries. Some expenditure, too, may be fixed in money terms, e.g. past hire-purchase commitments.

   (iii) *A 'Pigou' effect.* The rise in prices lowers the real value of cash balances, and people may maintain this real value by reducing consumption (*see* p. 64).

   (iv) *Real disposable income may fall because of progressive taxation.* All groups may accept this situation – which represents increased real saving by the government provided it does not increase its money expenditure accordingly.

(f) *There may be no increase in the supply of money.* If the government does not increase the supply of money, the extra demand for active balances will cause a rise in the rate of interest with some effect on the level of investment.

The above analysis suggests that although, in the absence of fresh 'shocks', inflationary pressure eventually works itself out, the effect on the price level may be considerable, especially if the passive groups in the economy are relatively small or if there is little decrease in real consumption as money incomes and prices rise. It is likely, therefore, that the government will have to intervene to check the price rise.

(2) A cost-induced process

As the level of unemployment decreases, certain income sections may move from the defensive to the offensive in seeking money income increases. Thus producers may seek higher real profit margins. But it is the trade unions who exert the chief pressure.

Trade unions are in a strong position. Employers generally see little point in resisting wage demands. For one thing, an individual employer knows that he will not be at a disadvantage for all other employers will have to grant similar wage increases. For another, when a number of large trade unions are obtaining wage increases there is a macro effect – the extra wages represent increased *AMD* to purchase output at the higher prices resulting from higher costs. And the government, committed to a full employment policy, expands the money supply until it is sufficient to finance the higher incomes.

Thus, as a result of the demand-pull inflation after the Second World War, trade unions have developed the habit of asking for wage increases regularly, even after demand has slackened. Indeed, in recent years, even an unemployment rate of 3 per cent has not halted the rise in prices. Trade unions have demanded wage increases beyond those justified by any price rise or increase in productivity. They may wish long-term settlements to take account of possible future price rises. More likely, they are seeking to improve their position relative to the rest of the community or to maintain particular wage differentials relative to other unions. Or they may simply be seeking to maintain wage-rates on a national level. Profits, and therefore wage-rates, may be high in one sector of the economy; trade union pressure transmits these higher wage-rates to other sectors where profits are not so high!

For a variety of causes, we thus have 'cost-push' inflation, where prices rise in the absence of excess demand. A rise in wage-rates shifts the Z curve upwards, followed by a rise in the D curve, *even though there is no excess demand to start with*. For example, in Fig. 72 we start from an equilibrium output ON, where the price level is AN/ON. A rise in wage-rates shifts the aggregate supply curve up to Z'; as a result the AD curve moves upwards to D'. There is thus a higher price level BN/ON, which leads to further wage increases and another rise in the Z curve.

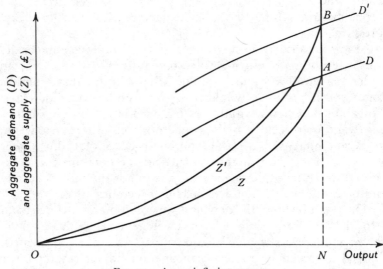

FIG. 72.—A cost-inflation process.

Again we have to ask whether the process will come to an end. In Fig. 72, the process is likely to continue indefinitely (unstable), since the Z and D curves have shifted up to the same extent. Where aggregate demand shifts up less, however, some unemployment will result. This may produce a moderating effect on wage demands. The process may also come to an end for the reasons given when we discussed demand inflation.

An import-induced inflation may be analysed by similar movements of the Z and D curves, a rise in import prices generally leading to wage demands to offset a rising cost of living, and hence leading also to a rise in the D curve.

Summary

A rise in prices can start an inflationary process. Such a rise is likely as full employment is approached, and can originate either on the demand side through increased spending not matched by increased output, or on the cost side through excessive wage demands, increased profit margins or a rise in the price of imports.

Both demand-pull and cost-push are interrelated in the inflationary process. It is likely that the rise in prices in Britain after the Second World War was initiated on the demand side; people spent balances accumulated during the war, and in addition government spending was high. Compensatory wage increases propagated the spiral. In recent years, however, it is cost-push which has been the initiating force, 'wage-drift' (through bonuses, guaranteed overtime at higher rates, etc.) and 'full-cost' pricing (a fixed percentage mark-up) adding to the price rise.

It should be noted that both types of inflation need an increase in AMD to keep them going; that is, demand influences are always present in inflation. They differ in that they have a different motive force, a difference which is important, as we shall see, as regards policy.

Expectations and the possibility of hyper-inflation

Once the process of rising prices is under way, it can be fed by expectations of further price rises. As we showed on p. 233, where the expected price rise is less than the actual price rise, the inflation process will eventually work itself out. But the opposite applies when the expected price rise is greater than the actual rise. Here we have an explosive situation. People hasten to spend money, for money as an asset is unattractive since it is expected to fall in value.

At first speculative balances are moved from bonds to shares (where profits rise with higher prices). But in a hyper-inflation, people will not retain money even for transactions purposes. (In the Austrian inflation of the 1920s, professors' wives called at the university on pay-days to collect salaries so that they could spend them before they had fallen in value during the rest of the day!) People economise on money balances by matching up receipts and expenditure, and buy real assets, e.g. antiques, Old Masters, and houses.

Nevertheless, the possibility of hyper-inflation should not be exaggerated. Before this happens, it is likely that some of the damping factors mentioned earlier will have come into effect. Most Western countries since the Second World War have experienced rising prices, but have managed to keep the rise at between 2 and 8 per cent per annum.

VII. WHY CONTROL INFLATION?

Rising prices affect the economy both interally and externally.

Internal effects

The effects of inflation on the internal situation in an economy are mixed. At first sight, some appear to be beneficial, but this view must be modified upon closer examination.

First, rising prices may make easier the task of the government in maintaining full employment. By improving the climate for investment, they help to ensure a high level of AD. This means that pools of unemployed are more easily absorbed by: (*a*) the movement of unemployed workers outwards to where demand is high, (*b*) the movement of firms inwards to where there are unemployed workers. In practice, however, immobilities lead to excess demand in certain sectors of the economy, and this has inflationary repercussions elsewhere, particularly through national wage agreements. Moreover, not only may mobility be thwarted by firms hoarding scarce labour and resources in case such factors should be needed later, but mobility may be of the wrong type – a high labour turnover through workers simply shifting jobs within the same occupation and area.

Secondly, rising prices may be conducive to growth. Investment and innovation by entrepreneurs may be encouraged. Buoyant demand for labour is likely to increase the labour supply through overtime and the entry of married women. Moreover, with no fear of the sack, workers may forsake restrictive practices.

Now while there may have been something in the above two arguments in the 1930s when unemployment was at a high level and remedies for curing it were unknown, the use of rising prices today as a means of encouraging a high level of AD cannot be accepted. In fact, for the following reasons, such a policy is self-defeating.

First, where inflation arises from increased consumption or government spending, investment may have to be restricted. Secondly, persistent inflation tends to encourage inefficiency. A buoyant seller's market means that competition loses its edge, for higher prices allow even the inefficient firms to compete and survive. Entrepreneurs are also able to hoard factors and, with plenty of vacant jobs available elsewhere, workers may not work so efficiently or may simply switch jobs for the sake of change.

Thirdly, inflation results in an arbitrary redistribution of income. People on fixed incomes lose – often those least able to bear it, e.g. pensioners. Those who can adjust incomes reasonably quickly in the face of rising prices, e.g. strong trade unionists and profit-takers, can hold their own or even gain. Similarly, those who have lent on fixed money terms lose; debtors gain. Thus the stability upon which all lending and borrowing depends is undermined. Saving tends to be reduced (thus adding to the inflationary pressure) and money rates of interest rise (since people seek to offset a possible capital loss). The government, as the largest debtor, gains as inflation reduces the real burden of servicing the national debt. If, for instance, the interest charge is £1,000 million a year, one-thirtieth of a money national income of £30,000 million has to be raised by taxation to pay the necessary interest charges. When inflation increases the money national income to £40,000 million, only one-fortieth is needed for this purpose. Alternatively, the government can increase its other expenditure without raising tax rates! Rising interest rates may, however, offset the price-level effect.

It should be noted, too, that the longer the price rise continues, the more difficult is the government's task of bringing it under control. People become 'inflation-conscious', reducing their demand for fixed-interest-bearing securities, and saving less. Indeed, if the price rise gathers momentum, hyper-inflation becomes a possibility.

External effects

Inflation can create serious difficulties for a country dependent on international trade, as Britain has discovered over the past twenty years. Where the level of domestic prices gets too far out of line with those of foreign competitors in world markets, there are repercussions on the balance of payments. Imports of consumer goods rise, as they become more competitive with home goods and as money incomes rise. Exports are discouraged; higher prices induce exporters to sell on the home market, and lead to a contraction of demand by foreigners. A balance of payments deficit on current account means a drain on the reserves or less net lending abroad.

But, in the case of the United Kingdom, this is not all. Because the reserves of sterling are so small relative to the size of her outstanding short-term obligations, rising prices in the United Kingdom undermine the confidence of the owners of such short-term balances. Should they start to cash them, a balance of payments crises develops even though, as in 1957, the current balance of payments may be in surplus.

The result has been that the British government has periodically been forced to take measures to reduce inflationary pressure. This has led to the policy known as 'stop–go'. Inflation thus proves inimical to sustained growth.

VIII. GOVERNMENT POLICY TO CONTROL INFLATION

The relationship between the rate of price changes and the level of unemployment

Our analysis indicates that the pressure on prices is likely to increase as the level of unemployment falls. This conclusion appears to be substantiated by research into the relationship between U.K. money wage-rates and the level of unemployment between 1816 and 1957, carried out by Professor A. W. Phillips. From it we obtain what has come to be known as the 'Phillips curve', which shows the relationship between the rate of change of wages (and therefore prices) and the level of unemployment (Fig. 73).

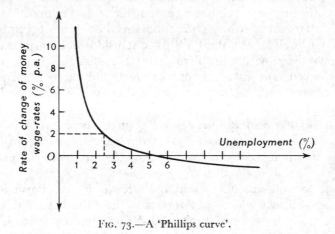

FIG. 73.—A 'Phillips curve'.

From the Phillips curve, it can be concluded that:

(a) given productivity increases of 2 per cent per annum, stable prices can be maintained with unemployment of about 2·5 per cent, for the rise in money wage-rates will be covered by increased productivity;

(b) stable wage-rates can be maintained only if an unemployment rate of about 5·5 per cent is acceptable.

We must further remember that the Phillips curve excludes certain exogenous causes of a rise in the price level, in particular increased import prices (resulting, for example, from a deterioration in the terms of trade or devaluation).

Policy alternatives

Full employment, therefore, is not a point (as conceived by Beveridge and Keynes), but a 'zone'. Such a zone arises because:

(a) a high level of AD can encourage overtime working and attract women into the labour force;

(b) the inflationary process begins before Keynes's full employment output – elasticity of supply is zero with respect to further increases in AD – is reached. Indeed, Professor Ohlin has suggested an alternative definition of full employment as 'the degree of employment that exists when the aggregate demand for commodities is at the highest level that is compatible with the condition that demand at *existing prices* is balanced by current supply'.

If our analysis and the Phillips conclusions hold, government policy is faced with a problem before Keynes's full employment is achieved. It has to choose between the three alternatives stated on p. 230. Among economists there are two main schools of thought.

The first considers that a level of unemployment of only 1·5 per cent must be the goal. Apart from humanitarian considerations, it is held that the fewer factors unemployed, the greater will be the national output.

The second school, of which Professor F. W. Paish is the best-known advocate, considers that the inflationary troubles of the U.K. are the result of running the economy at too high a level of employment. This has had two main effects: (a) excess demand develops in certain sectors which, through national wage agreements, is diffused through the economy in higher costs; (b) wage increases become larger and more frequent. Consequently, British prices get out of line with those of foreign competitors, balance of payments difficulties occur, and the 'stop' has to be imposed. Moreover, these economists do not admit that a higher rate of unemployment need necessarily produce a lower national product. The greater pool of unemployed resources would allow expanding industries to satisfy their demands more quickly and encourage employers to release supplies of labour. The efficient working of the price mechanism would not be hampered by extensive physical controls imposed by the government. The removal of windfall gains resulting from price rises would force inefficient firms out of business, concentrating production on the more efficient. Above all, a steady price level would enable the economy to work without the disrupting effects of 'stop–go'.

In practice, any decision has to take into account political considerations. No government could survive if it tried to work the economy at the level of unemployment required to eliminate price rises. These occur even if the level of unemployment is 3 per cent, as we saw with the squeeze during the second half of the 1960s. (The success of deflationary measures prior to this is doubtful, for price rises were probably moderated by the improvement in the terms of trade rather than by cutting back AD.)

Since the Second World War, government policy to combat rising prices has been along the following lines.

(1) *Exhortation*

Ministerial statements, publicity campaigns, etc., seek to moderate demand on the nation's resources and increase those resources by greater productivity. Thus we have the National Savings Campaign, requests to trade unions for 'voluntary restraint', pleas to companies to restrict dividend distributions, exhortations to workers and businessmen to increase productivity and particularly to export.

No harm is done by such exhortations (except when they act as a substitute for positive government measures), but the effect can be only marginal. In a private enterprise economy where the mainspring is the profit motive, it is unreasonable to expect persons to act continuously in the 'national interest', especially when there is no certainty that others will follow suit. It is far more effective to take positive measures, e.g. incentives for exports and productivity (thereby harnessing man's basic self interest).

(2) *Control of the level of AD*

Monetary and fiscal measures can be used to ensure that money AD is only just sufficient to buy the total output at constant prices. Such measures were examined in Chapters 13 and 14.

(3) *Direct controls*

Direct controls have been used to curb consumption and investment when the cause of inflation has been excess demand. Thus we have had price control and rationing of consumer goods, hire-purchase restrictions, building licences, controls over industrial building through Industrial Development

Certificates, controls over investment spending by the Capital Issues Committee and controls over spending by the local authorities and the nationalised industries.

Such a policy – often referred to as 'suppressed inflation' – either postpones demand or diverts it to non-controlled industries – the most likely result unless controls are applied vigorously to the whole economy, an administratively impossible task. If demand is postponed, consumers are put in possession of liquid funds which enable them to go on future spending sprees (e.g. after the Second World War); if demand is diverted to non-controlled goods, their prices rise and attract resources away from more essential goods. Suppressing inflation does not remove the cause but, by providing a break in the price–cost upward spiral, it may allow other measures to become effective.

Controls have also been placed on prices, wages and dividends in order to bring about a break in the sequence of the price–cost leapfrog. If the price rise can be checked, it removes the justification for inflationary wage increases. If dividend and wage increases can be prevented, then prices need not rise, except in so far as the prices of imports have risen. In practice, wage-freezes, 'periods of severe restraint', etc., have had only a temporary effect. When a freeze is imposed, some workers will just have received an increase in wages, where others will have their claims in the pipeline. The longer the freeze continues, the greater will be the grievance of this latter group of workers. Thus, unless the freeze is backed with legal powers of prohibition, it will eventually break down.

Furthermore, if wages and dividends are controlled, the allocating functions of the price mechanism are removed. How is labour to be attracted to those industries where it is most needed if wages are not permitted to rise? Similarly, how shall capital be allocated if charges in relative profitability are not indicated? Logically, if wage and profit controls are to work satisfactorily, there must also be central direction of labour and production!

Such criticisms do not apply with the same force to selective and temporary controls. These may be designed to contain a rush of hire-purchase spending, to limit spending in a particular sector (industrial building in congested or 'overheated' areas), to restrict a bunching of investment spending, or to phase local authority building programmes or investment by the nationalised industries. Thus such selective or temporary controls, in contract to those which are permanent, may play an important role in containing inflation.

SUGGESTED READING

*G. Ackley, *Macroeconomic Theory* (Macmillan, New York, 1961) ch. 16.

*R. J. Ball and P. Doyle (eds.), *Inflation: Selected Readings*, esp. Nos. 4 (S. Weintraub), 8 (M. Friedman), 13 (F. W. Paish) (Penguin, 1969).

*F. S. Brooman, *Macroeconomics*, 4th ed. (Allen & Unwin, 1970) ch. 13.

R. E. Caves, *Britain's Economic Prospects* (Allen & Unwin, 1968) ch. 3.

A. Day, *Outline of Monetary Economics* (Oxford U.P., 1957) chs 18–22.

E. Dean (ed.), *The Controversy over the Quantity Theory of Money* (Heath, 1965).

M. Fleming, *Introduction to Economic Analysis* (Allen & Unwin, 1969) chs 26–27.

R. F. Harrod, *Money* (Macmillan 1969) ch. 6.

J. M. Keynes, *The General Theory of Employment, Interest and Money* (Macmillan, 1936) ch. 21.

R. G. Lipsey, *An Introduction to Positive Economics*, 2nd ed. (Weidenfeld & Nicolson, 1966) ch. 51.

M. Stewart, *Keynes and After* (Penguin, 1967) ch. 8.

A. W. Stonier and D. C. Hague, *A Textbook of Economic Theory*, 3rd ed. (Longmans, 1964) ch. 24.

CHAPTER 16

THE BALANCE OF PAYMENTS

I. THE BALANCE OF PAYMENTS ACCOUNTS

THE analysis so far has been concerned with a 'closed' economy, that is, one which has no relationships with any other economy. We now remove this assumption, and deal with an 'open' economy, that is, one which imports and exports goods, buys and sells services, and lends to or borrows from other countries. We shall start by examining the 'balance of payments accounts'.

The balance of payments accounts of a country set out, in summary form, all the current and capital transactions which have taken place between the residents of that country and the rest of the world in a given period of time. This period is usually a year, though many countries now prepare quarterly accounts for forecasting purposes. The actual form in which the accounts are presented varies from one country to another. We shall describe that adopted by the United Kingdom in 1970 (Table 7).

(1) *The current account*

The current account is concerned with the foreign currency spent on importing goods and services from abroad in the course of the year and the foreign currency earned from goods and services exported. It is made up under two main headings – visible trade and invisibles.

Goods exported are termed 'visible exports', because they can be seen and recorded as they cross the political boundaries between countries. Services performed for people of other countries, however, are called 'invisible exports', because they cannot be seen and recorded as they cross frontiers. Examples are: government expenditure abroad, e.g. on overseas garrisons and diplomatic services; shipping services and civil aviation;

Table 7

Summary of the United Kingdom's Balance of Payments Accounts, 1963–9
(£ million)

	1963	1964	1965	1966	1967	1968	1969
A. Current account							
Visible trade	− 80	− 519	− 237	− 73	− 552	− 643	− 141
Invisibles	+194	+124	+160	+116	+240	+ 324	+557
CURRENT BALANCE	**+114**	**−395**	**− 77**	**+ 43**	**−312**	**− 319**	**+416**
B. Investment and other capital flows	− 103	− 289	− 308	− 564	− 560	−1,010	+ 48
C. Total currency flow and official financing							
Current balance	+114	− 395	− 77	+ 43	− 312	− 319	+416
Investment and other capital flows	− 103	− 289	− 308	− 564	− 560	−1,010	+ 48
Balancing item	− 69	− 11	+ 32	− 26	+201	− 81	+279
TOTAL CURRENCY FLOW	− 58	− 695	− 353	− 547	− 671	−1,410	+743
Financed as follows:							
(net drawing from (+)/net repayments to (−))							
I.M.F.	+ 5	+357	+489	+ 15	− 339	+ 506	− 30
Other monetary authorities	—	+216	+110	+294	+691	+ 790	−669
Transfer from dollar portfolio to reserves	—	—	—	+316	+204	—	—
Drawings on (+)/additions to (−) official reserves	+ 53	+122	−246	− 34	+115	+ 114	− 44
Total official financing	+ 58	+695	+353	+591	+671	+1,410	−743

tourist expenditure; receipts of banks, insurance companies, etc.; interest, profits and dividends from overseas investments; and private transfers, e.g. remittances to relatives abroad.

The difference between the values of goods exported and imported is known as the *balance of trade*. When we add payments and income on the invisible items, we have the *current balance*.

There is no special reason why earnings from goods and invisibles exported between 1 January and 31 December in any one year should equal expenditure on goods and invisibles imported during that period. In fact, it would be a extra-ordinary coincidence if they did so. The current account, therefore, is likely to show a difference between earnings and expenditure. Any surplus on current account (when the *value* of goods and invisibles exported exceeds the *value* of goods and services imported) adds to the United Kingdom's gold and foreign currency reserves; the opposite, a deficit, reduces them. The importance of a surplus or deficit, especially when looked at over a number of years, is that it indicates how a country is doing in its day-to-day dealings – whether it is spending less or more than it is currently earning.

(2) *Investment and capital flows*

If the current account transactions were a country's only dealings with the world, the balance of payments accounts would be quite simple. A surplus of £100 million, for example, would add that amount to the reserves or allow it to invest that amount overseas or to pay off short-term borrowings from the International Monetary Fund (I.M.F.) or other foreign creditors. A deficit of £100 million would reduce the reserves by that amount or have to be financed by disinvestment or short-term borrowing abroad.

However, there are other flows of money into or out of a country which affect its ability to build up reserves or to pay off government debts. These are flows of capital – leaving Britain for investment or loans abroad, and coming into Britain for similar purposes. Thus investment by private persons resident in the U.K. in factories or plant overseas (whether directly or by the purchase of shares), or a loan by the British government to an underdeveloped country, lead to an outflow of capital and the spending of foreign currency. Similarly, investment in the U.K. by persons overseas or borrowing from abroad by the British government, local authorities, nationalised industries or companies lead to an inflow of foreign capital and the receipt of foreign currency.

(3) *The total currency flow*

In the old form in which the U.K.'s balance of payments accounts was presented, the current balance was added to the balance of long-term investment to show the 'basic balance'. While this 'basic balance' was a good indication of the U.K.'s position over the longer term, it did, when in deficit, tend to overstate the pressure on the reserves, and this could have serious repercussions on foreign confidence in sterling.

The fact is that much of Britain's overseas investment is financed by short-term capital borrowed from foreigners, e.g. from the growing pool of Euro-dollars deposited in London. To the extent that this occurs, there is no net outflow of foreign currency. Britain's overseas investment which is undertaken in order to make a profit is, in fact, like private business ventures. And, just as the shopkeeper borrows from his bank to cover the holding of stocks before Christmas, so the U.K. borrows to finance investment overseas in factories, plantations, oil-wells, nickel-mines, etc.

The new form of the U.K.'s balance of payments accounts allows for this short-term borrowing, concentrating attention on the net amount of foreign currency which has to be found from official sources to cover the year's current balance and the net capital flows.

In practice, some transactions involving foreign currency, e.g. spending by British people on holidays abroad, cannot always be recorded accurately. There is then a difference between the recorded current balance plus the net capital flows and the exact amount of foreign currency which the Bank of England knows has been gained or lost. A *balancing item* is therefore added to make up for the difference. This balancing item is then added to the current balance and the investment and other capital flows to give the *total currency flow*.

The importance of the total currency flow is that it shows the money available for adding to the reserves or paying off the country's short or medium-term borrowing.

(4) *Official financing*

Any loss on the total currency flow has to be covered by the government by drawing on the reserves or by borrowing from the I.M.F. or other sources overseas. When there is a gain – a plus currency flow – the government can build up reserves or pay off such borrowing.

The items under 'Official financing' show how the government has covered a net loss or used a net gain. The + and – signs may seem rather confusing because + is usually taken as favourable and – as unfavourable, as with the current account. In fact the minus sign here means money going 'out' to pay off debts or into the reserves, and is therefore a good indication. A plus sign, on the other hand, means that the government has borrowed from abroad or 'borrowed' from the reserves – and we should rather not have to fall back on such money.

II. DISEQUILIBRIUM IN THE BALANCE OF PAYMENTS

When do corrective measures become necessary?

In the short period, a withdrawal from the reserves may not be serious. It may easily happen that, just prior to 31 December, the date usually chosen for drawing up the accounts, imports of raw materials are running at a high rate. Later, when the goods manufactured from these raw materials are sold abroad, the reserves will be replenished. Reserves of gold and foreign currencies are held for this very purpose – to provide a 'cushion' when current earnings are temporarily insufficient to cover payments abroad.

But the situation is different when year after year a country has an outward currency flow either through 'over-spending' on the current account or through 'over-lending' of capital. The latter is less serious, for the flow of lending can be quickly reduced. But over-spending on the current account means that country has been living beyond its means, and the correction involves some reduction in living standards. Nevertheless, if such a 'fundamental disequilibrium in the balance of payments' is not corrected, reserves will run out and other countries will refuse to lend because they doubt whether the spendthrift will ever be in a position to repay.

Alternative methods of correction

The prices of goods which enter into international trade have two components: (a) the domestic price, and (b) the rate at which the domestic currency exchanges for the foreign currency. Hence, if the U.K. is running a deficit, it can correct it either by (a) lowering the prices of domestically produced goods, that is, by lowering costs of production in the U.K.; or (b) lowering the exchange rate between sterling and other currencies. The next three sections discuss how a deficit can be removed if the exchange rate if flexible, if it is fixed, or if the economy adopts a compromise, the 'adjustable peg'.

III. FOREIGN EXCHANGE RATES

Occasionally, international trade may take the form of a barter arrangement, e.g. one country exchanges so much wheat for another country's lorries. Normally, however, exchanges are arranged by private traders who, according to relative prices, decide whether it is profitable to export and import goods.

But each country has its own currency, the U.S.A. (dollars), Spain (pesetas), France (francs), the United Kingdom (pounds sterling) and so on. This difference is important in international economics for two reasons: (a) as we have seen, sufficient foreign currency has to be obtained to pay for imports; (b) a rate has to be established at which one currency will exchange for another. Thus a pound sterling can be exchanged approximately for either 2·40 American dollars, 167 pesetas or 13·20 French francs. Basically, these rates of exchange are determined in the 'foreign exchange market'. This meets in no one place, but consists of all the institutions and persons – banks of all kinds, dealers and brokers – who are buying and selling foreign currencies. The foreign exchange market is a world market, dealers throughout the world being in constant contact with one another by telephone.

A free market

Let us suppose that the authorities do not intervene in the

foreign exchange market at all. In this case, the market will be a good example of 'perfect competition': each currency is homogeneous, knowledge is widespread among the expert dealers, there are large numbers of buyers and sellers and each dealer operates solely on the basis of price. The foreign exchange rate will therefore be determined by the forces of demand and supply. Suppose there are just two countries, the U.K. and the U.S.A., and we wish to determine the exchange rate between pounds and dollars. For simplicity, let us assume to start with that U.K. residents only demand dollars (i.e. supply pounds) when they wish to purchase goods from the U.S.A.; similarly the demand for pounds arises only because Americans wish to buy U.K. exports. The demand curve for pounds will tend to slope downwards because as fewer dollars have to be given up for each pound, it becomes cheaper to buy U.K. goods. The supply curve of pounds will slope upwards because as more dollars can be obtained per pound, so it becomes cheaper to buy American exports.

In Figure 74, the equilibrium rate of exchange at which the demand for pounds equals the supply of pounds is \$2·40. Let us suppose that there is, in addition, balance of payments equilibrium for both the U.K. and the U.S.A.

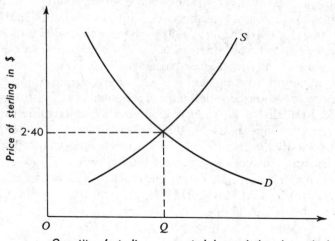

Quantity of sterling per period demanded and supplied

FIG. 74.—A free foreign exchange market.

What will be the effect on the exchange rate if the U.S.A.'s demand for U.K. exports decreases, and the balance of payments of the U.K. therefore becomes adverse? The decreased demand for U.K. goods will cause a decreased demand for pounds, e.g. curve *D'* (Fig. 75). At the existing rate of exchange, there is an excess supply of sterling on the market, and this will cause the rate to depreciate. As the rate depreciates, two changes tend automatically to correct the balance of payments deficit: (*a*) the demand for pounds expands along *D'* from *OQ'* to *OQ''*, and (*b*) the supply of pounds contracts along *S* from *OQ* to *OQ''*. In other words, the market forces automatically *eliminate any deficit* by expanding exports and contracting imports. (At the same time, the U.S.A. will have developed a surplus. The exchange rate will appreciate, and this will eliminate the surplus by contracting exports and expanding imports.)

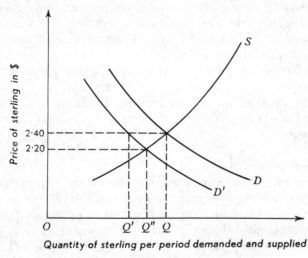

FIG. 75.—A depreciation of the exchange rate.

From this simple model it would appear that the problem of balance of payments deficits/surpluses simply does not arise if foreign exchange rates are allowed to fluctuate freely. Moreover, domestic prices remain constant. Why, then, in practice do most countries intervene in the foreign exchange market? There are four basic reasons:

(1) *To offset temporary autonomous capital movements*

By concentrating only on currency flows in return for imports and exports, our model drastically oversimplifies. The demand for pounds may arise because foreigners (i) wish to buy U.K. goods or services; (ii) want other 'invisible' imports, e.g. foreign holdays in the U.K.; (iii) make long-term capital movements; (iv) make short-term capital movements. This means that the exchange rate may fluctuate simply because of autonomous capital movements. Yet this will affect the values of imports and exports on the current account! This is an unnecessary complication if the capital movements are of a temporary nature.

(2) *To eliminate the effects of speculation*

In particular short-term capital movements may be speculative. If foreigners who have imported British goods expect the pound to depreciate, they will delay as long as possible before paying, whereas British residents who have imported goods will pay as quickly as possible. These 'lags' and 'leads' may be quite important in magnitude, and will have an adverse effect on the sterling exchange rate. In addition, holders of sterling become less willing to hold it if they expect its value to depreciate.

(3) *To give stability to the exchange rate*

Suppose that the demand for sterling decreases from D to D' (Fig. 75), causing the exchange rate to depreciate to \$2·20. The depreciation itself may cause holders of sterling to think that a further fall is likely. If they do, they will react by selling sterling, that is, the supply curve S will shift to the right. This causes the exchange rate to fall even further: the expectations of the sellers come to be justified! If more and more holders of sterling act in this way, a crisis can easily develop. In this case, the exchange rate is unstable. (It should be noted, however, that speculation is not necessarily destabilising; provided movements in the rate are not too large, a rise in the rate will usually cause people to expect a future fall, and a fall will cause them to expect a rise. They will therefore tend to sell or buy respectively, and this will stabilise the rate.)

(4) *To prevent frequent fluctuations in the exchange rate*

An unstable exchange rate will obviously have adverse effects on international trade and investment. But even if the rate is stable, frequent changes will tend to inhibit trade and investment. For example, by the time an exporter receives payment for his good, the exchange rate may have moved against him so much that his expected profit has been turned into a loss. In such circumstances he may prefer not to take the risk of trading with somebody in another country. Although arrangements can usually be made with a dealer to supply 'forward exchange' (that is, the foreign currency can be obtained at a given future date at an agreed price), the additional cost involved may make trade unprofitable.

Because of these disadvantages, most economies have avoided freely fluctuating rates. In the next section we analyse an alternative – a 'full' gold standard system – in which each country maintains a fixed exchange rate.

IV. THE GOLD STANDARD SYSTEM

The meaning of the 'gold standard'

A country is said to be 'on the gold standard' when its standard monetary unit can be exchanged for gold at a fixed rate and without restriction. Thus, in 1914, the pound sterling was exchangeable for 113·0016 grains of fine gold, and the American dollar for 23·22 grains.

The mechanism of the gold standard

Suppose that the value of Britain's imports from the U.S.A. exceeded the value of her exports. Dollars would be required to pay for these imports and the price of the dollar would rise relative to the pound on the foreign exchange market.

Now £1 sterling would buy 113 grains of fine gold, and this quantity of gold could also be exchanged for $4·86. Therefore, £1 = $4·86. If, on the the exchange market, a British importer could obtain only $4·70 for a pound, it would be cheaper for him to change his sterling into gold at the fixed price, and then ship this gold to the American exporter in order to pay for the goods. In practice, therefore, £1 could never exchange for less than $4·86 minus the cost of buying gold and shipping it to America (about ½ per cent). Similarly, if exports were greater in value than imports, £1 could never exchange for more than $4·86 plus the cost of buying and shipping gold from America. Thus the rate of exchange between the pound and the dollar could only fluctuate within very narrow limits – the gold points shown in Fig. 76.

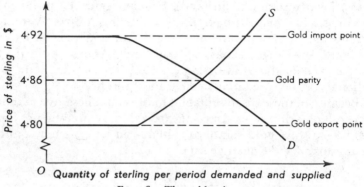

FIG. 76.—The gold points.

The first major advantage of the gold standard was therefore the encouragement given to international trade and investment, because: (a) a country's currency was virtually equivalent to gold; (b) exchange rates were fixed through the common link with gold; (c) gold was a world currency.

The second major advantage was that the gold standard provided a mechanism for correcting balance of payments disequilibria. In the case of a U.K. deficit, purchases of gold were paid for by cheques drawn on the commercial banks. The commercial banks drew the gold from the Bank of England, thereby lowering the balances they held there. This reduced their cash ratio, and so, unless the Bank of England restored the position by buying securities on the open market, the commercial banks had to reduce their lending activities.

Furthermore, the Bank of England's power to issue notes was

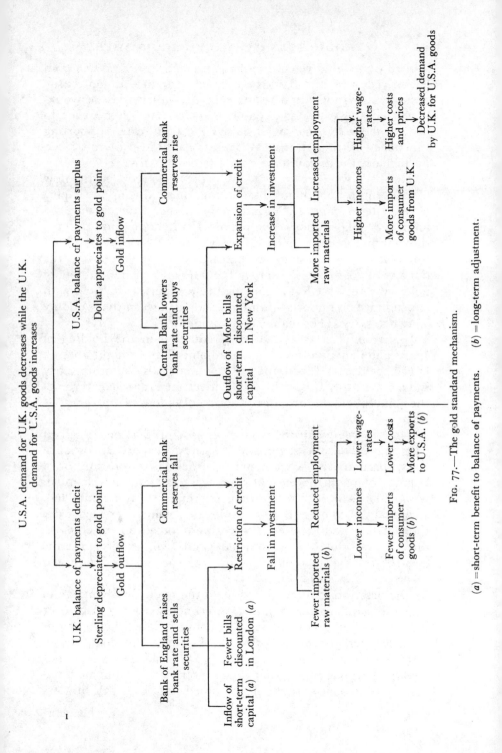

U.S.A. demand for U.K. goods decreases while the U.K. demand for U.S.A. goods increases

U.S.A. balance of payments surplus

Dollar appreciates to gold point

Gold inflow

Commercial bank reserves rise

Central Bank lowers bank rate and buys securities

Expansion of credit

Outflow of short-term capital

More bills discounted in New York

Increase in investment

More imported raw materials   Increased employment

Higher incomes

More imports of consumer goods from U.K.

Higher wage-rates

Higher costs and prices

Decreased demand by U.K. for U.S.A. goods

U.K. balance of payments deficit

Sterling depreciates to gold point

Gold outflow

Commercial bank reserves fall

Bank of England raises bank rate and sells securities

Inflow of short-term capital (a)

Fewer bills discounted in London (a)

Restriction of credit

Fall in investment

Fewer imported raw materials (b)   Reduced employment

Lower incomes

Fewer imports of consumer goods (b)

Lower wage-rates

Lower costs

More exports to U.S.A. (b)

Fig. 77.—The gold standard mechanism.

(a) = short-term benefit to balance of payments.   (b) = long-term adjustment.

I

limited by its gold reserve and the fiduciary issue. When gold left the country, the Bank was forced to reduce its note issue because any application to increase the fiduciary issue would have been regarded as a panic measure. Hence in order to protect the gold reserves, it raised the bank rate, supporting this policy with open-market operations. Other interest rates, particularly the discount rate, moved in sympathy.

This had two effects. First, the higher rate reduced the flow of bills sent to London for discounting, thus reducing the export of short-term capital. Secondly, the higher rate encouraged foreigners to keep short-term balances in London and attracted short-term foreign capital. The two taken together had an immediate, first-aid effect of halting, and even reversing, the outflow of gold. But to remove the *real* cause of the outflow of gold – the decrease in the earnings from exports compared with expenditure on imports – fundamental changes in the economy were necessary. These came about as follows.

Higher interest rates led to a reduction in the holding of stocks and in capital investment at home. This brought about a fall in the demand for imported raw materials – another fairly immediate benefit. But the fall in investment also led, through the multiplier, to an all-round contraction of incomes at home.

This, it was assumed, would bring a proportionate fall in costs and home prices, making it easier to export. In practice costs, particularly wages, proved sticky. Restoration of a balance of payments equilibrium was restored, not so much by greater exports, as by reduced imports as incomes fell. Eventually, however, the unemployment which resulted from the deflation had its effect. Wages were forced down, costs reduced, prices of home-produced goods fell, exports became cheaper relative to foreign goods, and the flow of trade was reversed.

The description above leads us to the main disadvantage of the gold standard mechanism: an economy loses control over its domestic economic policy. It should inflate when it gains gold, and deflate when it loses gold. In particular, deflation results in unemployment (because wages and prices are not flexible downwards), so that the economy cannot pursue a full employment policy. It should be noted, too, that gold inflows and outflows may be the result of speculation, rather than of any fundamental change in the structure of the economy.

We have seen that, while freely fluctuating rates have the advantage of correcting an imbalance without altering the domestic cost–price structure, they tend to inhibit trade. On the other hand, fixed rates encourage trade, but can only correct imbalances through inflation or deflation. In the post-war world, countries have tried to obtain the best features of both free and fixed rates by using the adjustable peg system.

V. THE ADJUSTABLE PEG SYSTEM

The main argument against a freely fluctuating rate is that the rate can be influenced by many factors (particularly short-term speculative capital movements) which bear little relation to the basic condition of the balance of payments. Consequently most countries now 'peg' their currencies at fixed rates. For example, the U.K. has agreed a par value of $2·40 with the I.M.F., although fluctuations are allowed to take place between the limits of $2·38 and $2·42 as shown in Fig. 78.

Suppose the market forces are represented by D and S,

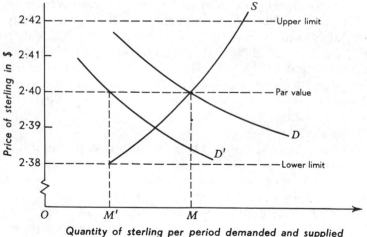

Quantity of sterling per period demanded and supplied

FIG. 78.—A 'pegged' exchange rate.

giving a rate of $2·40. Now the demand for sterling decreases to D', causing the pound to depreciate. As soon as the rate approaches anywhere near the lower limit, the authorities will have to take action to 'support the rate'. Thus, in the U.K., the Bank of England, through the Exchange Equalisation Account, will counteract the lower demand by buying on the market with some of the convertible currency reserves. In Figure 78, if it wished to maintain the rate at £2·40, it would have to buy MM' sterling.

Countries are expected to maintain the pegged rate as long as possible, so that the advantages of fixed rates for the world economy are obtained. But obviously the authorities can only support the rate from the reserves for a limited time: the U.K. reserves, for example, are small relative to the size of her imports and exports. In short, having chosen a fixed rate, the authorities have to accept the implication of fixity: adjustment to the balance of payments must come, as we saw in section III, from changes in income and employment (unless the government places restrictions on trade).

However, no government today is prepared to accept large changes in income (and hence in employment) simply to maintain the exchange rate at a certain level. Hence the rules of the I.M.F. allow some flexibility in order to avoid undesirable levels of unemployment. This flexibility takes two forms: (a) in the short run, member countries can draw foreign currency from the Fund so that they are not forced to support the parity entirely from their own reserves; (b) in the long run, if there is 'a fundamental disequilibrium', the peg can be adjusted, that is, the par value can be altered. For example, the pound sterling was devalued in 1967 and the German Deutschmark was revalued in 1968.

Summary

The balance of payments can be said to be in equilibrium if the foreign payments required for autonomous imports are equal to the foreign receipts gained from autonomous exports (where 'imports' and 'exports' are used in the widest sense of the term, to include both current and capital transactions). If the demand for foreign exchange is just equal to the supply at the current exchange rate, this implies balance of payments equilibrium. When demand and supply are unequal at the current exchange rate, this implies disequilibrium.

The basic problem for policy-makers with regard to the balance of payments is therefore to manage the foreign exchange market: pressures on the exchange rate must be identified and removed.

Under a managed currency, there are basically two correcting mechanisms: (a) an adjustment of the income level, or (b) a policy designed to switch expenditure. The latter may include a change in the exchange rate to a more appropriate level. These mechanisms are discussed in the next two chapters.

SUGGESTED READING

T. F. Dernburg and D. M. McDougall, *Macro-economics*, 3rd ed. (McGraw-Hill, 1968) ch. 14.
R. F. Harrod, *International Economics*, 4th ed. (Macmillan 1957) chs 5 and 6.
R. F. Harrod, *Money* (Macmillan, 1969) chs 3 and 4.
C. P. Kindleberger, *International Economics*, 4th ed. (Irwin, 1968) chs 2–5.
W. M. Scammell, *International Monetary Policy*, 2nd ed. (Macmillan, 1967) chs 2–10.

CHAPTER 17

BALANCE OF PAYMENTS ADJUSTMENT THROUGH INCOME CHANGES

I. INTRODUCTION

IN Chapter 16, section III, we saw how a balance of payments deficit was corrected under the gold standard. The gold outflow led to action by the central bank which caused a deflation of costs and prices, or unemployment. The classical economists emphasised the role of price changes; the deficit would be corrected by a greater demand for cheaper exports and a reduced demand for dearer imports. In practice, as we have seen, costs and prices were fairly rigid; workers preferred to be unemployed rather than accept a cut in money wages. Hence the correction in the balance of payments was achieved more by reduced demand for imports (as incomes fell) than by a change in the relative prices of imports and exports.

There are therefore two mechanisms which can be used to restore equilibrium in the balance of payments:

(1) *Relative price changes*

These are caused by changes in costs and prices within an economy, or by changes in the exchange rate. They lead to what is essentially *expenditure switching* (*see* Chapter 18).

(2) *Relative income changes*

Here the basic principle is to treat imports and exports on Keynesian lines. For the U.K., export receipts are part of her income, swelling the circular flow in the same way as investment expenditure. Import payments, however, increase the incomes of *other* countries: they constitute a leak out of the circular flow, in the same way as savings do. Consequently, if a country's exports increase in value, national income will rise; if they fall, national income will fall. At the same time, if imports are related to income, changes in income will cause changes in import payments.

There is therefore a two-way connection: the balance of payments affects income, and income affects the balance of payments. These relationships form the subject-matter of this chapter.

II. THE BALANCE OF PAYMENTS AND THE LEVEL OF INCOME

In order to exclude the effects of saving, investment and government activity on the level of income, and to concentrate entirely on the balance of payments, we shall take a very simple model.

We assume:

(1) A is a country whose international trade is small relative to total world trade. This enables us to ignore the repercussions (or 'feedbacks') of changes in A's exports or income on the rest of the world (R.O.W.).

(2) A is producing at less than full employment.

(3) Increased activity does not affect the price level up to full employment.

(4) Exchange rates remain fixed.

(5) There is no change in the rate of interest as a result of a change in activity. Thus induced changes in capital movements can be ignored.

(6) There is no investment spending, government spending, or taxation.

(7) All figures are expressed in £ million.

(8) Income is in equilibrium at 1,000.

(9) The whole of income is consumed (C), i.e. there is no saving. However, consumption can either be on domestic output (C_d) or on imports (M). Hence we have $Y = C = C_d + M$. All importing is performed by households, none by firms.

(10) $M = mY$, where m is the fraction of income spent on imports, i.e. the propensity to import. Similarly c_d is

the propensity to spend income on domestic consumer goods.

(11) $m = 0.2$ at all levels of income, i.e. the marginal and average propensities to import are equal. Thus $c_d = 0.8$.

(12) The volume of exports (X) is independent of income.

The circular flow of income is therefore as shown in Fig. 79.

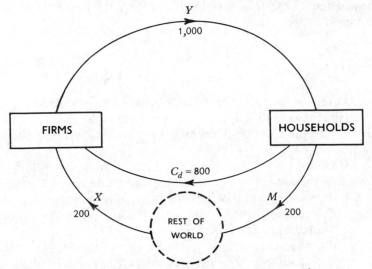

FIG. 79.—The circular flow of income including imports and exports.

In general, $Y = C_d + X$

$$= c_d Y + X$$

$$\therefore Y(1 - c_d) = X$$

$$\therefore \qquad Y = \frac{X}{(1 - c_d)}.$$

Since $(1 - c_d) = m$, $Y = \dfrac{X}{m}$.

The effect of a change in the balance of payments on the level of income

Suppose exports increase to 400, causing a balance of payments surplus of 200 and an initial expansion of income to 1,200. This will not be the final position. The expansion of income will continue until the balance of payments is once more in equilibrium. In other words, it is the change in income, not a change in relative prices, which, in this model, brings about equilibrium.

What new equilibrium level of income will result? We can follow through the circular flow of income (Fig. 80).

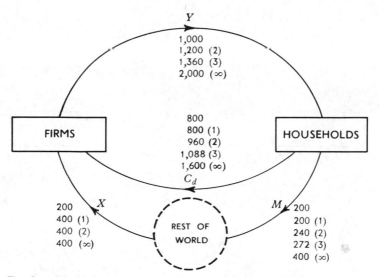

FIG. 80.—The result of an increase in exports on the circular flow of income.

The change in exports is subject to the multiplier $(1/m)$

so that $\Delta Y = \dfrac{\Delta X}{m} = \dfrac{200}{0\cdot2} = 1,000.$

Hence the new level of income is 2,000, and imports rise to 400. (Balance of payments equilibrium is maintained in this model because imports constitute the only leakage out of the circular flow.)

To sum up, the balance of payments and income interact in two ways: (1) the balance of payments affects Y; (2) changes in

Y affect the balance of payments through the relationship between M and Y.

Does the balance of payments always balance when income is in equilibrium?

In practice, the interaction between the balance of payments and the level of Y is not quite so simple. We have to consider

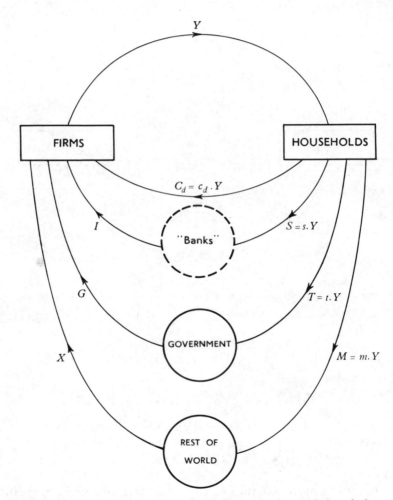

FIG. 81.—The circular flow of income with three injections and three leakages.

the whole range of leaks out of, and injections into, the income flow.

Assume:

(1) X, I and G are autonomous.

(2) C_d, M, S and T are each a fixed proportion of income, with propensities c_d, m, s and t.

The resulting circular flow of income is shown in Fig. 81. The income-generating equation is:

$$= C_d + I + G + X$$

$$= c_d.Y + I + G + X.$$

Hence $\qquad Y(1 - c_d) = I + G + X.$

Hence $\qquad Y = \dfrac{I + G + X}{(1 - c_d)}.$

Alternatively, since $c_d + s + m + t = 1$, this can be rewritten

$$Y = \frac{I + G + X}{(s + m + t)}.$$

Alternatively, we can rewrite this as an equilibrium condition by cross-multiplying:

$$(s + m + t)Y = I + G + X$$

or $\qquad S + M + T = I + G + X.$

This turns out to be the familiar condition (*see* Chapter 7) that, in equilibrium, the sum of the injections exactly matches the sum of the leakages.

Note that it is not necessary for any given pair of injections and leaks to be equal. Suppose, for example, that $I = G = X = 120$, so that total injections are 360. Suppose that $s = 0.05$, $m = 0.2$ and $t = 0.15$. Then:

$$Y = \frac{360}{0.4} = 900.$$

Out of this income, $S = 45 <$ investment, 120

$$M = 180 > \text{exports, } 120$$

and $T = 135 >$ government spending, 120.

Thus there is a big excess of private investment spending over saving, but this is offset by a budget surplus and an import surplus (balance of payments deficit).

The analysis can be illustrated by the familiar 45° diagram. In Figure 82 we start with the consumption function C. Now this is composed of two elements: consumption on domestic goods (C_d) which adds to the circular flow, and consumption of foreign goods (imports M) which is a leakage. In order to build up the aggregate demand schedule, we therefore subtract the import component from total consumption. Now we assumed that the propensity to consume, c, is composed of the

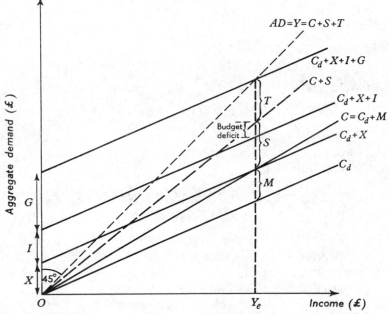

Fig. 82.—Equilibrium national income with balance of payments equilibrium.

propensity to consume domestic goods, c_d, and the propensity to import, m. If these propensities are constant fractions, and the average and marginal propensities are equal, both C and C_d will be straight lines through the origin, but of different slope, as shown. To the domestic consumption function C_d are added the other components of aggregate demand: exports, investment and government expenditure. Since these are assumed to be independent of income, the aggregate demand curve moves upwards, parallel to C_d, to (C_d+X), to (C_d+X+I), and to $(C_d+X+I+G)$.

Equilibrium national income is therefore Y_e, from the intersection of the AD function with the 45° line. In our diagram, there is also balance of payments equilibrium as exports X are exactly equal to imports M (the gap between C and C_d). The relationships between S and I and between T and G are shown by adding savings to consumption (curve $C+S$). We then see that there is an excess of saving over investment, and this is exactly offset by a budget deficit, for G is greater than T.

A change in an injection

A change in exports, investment or government spending will be subject to the multiplier $[1/s+m+t]$. If follows from this that:

(1) The balance of payments does not improve by the full amount of an increase in exports (ΔX) because imports also increase through the expansion of income.

(2) Exports will increase income, according to the compound multiplier. If, therefore, there is unemployment, the situation can be improved by pushing exports (by dumping, if necessary!). But these exports represent other countries' imports, and a reduction in their income follows, giving them unemployment. This policy of 'exporting' unemployment was attempted by many countries in the 1930s. As a result of the retaliatory measures which followed, all countries lost because international trade was progressively reduced. The rules of the I.M.F. (International Monetary Fund) and GATT (General Agreement on Tariffs and Trade) seek to prevent this from happening by regulating devaluation, tariff barriers, etc.

(3) If the balance of payments was previously balanced, and there is an increase in income (from any cause except an increase in exports), this will have the effect of creating a balance of payments deficit. Similarly a reduction in income will create a surplus. This is the reason for

deflating in order to reduce a balance of payments deficit (plus the hope that price rises will be kept in check relatively more than in other countries!).

Full employment and the balance of payments

To sum up, there is no reason why a balance of payments equilibrium should be achieved at the equilibrium level of income. We have also seen (Chapter 4) that there is no automatic tendency for the equilibrium level of income to coincide with full employment. It follows that government policy directed to achieving full employment may conflict with the goal of balance of payments equilibrium. In our model, for example, given the fixed level of exports X, imports increase with income according to the value of m. If the government budgets for a deficit to remove unemployment, Y will rise, and hence M will also rise. If the payments position was in balance so start with, a deficit will now appear; if there were an existing deficit, it will get worse; any original surplus will diminish.

(Note that in both models we have excluded the effects of feedbacks on the incomes of other countries as a result of the changes in A's income, exports and imports. These are examined in the Appendix.)

III. BALANCE OF PAYMENTS ADJUSTMENT

The analysis above explains in more detail how the gold standard mechanism worked: the deficit country adopted a deflationary monetary policy, which tended to cut investment. This had multiplier effects on income, and resulted in unemployment. Because imports were related to income, import expenditure fell with national income. It was this income effect, rather than any change in the prices of exports and imports, which restored equilibrium to the balance of payments.

The analysis also applies, of course, to deflationary (or inflationary) policies today. As we have already explained, however, the commitment to 'a high and stable level of employment' puts a limit on the amount of deflation the government will wish to carry out. There is a 'trade-off' between unemployment and a balance of payments deficit. A government will be prepared to cure its deficit by deflating incomes so long as unemployment does not rise above, say, 3 per cent; but if the deficit is so large that the requisite degree of deflation would cause unemployment to rise above 3 per cent, it will either (a) use a switching policy instead of deflation, or (b) combine some element of deflation with a switching policy.

We now turn to an analysis of expenditure-switching policies.

APPENDIX 1: FEEDBACK EFFECTS

In the analysis of this chapter, we ignored feedback effects. Let us now consider a case where country A is so important in world trade that changes in her income or exports have significant repercussions on the incomes of other countries, with consequent feedbacks.

Suppose there are only two countries in world trade, A and B. What effects will follow from a change in A's income?

Suppose A's income increases as a result of an increase in investment, government spending or autonomous consumption. What will be the sequence of events when we allow for international trade?

(a) The increase in A's income leads to an increase in A's imports.

(b) That is, B's exports increase.

(c) B's income therefore increases, and so she imports more from A.

(d) That is, there are induced exports for A.

(e) This will still further increase A's income, and so on, until the whole multiplier effect has worked out.

The extent of the final increase in A's income will depend upon:

(a) The initial increase in B's exports, i.e. upon A's marginal propensity to import (m_a).

(b) How much B's income originally increased owing to her extra exports, i.e. it depends upon B's marginal propensity to save (s_b).

(c) B's marginal propensity to import (m_b) – the larger this is, the greater will be the induced exports of A.

(d) A's marginal propensity to save (s_a) – the larger this is, the smaller the multiplier effect.

For a formal exposition, assume: (i) I and G are autonomous and unrelated to a change in Y's income; (ii) there is a change I and G. Let $\Delta I + \Delta G = R$.

A's increase in income is:

$$\Delta Y_a = c_a \Delta Y_a + R + \Delta X_a \text{ (induced from B)} - m_a \Delta Y_a. \tag{17.1}$$

B's increase in income is:

$$\Delta Y_b = c_b \Delta Y_b + m_a \Delta Y_a - m_b \Delta Y_b. \tag{17.2}$$

But $\Delta X_a = m_b \Delta Y_b$

$\therefore (17.1)$ becomes:

$$\Delta Y_a = c_a \Delta Y_a + R + m_b \Delta Y_b - m_a \Delta Y_a. \tag{17.3}$$

From (17.2), $\Delta Y_b (1 - c_b + m_b) = m_a \Delta Y_a$

$$\therefore \Delta Y_b = \frac{m_a \Delta Y_a}{1 - c_b + m_b}.$$

Substitute this in (17.3),

$$\Delta Y_a = c_a \Delta Y_a + R + \frac{m_b m_a \Delta Y_a}{1 - c_b + m_b} - m_a \Delta Y_a$$

$$\therefore \Delta Y_a = \left\{ 1 - c_a + m_a - \frac{m_b m_a}{1 - c_b + m_b} \right\} = R$$

$$\therefore \Delta Y_a = \frac{R}{s_a + m_a - \dfrac{m_a m_b}{s_b + m_b}}.$$

This can be compared with the multiplier given on p. 267: $(1/s_a + m_a)$. That is, the result of the feedback effects is an increase in the size of the multiplier. For example, if $s_a = s_b = 0.2$ and $m_a = m_b = 0.1$,

$$\left(\frac{1}{s_a + m_a} \right) = \frac{1}{0.2 + 0.1} = 3.3,$$

whereas $$\left(\frac{1}{s_a + m_a - \dfrac{m_a m_b}{s_b + m_b}} \right) = \frac{1}{0.3 - \dfrac{0.01}{0.3}} = 3.75.$$

This means that A's income will increase more than in the

simple case because it will be fed by induced exports as well as by the original injection.

A similar analysis can be applied to a rise in A's exports, the significant point here being that these represent increased *imports* for B, and hence a fall in B's income. There will be feedbacks: (*a*) as A's income increases due to the initial rise in exports, and she imports more from B; (*b*) as B's income falls due to her increased imports, and she imports less from A; (*c*) as B's income recovers due to the induced exports to A; and (*d*) as A's income falls again due to the induced fall in exports to B. The final result again depends upon the relative values of s_a, s_b, m_a and m_b.

APPENDIX 2: THE 'ABSORPTION' APPROACH

While the classical approach to balance of payments problems stresses the importance of price elasticities in 'switching' expenditure policies, the Keynesian approach stresses income effects. The latter can be explained algebraically as follows.

In equilibrium, $Y = C + I + G + X - M$.

This can be rewritten as: $X - M = Y - (C + I + G)$, or as:

$$B = Y - A,$$

where B is the balance of payments position, and A is the sum of the expenditures $C + I + G$, which can be called 'absorption'. Thus the balance of payments on current account is equal to national income minus absorption.

Similarly, a change in the balance of payments ΔB can be expressed as $\Delta B = \Delta Y - \Delta A$; that is, the change in the balance of payments position is equal to the change in national income (output) minus the change in absorption.

From the above, two propositions follow:

(*a*) *If there is less than full employment, the balance of payments can be improved by increasing output more than absorption*

For example, if we ignore government expenditure and taxation, in equilibrium:

$$X + I = M + S,$$

or

$$X - M = S - I.$$

Given a fixed level of investment and a linear savings function, the curve of $(S - I)$ will be upward-sloping, as in Fig. 83. Similarly, given a fixed level of exports and imports a linear

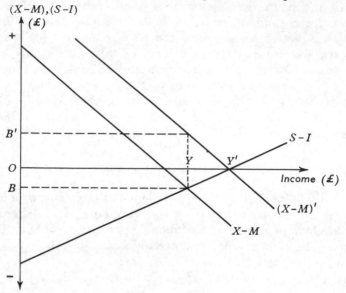

FIG. 83.—The effect of devaluation on national income and the balance of payments.

function of income, the curve of $(X - M)$ will be downward-sloping. Income will be in equilibrium at Y, where $X - M = S - I$; here there is a balance of payments deficit of OB.

A devaluation which successfully increases demand for exports and decreases demand for imports (because changes in the relative prices of exports and imports leads to a 'switching' of expenditure) will shift the $(X - M)$ curve to the right. If the curve shifts to $(X - M)'$ as in Fig. 83, the balance of payments deficit is exactly eliminated. At the same time, income has risen from OY to OY'.

It should be noted that the *initial* effect on the balance of payments appears much more favourable: switching at the orignal income level OY produces a surplus of OB'. But as exports generate a higher level of income, the propensity to import operates, and the initially favourable balance is modified. The extent to which income rises – and hence the extent to which the *impact-switching* effect of devaluation is cut down by subsequent *indirect* income effects – will depend on the marginal propensity to save, for this determines the slope of $(S-I)$.

Putting this in terms of absorption, we have:

$$\Delta B = \Delta Y - \Delta A.$$

If s is relatively high, the multiplier will be low so that ΔY will be relatively small. But absorption will be relatively smaller still, so that the improvement in the balance of payments will be greater.

(*b*) *If there is full employment, any improvement in the balance of payments must be obtained by reducing absorption*

With full employment, Y cannot be increased $(\Delta Y = 0)$. We have, therefore: $\Delta B = -\Delta A$. That is, an improvement in the balance of payments must come about by reducing absorption.

Professor Alexander has suggested that such a decrease could

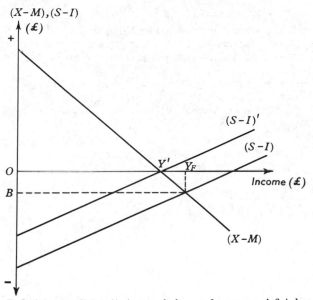

FIG. 84.—Deflationary policies eliminate a balance of payments deficit but create unemployment.

come about in various ways. For instance, it might come about automatically by a redistribution of income. If import prices are important in the cost of living, a devaluation will reduce the real incomes of those on fixed incomes or in a weak bargaining position. At the same time, profits in exporting industries will rise. There will thus be a decrease in absorption if the extra savings of profit-receivers exceed the reduced savings of the other group.

The argument suggests that, where there is full employment, devaluation will be unsuccessful unless it is accompanied by some deflationary measures. In Figure 84, $(S - I)$ and $(X - M)$ give equilibrium at full employment income Y_F, where there is a deficit OB. Deflationary policies shift autonomous consumption downwards, and hence $(S - I)$ upwards to $(S - I)'$. This creates unemployment equivalent to $Y'Y$, but eliminates the deficit. If devaluation were undertaken simultaneously, $(X - M)$ would shift to the right (because of the switching effects of relative price changes), and this would raise income and improve the balance of payments still further.

SUGGESTED READING

S. Alexander, 'The Effects of a Devaluation on a Trade Balance', *International Monetary Fund Staff Papers*, II, No. 2 (April 1952).

*F. S. Brooman, *Macroeconomics*, 4th ed. (Allen & Unwin, 1970) ch. 8.

B. J. Cohen (ed.), *Balance-of-Payments Policy* (Penguin, 1969).

R. F. Harrod, *Money* (Macmillan, 1969) chs 9 and 11.

*C. P. Kindleberger, *International Economics* (Irwin, 1968) chs 9-11, 16.

CHAPTER 18

BALANCE OF PAYMENTS ADJUSTMENT THROUGH EXPENDITURE SWITCHING

EXPENDITURE switching may be either (1) forced, or (2) voluntary or induced.

I. FORCED SWITCHING

Here people are forced to switch expenditure through some form of government regulation or control.

(1) *Import controls*

Import duties or quotas may be imposed to limit imports and thus reduce the balance of payments deficit. The former increase the price of imports. But if demand is inelastic, as it may well be for foodstuffs and raw materials, imports will not be greatly discouraged. In this case, expenditure of foreign currency may hardly decrease. Consequently, a quota in terms of volume may be fixed beyond which further imports are not allowed.

There is a case for the above controls if exchange rates are unstable (*see* p. 254), for in such circumstances a devaluation would only make the balance of payments worse. Furthermore, controls can be made discriminatory.

Otherwise the disadvantages of the policy are serious:

(*a*) Controls reduce the advantages of international specialisation.

(*b*) The protection of domestic industries from competition may impair their efficiency.

(*c*) Since Britain is a major importer, controls reduce the incomes of other countries.

(d) The policy invites retaliation by other countries, thereby still further reducing trade.

(e) It does nothing to remove the cause of the balance of payments deficit. Indeed, import duties, by raising prices, may give a twist to the inflationary spiral, while quotas will merely divert demand to the home market.

(f) It suffers from all the defects of controls – administrative costs, evasion, black markets, etc.

(g) It may offend international agreements, e.g. the I.M.F. and GATT, and certainly conflicts with the spirit of these agreements.

For these reasons, the U.K. has avoided import controls in recent years, with the exception of the temporary 15 per cent surcharge imposed in 1964.

(2) Exchange control

Exchange control may be introduced:

(a) to limit the amount of foreign currency spent on imports;

(b) to discriminate against those countries whose currencies are 'hard' (that is, cannot easily be earned by exporting to them), and to favour those countries whose currencies are 'soft' (because they buy exports from the country concerned);

(c) to distinguish between essential and non-essential goods;

(d) to control the export of capital.

All earnings of foreign currency or claims to foreign currency have to be handed over to the government or its agent (in the case of the U.K., the Bank of England), who alone can authorise withdrawals for the purpose of making foreign payments. Often licences are required to import certain goods.

Exchange control is essential when a country's currency is over-valued – that is, the pegged rate is higher than the free market rate would be. What this really means is that foreign currencies are valued below the market price – and so they have to be rationed.

Pegging the rate at a high level, however, may be advantageous if the demand for imports and the supply of exports is inelastic. In such circumstances, the balance of payments will not be improved by a devaluation (see p. 281).

This was the position facing the U.K. after the war. Imports of foodstuffs and raw materials were essential, but her productive capacity was such that she could not deliver all the exports on order. Because foreign currency was scarce, the purposes for which it was required had to be carefully scrutinised. Imports from hard-currency areas, such as the U.S.A. and Switzerland, were severely curtailed. Spending on nonessentials, such as foreign travel, was strictly limited. Even today exchange control still operates for certain capital movements.

Nevertheless, exchange control suffers from many of the disadvantages associated with rationing. Inefficient home firms are protected from foreign competition; regulations are evaded, and 'black markets' in currencies occur; many administrators are needed who could be employed more productively elsewhere. Moreover, it can lead to uncertainty in international trade. Countries may find their regular markets closed, and firms cannot plan ahead because they do not know whether they will be able to purchase their raw materials from a hard-currency area. Furthermore, .the confidence of foreigners is impaired if any attempt is made to prohibit the movements of their funds out of a country. Finally, when people are prevented from buying in hard-currency countries, it often means that they are forced to purchase dearer or inferior goods elsewhere.

II. VOLUNTARY SWITCHING

With voluntary switching, people are induced to switch expenditure via market forces through a change in the relative prices of imports and exports. Such a change can come about through: (a) a change in the cost–price structure of a country; (b) a change in the exchange rate. Policies are usually adopted in the following order.

(1) *Measures to promote exports*

Governments may pursue a vigorous policy to promote exports. Thus the British government guarantees payment through the Export Credits Guarantee Department and gives information on the possibility of developing markets abroad. Moreover, in granting loans, banks are asked to discriminate in favour of exporters. Here there is an element of forced switching. Although, under the terms of GATT, it is impossible to grant direct tax reliefs, incentives can be incorporated in indirect taxes, as for instance through an added-value tax.

(2) *Mild deflation*

We have already seen that a severe deflation is nowadays ruled out because it conflicts with full employment and economic growth. However, a mild dose of deflation can be used: (*a*) to damp down inflationary pressure so that the rise in costs and prices is reduced, thus improving the country's competitive position relative to other countries; (*b*) to reduce the pressure of domestic demand so that resources are switched to producing for the export market instead of for the home market.

(3) *A prices and incomes policy*

The rate of increase of costs and prices may be checked by 'moral suasion' from the government. 'Guideposts', such as an annual wage increase of $4\frac{1}{2}$ per cent, indicate the rises in wages and prices permissible, which are only to be exceeded for special reasons, such as an abnormally low level of income, a rise in productivity above the average or higher costs (notably of imported raw materials). If the policy is a voluntary one, its success depends on the acceptability of the guideposts, co-operation by trade unions and employers, and the degree to which trade unions and employers trust each other.

So far voluntary policies have not been conspicuously successful, and governments have had to take steps to impose wage and price settlements.

(4) *Altering the pegged rate – devaluation*

This is analysed in detail below.

III. DEVALUATION

As we have seen, under the I.M.F. agreement, countries endeavour to get the best of both worlds – stable exchange rates but without the need for deflation to correct a balance of payments deficit. Under the agreement:

(*a*) Currencies are to be convertible at declared rates.

(b) Each country is to maintain a high level of AD so that there are no adverse repercussions on the incomes of other countries through a reduction in their exports.

(c) Short-term loans are available to tide over temporary deficits in the balance of payments.

(d) Although exchange rates are 'pegged', the peg is movable, devaluation and revaluation being possible by up to 10 per cent without the agreement of the Fund, and by more with its agreement.

Devaluation, unlike depreciation, is a once-for-all reduction in the declared gold value of a country's currency by deliberate government decision. This means that the exchange value of the currency in terms of other currencies falls. Hence devaluation works in the same way as depreciation – not by bringing down the internal price level, but by reducing the rate at which the home currency exchanges for other currencies.

To analyse whether devaluation will produce an improvement in the balance of payments we must work either in terms of the home currency (sterling) or in terms of foreign currency (dollars). Let us examine the effects on the balance of payments of an assumed 50 per cent devaluation of sterling. The following are the main questions which have to be answered:

(1) *How will the elasticities of demand for imports and exports affect the balance of payments?*

(a) *In terms of sterling*

(i) *Imports.* A given quantity of imports now costs twice as much in sterling as previously. The supply curve moves from S to S_1 (Fig. 85(a)).

It will be observed that if the demand for imports is perfectly elastic, the price of imports in sterling remains the same, but the quantity bought falls. Thus the value of imports falls. On the other hand, if the demand for imports is absolutely inelastic, the price rises but the quantity bought remains unchanged. Thus the value of imports rises. If the elasticity of demand for imports = 1, there will be no change in the value of imports. Thus the effect of devaluation on the amount of sterling spent on imports depends upon the elasticity of demand for imports (provided that the supply of imports is not absolutely inelastic – see later). Thus, in Fig. 85(*a*), expenditure on imports increases or decreases according to whether *A* is greater or less than *B*, that is, according to whether demand is inelastic or elastic.

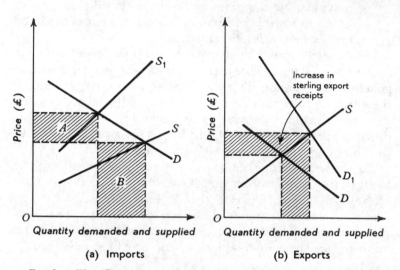

| (a) Imports | (b) Exports |

FIG. 85.—The effects of a devaluation of the pound, in terms of sterling.

(ii) *Exports*. Devaluation of sterling makes no difference to the supply of exports in sterling: the supply curve remains unchanged. But to American buyers it means that a given quantity of exports costs them half as much as formerly, since they are concerned with the price of those exports in dollars. Thus the demand curve shifts from *D* to D_1 (Fig. 85(*b*)). Hence, unless demand is absolutely inelastic, both the volume and price of exports in sterling increase, and the value of exports in sterling must increase.

It can be shown that, if we start from a balance of payments equilibrium, devaluation will result in a surplus provided that the sum of the elasticities of demand for imports and exports is greater than 1.

(b) *In terms of dollars*

    (i) *Imports*. Britain's devaluation makes no difference to the supply curve of American exports in terms of dollars; the price structure in the U.S.A. remains the same. But for British importers, imports are twice as expensive in terms of dollars. Thus the demand curve falls from D to D_1 (Fig. 86(a)). Hence, unless demand is absolutely inelastic, both the volume and price of imports in dollars fall, and the value of imports in dollars must decrease.

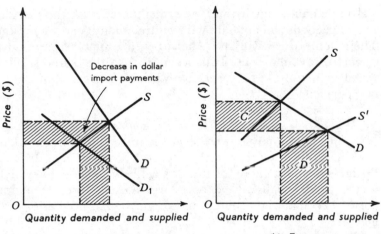

FIG. 86.—The effects of a devaluation of the pound, in terms of dollars.

    (ii) *Exports*. Devaluation means that, in terms of dollars, Britain's exports are halved in price. Thus the supply curve falls from S to S_1 (Fig. 86(b)). The change in dollar expenditure on exports therefore depends upon the elasticity of demand for exports. If demand is elastic, expenditure increases (D is greater than C); if it is inelastic, expenditure decreases (D is less than C).

What is the probable situation in the real world for the U.K. as regards the elasticities of demand for imports and exports? Demand for imports is likely to be fairly inelastic. Most of Britain's imports are necessities – foodstuffs and raw materials. Offsetting this is a likely fall in British demand for luxuries and foreign travel, as home-produced goods and holidays are now more competitive.

On the other hand, the demand for British exports as a whole is probably elastic. Not only could she undersell her competitors, e.g. in cars, electrical equipment, etc., but the lower export prices resulting from devaluation would convert what were formerly 'potential exports' into real exports. Moreover, such items as tourism are likely to have a highly elastic demand. But it must be remembered that the price of exported goods will not fall by the entire amount of devaluation. Their home price will rise when they are made from dearer imported raw materials. Thus when in 1967 the pound sterling was devalued by 14 per cent, many export prices fell by only 4 or 5 per cent.

(2) *Will there be any change in the conditions of demand?*

In the above analysis it has been assumed that the conditions of demand for imports and for exports do not change. In fact, Britain's demand curve for imports is likely to show some shift to the right because, as exports are manufactured from imported raw materials, more imports will be required as exports increase.

On the other hand, we have to allow for the effect of increased spending on imports by the U.S.A. if her demand for British exports is elastic. This will tend to reduce income in the U.S.A., causing her demand curve for British exports to shift somewhat to the left.

(3) *What are the elasticities of supply of imports and exports?*

(*a*) *Imports.* If foreigners are dependent on the British market, and supply is very inelastic, then they may be willing to lower their prices. This may reduce Britain's expenditure of foreign currency, although in volume imports are almost as great. If Britain's demand for imports is inelastic, this will be particularly advantageous.

(b) *Exports.* It is on the supply side that the greatest obstacles to a successful devaluation are likely to be encountered. The fall in the price of exports will probably lead to an expansion of demand, but this will be of no advantage if the supply of exports cannot be increased.

Two important questions have to be asked. (i) Has devaluation become necessary because prices have risen in conditions of full employment? If so, exports can only be increased by diverting goods from the home market (though increased productivity will help in the long term). This diversion can be achieved by physical controls, increasing the prices of home goods by indirect taxation, or by a reduction of incomes through a deflationary policy. In full employment, therefore, devaluation should be accompanied by one or all of these measures. (ii) What will be the reaction of the trade unions following devaluation? An increase in the cost of imports, together with any addition to indirect taxes, raises the cost of living. There is thus a strong temptation to demand wage increases. Moreover, labour is in a strong position, for the demand for exports is running at a high level following devaluation. If the trade unions exploit their position, the resultant rise in wages will soon wipe out the cost advantage gained by Britain through devaluation. In these circumstances, devaluation is self-defeating, for a country will soon be back in the position from which she started – exports insufficient to pay for imports.

It should be noted, however, that where the demand for British exports is inelastic, inelasticity of supply may not be detrimental. The higher costs of production at home will be paid by foreign importers, and British earnings of foreign currency may not fall.

(4) *What is the nature of British and American investment with each other?*

Suppose British investments in the U.S.A. are mostly in the form of shares in companies there. Profits will be earned in dollars, and so there will be no loss of foreign currency after devaluation.

On the other hand, if American investments in the U.K. are in stock with interest fixed in sterling, the U.S.A. will lose by British devaluation, for fewer dollars will now be obtained from the same investments.

(5) *Will countries regard devaluation as a once-for-all measure, or will they fear further devaluation?*

Devaluation by Britain reduces the value of sterling securities held by foreigners, including the sterling balances held in London. In the first place, this may destroy confidence in sterling, undermining London's position as a banking centre. Business is transferred elsewhere, and invisible earnings are lost. Secondly, unless devaluation is accompanied by positive measures (including a wages policy) to correct the underlying inflation, foreigners will fear a further devaluation and so hasten to remove their capital from London. This will mean a further depletion of the reserves, and make a new devaluation even more likely.

(6) *Will the U.S.A. retaliate by itself devaluing?*

If the U.S.A. retaliates it will wipe out Britain's advantage. The rules of the I.M.F. are designed to prevent such competitive devaluation: devaluation is permissible only if there is a chronic balance of payments deficit.

The above arguments suggest that Britain will turn to devaluation only as a last resort. Not only does it involve loss of face, but it represents a deterioration in the terms of trade, a large amount of additional exports having to be given to achieve a small gain in the balance of payments.

IV. ALTERNATIVES TO THE 'ADJUSTABLE PEG'

The adjustable peg system has worked reasonably well since it was established in 1944, although there have been occasional crises. It can be argued, however, that these were due more to a general insufficiency of international liquidity than to the peg system itself (*see* Appendix 2).

Nevertheless, in recent years, several economists have advocated that Britain (and other countries) should let their exchange rates float in the free market. The major advantage here is that no income adjustments are necessary in the event of, say, a decreased demand for exports; the exchange rate does the adjusting instead. There is consequently no need for a 'stop–go' policy such as Britain has experienced since the war, and therefore economic growth should be smoother and faster.

However, as we have already seen, floating rates have numerous disadvantages. The uncertainty they cause tends to reduce trade and investment. Moreover, the policy would mean dismantling the whole system of international co-operation built up so laboriously since the war. Finally, if the real cause of a country's successive payments crises is an excessive rate of inflation (compared with its competitors), exchange depreciation provides no answer: the currency will go on depreciating – floating downwards. Speculative capital movements would add to this downward trend, giving rise eventually to the same sort of crises as under the pegged system.

Another suggestion is a 'crawling' peg. Here the exchange rate would, if necessary, be adjusted annually. This would reduce the upheaval which occurs when there has to be a major change in the peg which has been supported as long as possible. Once again, however, the policy is open to speculative pressure, while it may also encourage countries to delay taking the appropriate domestic measures to deal with inflation.

APPENDIX I: A NOTE ON THE DEMAND FOR AND SUPPLY OF IMPORTS AND EXPORTS

In the text we have spoken about the 'demand for imports', the 'supply of imports', etc. What we now investigate are the factors which give rise to this 'demand' and 'supply', and to their respective elasticities.

Let us assume that we are examining the balance of payments in terms of sterling.

Between a certain range of prices, if Britain is to import from the U.S.A., there will be an excess demand over supply in the U.K. and an excess supply over demand in the U.S.A. This is shown in Fig. 87(a) and (b). The equilibrium price OP is where the excess demand of the U.K. is just equal to the excess supply of the U.S.A.

This price can be determined directly by plotting the demand for imports against price (that is, the U.K.'s excess of demand over supply) and the supply of exports against price (that is, the U.S.A.'s excess supply over demand at corresponding prices). Thus $mn = m'n'$ and $pq = p'q'$. The demand for imports is shown by the curve $m'M$, and the supply of exports by the curve $p'X$ (Fig. 87(c)).

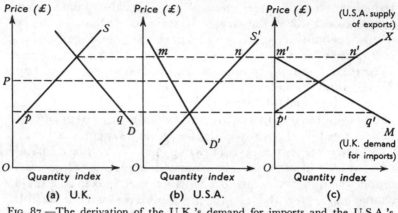

FIG. 87.—The derivation of the U.K.'s demand for imports and the U.S.A.'s supply of exports.

It can be seen that the demand of the U.K. for imports is compounded from the home demand for her imports and the home supply of the same goods. The more inelastic this home demand and the more inelastic the home supply, the more inelastic will be her demand for imports.

Similarly, the supply of the U.S.A. of exports is compounded from the home demand for goods which are also exported and the home supply of these goods. Again, the more inelastic is this home demand and supply, the more inelastic will be her supply of exports.

APPENDIX 2: INTERNATIONAL LIQUIDITY

One of the major difficulties resulting from Britain's devaluation of 1967 arose because insufficient weight was given to possible international repercussions. It illustrates how attention must be paid to *all* the factors mentioned above for the success of devaluation, and not merely to the elasticities of demand for exports and imports. The nature of international liquidity is such that no major country can act in isolation.

The trouble arises because world trade is increasing faster than the means for paying for it. As with our everyday financial transactions, payments and receipts do not coincide. Reserves are therefore needed for the transactions motive. In addition, creditors finance deficits by holding reserves. Such reserves have to be held in an acceptable form.

The one form that is always acceptable is gold. Unfortunately, the supply of gold is not increasing fast enough to keep up with the expansion of world trade and the corresponding need for larger reserves. In the past the difficulty has been overcome by countries holding reserves in other currencies – dollars and sterling, the 'reserve currencies' which are convertible into gold. In fact this has had the extra advantage that a rate of interest can be earned whereas there is no return on holding gold.

Britain's devaluation led to a loss of confidence in sterling because of the fear of further devaluation. Nor did the dollar look a satisfactory alternative in view of the strain on the U.S. economy of the Vietnam war. The result was that dollar balances held by foreigners were changed into gold.

To some extent the shortage of international liquidity has been made good by economising in the reserves through pooling arrangements, e.g. in the I.M.F. and by central banks. Other remedies proposed include the devaluation of the dollar in terms of gold, which would enable gold-holding countries to obtain more dollars and thus indirectly increase the acceptable means of international payment. For prestige reasons, the U.S.A. will not agree to this. It is likely, however, that the eventual solution will lie in 'demonetising' gold, using instead an internationally accepted line of credit, such as 'Bancor'.

SUGGESTED READING

S. Brittan, *The Price of Economic Freedom* (Macmillan, 1970).
P. Einzig, *The Case against Floating Exchanges* (Macmillan, 1970).
C. P. Kindleberger, *International Economics*, 4th ed. (Irwin, 1968) chs 15 and 17.
*E. Schneider, *Money, Income and Employment* (Allen & Unwin, 1962) pp. 242–79.
M. Stewart, *Keynes and Aftee* (Penguin, 1967) chs 9–10.

CHAPTER 19

ECONOMIC GROWTH
I. THE NATURE OF ECONOMIC GROWTH

The meaning of 'growth'

Britain's immediate post-war policy was mainly concerned with preventing a return to the depression conditions of the inter-war period. By the 1950s, however, it was realised that a high and stable level of employment could be maintained. This meant that policy could turn its attention to 'economic growth'. What does this mean?

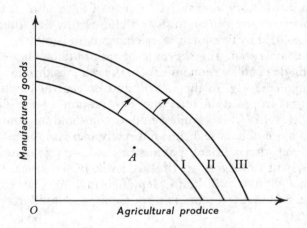

Fig. 88.—Economic growth pushes the production possibility curve outwards.

When there are unemployed resources, the economy's *actual* output is below its *potential* output; in terms of Fig. 88, the economy is producing inside the production possibility curve, e.g. at point *A*. Here output can be increased by the essentially short-run policy of increasing aggregate demand in order to absorb unemployed resources.

But, by itself, full employment of an economy's resources does not necessarily mean that the economy will grow. Growth is essentially a long-run phenomenon – the *potential* full employment output of the economy is *increasing* over time. In terms of Fig. 88, whereas full employment simply means that the economy is producing on a point on the production possibility curve I, growth means that, over time, the curve is pushed outwards to II and III.

Measuring growth

Growth means increased output over time, and output is most usually measured by gross national product. In using this figure, however, we must bear in mind certain qualifications.

First, it must refer to output in *real* terms. Corrections have to be made, therefore, for any changes in the general level of prices which may have occurred over the period.

Secondly, when people talk about 'growth', they are thinking chiefly of the difference it makes to the standard of living rather than to output itself. While the overall figure for real gross national product must be regarded as the best approximation available, allowances have to be made for changes in the size of the population, the proportion of output going to investment or defence as opposed to consumption, the distribution of increases in output, changes in hours of work and any social costs (such as river pollution) which do not enter into the calculation of G.N.P.

We can sum up, therefore, by saying that growth means an increase in the productive capacity of the economy over time and that this increase is usually measured by calculating the *rate* of change of G.N.P., or, more accurately, of real G.N.P. per head.

The importance of growth

Over the past ten years, the U.K.'s rate of growth has been about $2\frac{1}{2}$ per cent per annum. What difference to output (and thus to the standard of living) would it make if this rate were increased? We can illustrate by a simple example.

The important point is that the rate is *compound*. Thus, if we start off with a G.N.P. of £30,000 million, twentyfive years later we shall have:

Rate of growth (%)	G.N.P. (£m.)
2½	$30,000 \times (1·025)^{25} = 55,620$
3	$30,000 \times (1·03)^{25} = 62,282$
3½	$30,000 \times (1·035)^{25} = 70,890$
4	$30,000 \times (1·04)^{25} = 79,980$

It can be seen that, if the U.K. could achieve a growth rate of 3 per cent, output would double every twentyfive years; if it were pushed up by a further 1 per cent, output would increase two and a half times. Even a small change of ½ per cent makes an appreciable difference over the long run.

II. HOW IS GROWTH ACHIEVED?

There are three basic causes of growth:
(1) a rise in the productivity of existing factors of production;
(2) an increase in the available stock of factors of production;
(3) technological change.

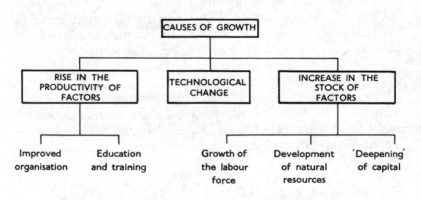

FIG. 89.—Factors leading to growth.

(1) A rise in the productivity of existing factors

In the short run, productivity may be raised by improvements in organisation, which secure, for example, more division of labour and economies of large-scale production or a more intensive use of capital equipment (e.g. the adoption of shift-working). Physical improvements for the labour force, e.g. better food and working conditions, may also increase productivity.

In the longer run, more significant increases can come with education and the acquisition of capital skills. This really represents, however, an increase in the capital invested in labour.

(2) *An increase in the available stock of factors of production*

(a) *A rise in the labour input.* What we really have to look for as a cause of growth is an increase in the size of the labour input to the total population. This ratio can increase through: (i) an increase in the number of hours worked per worker; (ii) an increase in the percentage of the working population to total population. The first is hardly likely to be a cause of growth in normal conditions, for as living standards improve the tendency is to demand more leisure. The second, however, may come about by an increase in the percentage of the population of working age and by changing attitudes to work. An increasing population tends to raise the percentage of workers, especially if this is brought about by immigration, for quotas can be operated to obtain young adult workers and those with particular skills. Participation in the working force depends upon the attitude of married women to work, the number of people who can afford to live on unearned income, the age at which people can retire on pension, etc.

(b) *Development of natural resources.* Productivity has increased, for instance, by the discovery of iron ore and nickel deposits in Australia and of natural gas in the North Sea off Britain. In the first case, resources can be transferred to more productive output (measured in value terms), and in the second, fuel supplies can be obtained with fewer factors of production, thereby freeing factors for other output.

(c) *Additional capital equipment.* Here we must distinguish between 'widening' and 'deepening' capital. Widening capital – adding similar capital equipment – is necessary if the labour force increases in order to maintain the existing capital–labour ratio and thus output per head. Suppose 10 men, digging a long ditch, have 5 spades between them. If the labour force is increased to 20 men the capital–labour ratio falls from 1:2 to 1:4 unless 'widening' takes place, that is unless another 5 spades are provided to maintain the existing ratio. 'Widening' does not increase productivity; it simply prevents diminishing returns to labour setting in.

'Deepening' capital occurs when the capital–labour ratio is increased. If, for example, when there were 10 spades to 20 men, the men were given a further 10 spades, the capital–labour ratio would be raised to 1:1.

(3) *Technological change*

All we have done in our example so far has been to increase the stock of a given kind of capital equipment, spades. Over time, however, productivity can be raised much more significantly by technological improvements. Thus the 20 men and their spades may be replaced by a single trench-digger and its driver. Because this does the job more quickly and efficiently, the remaining 19 men are released for other kinds of output.

In practice, all three causes are usually operating at the same time to increase productivity. Thus, as the labour force or natural resources are expanded, new capital is required, and this allows for the introduction of new techniques.

The speed with which new capital and improvements are introduced also depends upon the price of capital equipment relative to the wages of the labour for which it can be substituted. Over time, wages have tended to rise relative to the cost of capital equipment. This has been marked since the Second World War, where the effect has been to increase the rate of technological change in such industries as agriculture, cargo handling, transport, shipbuilding and mining.

III. CONSTRAINTS UPON GROWTH

The preceding section may have suggested that the attainment of growth is easy; all we have to do is to import the right type of labour, invest more in education, capital equipment and research, and encourage technological change. In practice, however, as Britain has discovered, a high growth rate is often difficult to achieve. Why is this?

The main reason is that, if the economy is functioning at or near full employment, growth through investment means less current consumption. If we want more factories, machines, roads, etc., we must be prepared to have fewer houses, cars, washing-machines, and so on. Now if people *voluntarily* decide to save a higher proportion of their incomes, more resources will automatically be set free for investment. But if people prefer a higher current standard of living, growth through investment can occur only if they are 'forced' to save, e.g. by higher taxation or rising prices.

The basic choice can be illustrated by a production possibility diagram. In Figure 90(*a*), the economy chooses combination *A* of investment and consumption. Here, we shall

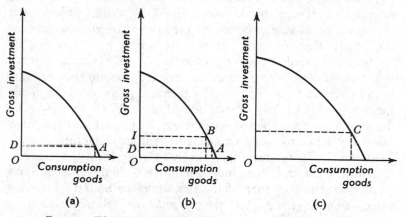

Fig. 90.—The importance of positive net investment for growth.

assume, investment is so low that the economy is just maintaining its capital stock intact; that is, net investment is zero. Consequently, if we ignore the other factors which can produce growth, we may expect this economy to 'stand still' over time. It has sacrificed future growth for a higher standard of living now. In (*b*), the economy has chosen position *B*, with net investment (*OD* representing depreciation of the capital stock in each diagram). The result is that, nine years later, the production possibility curve has been pushed outwards (*c*) and the standard of living has been raised, for at *C* both more consumption goods and more investment are obtained.

Other constraints upon growth are the desire for leisure, an ageing population, the rate at which immigrants can be absorbed and the level of research which determines technological change. But, for the U.K., the balance of payments has been particularly important. The U.K. is particularly dependent upon imports of raw materials for her industrial production. When the rate of growth rises, therefore, her demand for imports rises sharply, whereas exports increase only when production has been completed. This time-lag tends to cause a short-run deficit. But the situation is aggravated by the low level of the U.K.'s convertible currency reserves and sterling's role as a reserve currency. A deficit tends to give rise to speculation, leading to an outflow of short-term capital from the U.K. and thus a sterling crisis. The government then has to protect the reserves by raising bank rate and taking other deflationary measures. As a result, the 'go' of growth is quickly checked by the 'stop' of the balance of payments restraint.

Finally, it should be noted that growth entails costs additional to the sacrifice of current consumption necessary to the accumulation of capital. Growth usually means change, and the more rapid the growth, the greater the change. Thus in the U.K. during the post-war period, even when the growth rate has been relatively low, uneconomic coal-mines, cotton factories, shipyards and railways lines have been closed, while the plastics, electronics, car and other industries have been developed. Such changes in the structure of the economy are bound to lead to some unemployment. The process may be relatively painless if young workers can move into the expanding industries, for then the declining industries contract by natural wastage; but it is unlikely that all the changes can take place in this way.

A higher growth rate, therefore, means that people may have to accept the possibility of changing jobs quite radically, three or four times in a lifetime. This will entail retraining and probably moving around the country – and, as techniques change more rapidly, to a far greater extent than at present.

IV. A MODEL OF ECONOMIC GROWTH

The effect of investment over time

The theory of income determination (Chapter 6) showed

that income will expand or contract until the flow of saving generated is just equal to the level of investment. Thus if the rate of investment rises from I to $(I+\Delta I)$, income will rise from Y to $(Y+\Delta Y)$, and $\Delta Y = \Delta I/s$, where s is the marginal propensity to save.

This is essentially a short-run theory for it is based on assumptions which only hold over a short period of time. For example, it assumes a given population, a given state of technology, and given productive capacity. Now if the last assumption is to hold, the current rate of investment must be small relative to the existing stock of capital, for each year net investment is adding to this stock. Thus, if the stock of capital at the beginning of the year is K and the annual rate of net investment is I, the capital stock at the end of the year will be $(K+\Delta K)$, where $\Delta K = I$.

If, year by year, the capital stock is enlarged in this way, the productive capacity of the economy will grow larger. Thus, if the capital stock K is capable of producing a flow of output O each year, we should expect a capital stock $(K+\Delta K)$ to be capable of producing a larger flow $(O+\Delta O)$. When we move from short-run to long-run considerations, therefore, we must remember that net investment has other effects on the economy besides that of raising income to an equilibrium level where saving equals investment. The theory of income determination is essentially one that considers two static equilibrium positions by concentrating on changes which are taking place on the demand side. When we turn to the longer term, we have to consider the dynamic effects, particularly as regards what is happening on the supply side – the growth in productive capacity.

This is shown in Fig. 91. It is assumed that:

(1) The economy has a capital stock of K in year 0 and that the subsequent annual rate of investment is I. The capital stock therefore rises to $(K+I)$ in year 1, to $(K+2I)$ in year 2, and so on.

(2) There is a definite relationship between increments to the capital stock (net investment) and the resulting increments in the full employment output. This ratio, $\Delta Y/\Delta K$, is known as the output/capital ratio.

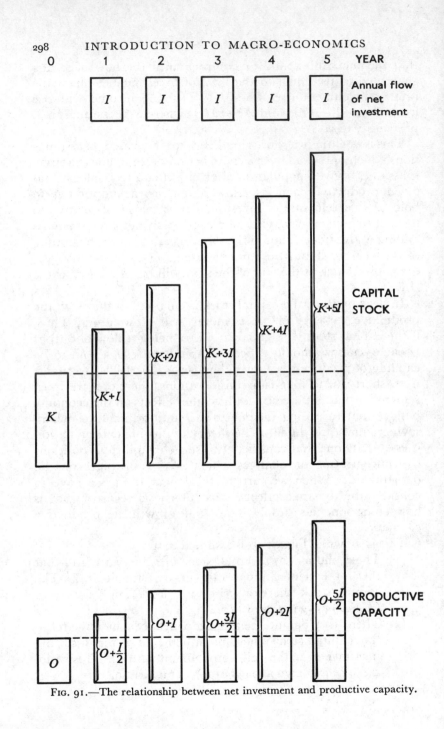

FIG. 91.—The relationship between net investment and productive capacity.

(3) The marginal output/capital ratio is constant over time and equal to the average output/capital ratio.

(4) The output capital ratio $= 0.5$. Thus, in year 0, with a capital stock K, output will be $K/2$. In year 1, the capital stock has increased to $(K+I)$, and so the full employment output is $(K+I/2)$, and so on.

Figure 91 shows the effect of positive net investment on the capital stock and thus on potential output.

Growth and full employment

We can link this growth in capacity and full employment output in a numerical example, using the same assumptions as above. Initially, it is assumed, the economy has a capital stock of 1,000. Hence output is 500. If the propensity to save is 0.2, saving will be 100. Thus, for the economy to be in equilibrium, investment must be 100.

Let us suppose that this rate of investment is maintained; the resulting rise in the capital stock is shown in column 2, and the rise in potential output in column 3 (Table 8).

But given the constant rate of investment and a constant propensity to save, the equilibrium level of income must remain at 500, with $S = I = 100$. Column 4 therefore shows the widening gap between the potential output of column 3 and actual output, which is determined by aggregate demand $= 500$.

TABLE 8

GROWTH AND FULL EMPLOYMENT

Period	(1) Investment	(2) Capital stock	(3) Full employment output	(4) (3) − 500
0	100	1,000	500	0
1	100	1,100	550	50
2	100	1,200	600	100
3	100	1,300	650	150
4	100	1,400	700	200

Column 4 shows that, if the rate of investment were maintained at 100, aggregate demand would be insufficient to keep factors fully employed, and workers would be laid off. Consequently, the economy would not pursue the steady path indicated in column 3 (even though this is in fact a diminishing *rate* of growth). Firms, with unemployed capital, would cut investment below 100 and the economy would be in the down-turn of a recession.

Our model suggests, therefore, that if full employment is to be maintained and the economy to grow, a *constant* rate of investment is insufficient. At first sight, it may seem that the remedy is to increase investment by 50 in each year in order to eliminate the gap in column 4. But this too is incorrect for, when investment is raised, the multiplier will operate to increase actual demand still further. For instance, an invest-ment of 150 in period 2 would generate a demand of 750. The capital stock would now be 1,250, giving a full employment output of only 625. In order to satisfy such a demand for goods, investment must evidently rise even faster! We thus have the 'paradox' of growth:

(a) Investment is necessary to generate aggregate demand but, at the same time, it may so increase productive power that output potential outstrips AD, causing investment to decrease again.

(b) Investment may generate aggregate demand to such an extent that it exceeds the possible full employment output, necessitating even greater investment if demand is to be satisfied.

If then we want *steady growth at full employment*, we have to steer a course between the Scylla of over-capacity and the Charybdis of excess demand. The appropriate rate of invest-ment can be found by examining the above model in general terms. We outline Professor E. Domar's exposition.

Domar's equilibrium growth path

Let I be the current rate of net investment and σ the output/capital ratio. Then the increase in output resulting from the current rate of net investment is:

$$\Delta O = \sigma . I.$$

Thus, if $\sigma = 0.5$ and $I = 100$, the increase in potential output is $\Delta O = 50$. In other words, if today's investment is 100, there will be extra capacity tomorrow of 50.

Now if this extra capacity is to be utilised, additional aggre-gate demand of 50 (that is, $\sigma . I$) must be forthcoming tomorrow.

Some of this additional capacity will be used to produce consumption goods (depending on the propensity to consume); but the remainder will have to be used for additional investment, ΔI. Given that the marginal propensity to save is s, the savings gap to be plugged by extra investment will be $s.\sigma.I$.

Hence $\Delta I = s.\sigma.I$. Dividing through by I, we have:

$\Delta I/I = s.\sigma$. That is, the rate of growth of investment must be $s.\sigma$.

We can illustrate by our original numerical example where $s = 0 \cdot 2$ and $\sigma = 0 \cdot 5$. Thus $\Delta I/I = 0 \cdot 2 \times 0 \cdot 5 = 0 \cdot 10$. The results of this rate of growth of investment of 10 per cent are shown in Table 9 and in Fig. 92. In period 0, investment is 100 and the economy is in equilibrium. This investment raises the capital stock in period 1 to 1,100 and potential output to 550. In this period, however, the new rate of investment is 110 (110 per cent of period 0). Since the multiplier is 5, the equilibrium level of income is now 550.

TABLE 9

THE RATE OF GROWTH OF INVESTMENT
AND FULL EMPLOYMENT

	(1)	(2)	(3)	(4)	(5)
Period	Investment	Capital stock	Full employment output	Actual output	(3) − (4)
0	100	1,000	500	500	0
1	110	1,100	550	550	0
2	121	1,210	605	605	0
3	133·1	1,331	665·5	665·5	0
4	146·41	1,464·1	732·05	732·05	0

It can be seen from the table that actual output is growing at 10 per cent – the same rate as net investment.

The effects of different propensities to save and different output/capital ratios

Table 10 shows how different marginal propensities to save and different output/capital ratios affect the rate of growth required for a 'moving' equilibrium.

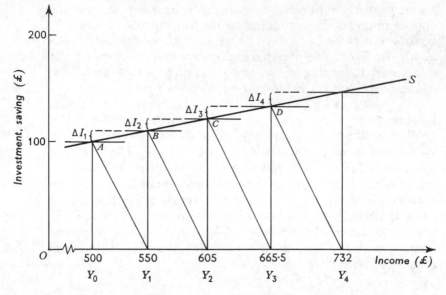

Fig. 92.—Domar's equilibrium growth of income. (Note that σ is the *slope* of AY_1, BY_2, CY_3, etc.)

TABLE 10

THE REQUIRED RATE OF GROWTH FOR SELECTED MARGINAL PROPENSITIES TO SAVE AND OUTPUT/CAPITAL RATIOS

σ \ s	·05	·1	·2	·5
·25	1·25	2·5	5	12·5
·5	2·5	5	10	25
·75	3·75	7·5	15	37·5
1·0	5	10	20	50

The table shows that:

(*a*) A country with a low *s* and a low σ will have a low equilibrium growth rate – conditions which are experienced in most underdeveloped countries.

(*b*) Given any value of σ, the growth rate can be raised by increasing the marginal propensity to save.

(*c*) Given any value of s, the growth rate can be raised by technological improvements which increase σ, the output/capital ratio.

Summary

Net investment, by increasing capacity, creates the necessity for even more investment in order to maintain aggregate demand. We have to discover the *steady* rate of growth which is possible, given the current propensity to save and the output/capital ratio. If growth is too fast, there is insufficient capacity and inflation because demand is continuously outstripping supply. If growth is too slow, there is surplus capacity and unemployment, because supply outstrips demand. Although these conclusions do not tally very closely with experience, they do highlight two extreme possibilities.

Nevertheless, we must recognise that Domar's model is based on simple assumptions. Once these are modified, his 'razor's edge' between excess demand and excess supply may not appear. For example, Domar assumes that the output/capital ratio is constant, implying that capital and labour inputs are retained in a fixed proportion. In contrast, the 'neo-classical' theory of growth associated with Professor R. M. Solow allows for a variable output/capital ratio, which occurs through diminishing returns to capital as capital is increased relative to labour.

Diminishing returns to capital can undermine the Domar conclusion that growth depends upon the current willingness to save. According to Domar, the equilibrium rate of growth is $\sigma.s$. On the neo-classical assumptions, as s is increased and the stock of capital rises accordingly, diminishing returns cause σ to fall. Consequently the rate of growth ($\sigma.s$) may be unchanged. Here technical progress is necessary to offset the tendency to diminishing returns as the capital stock rises.

SUGGESTED READING

*G. Ackley, *Macroeconomic Theory* (Macmillan, New York, 1961) chs 18-19.

S. Bober, *The Economics of Cycles and Growth* (Wiley, 1968) ch. 7.

F. S. Brooman, *Macroeconomics*, 4th ed. (Allen & Unwin, 1970) ch. 15.

R. L. Heilbroner, *Understanding Macroeconomics* (Prentice-Hall, 1965) ch. 12.

*E. Schneider, *Money, Income and Employment* (Allen & Unwin, 1962) pp. 185–92.

A. W. Stonier and D. C. Hague, *A Textbook of Economic Theory*, 3rd ed. (Longmans, 1964) chs 25-27.

CHAPTER 20

PLANNING FOR GROWTH

I. THE MEANING OF 'INDICATIVE PLANNING'

MANY countries, e.g. the U.S.S.R., China and Cuba, have increased their growth rate by a severe restriction of consumption so that resources are set free for the production of capital goods. This is possible in collectivist economies, where the government decides what shall be produced, lays down target output figures, and directs factors of production accordingly.

Such planning, however, is unacceptable in peace-time in countries where the individual retains the right to decide his type and place of work, how he will spend his income, and who shall govern him. In these economies, policy has to rely on persuasion, with the government exercising an overall control.

Even so, there are still many ways in which the government in a mixed economy can influence growth. Fiscal policy can be designed to increase saving and investment. Specific measures (e.g. the Industrial Reorganisation Corporation, soon to be wound up) can promote mergers which will yield economies of scale and better organisation. Education may be expanded. Research can be undertaken or sponsored by the government itself, or encouraged by patent protection or tax concessions.

In recent years, however, there has been a development of policy. As we saw in Chapter 19, given the propensity to save and the output/capital ratio, a certain rate of growth is essential if full employment is to be maintained. Policy is now being directed to ensure that this potential growth rate does not fall short through imperfections in the operation of the price system.

Even when the economy is operating at the full employment level, the private enterprise system works to some extent by trial and error. Because production takes place in advance of demand, it may be based on incomplete information. The result is that the plans of different industries do not harmonise. If, for instance, the production of cars increases, more sheet steel and power will be required. But will these industries have the right capacity? If they have too little, there will be bottle-necks; if too much, there will be a waste of resources. In the long period, the price system brings about the necessary adjust-ment, but it would be more satisfactory if the plans of all in-dustries were indicated in advance so that they could be harmonised.

The major aim of 'indicative' planning is to dovetail con-sumption and production decisions. It is called 'indicative' planning because, in contrast to those economies where the State dictates output targets, the government merely indicates appropriate targets to guide producers. Such estimates are based on discussions with industrialists themselves. The dif-ference between the two forms of planning has been illustrated by likening it to a road system. Under authoritarian planning, road users are permitted to travel only when, where and how they are directed by the State planning authority. With free enterprise 'indicative' planning, the State leaves every one to travel where he likes, and introduces a few rules, regulations, traffic signs, etc. – that is, policy measures backed by sanctions – to restrict freedom of travel.

Apart from dovetailing production decisions, such indicative planning enhances growth in other ways.

First, it forces the government to harmonise growth with its other policies, particularly price stability and the balance of payments, If, for instance, the steel industry cannot expand fast enough to cope with all the demands which are going to be made on it, firms will have to import steel or alter their plans. Thus, by collecting information on how industries depend on each other and on supplies from abroad, planning can help to prevent the steep falls into deficit on the balance of payments which have been the main cause of the 'stop–go' policies of the post-war period.

Secondly, planning makes the government examine its own expenditure policy. Not only is such expenditure partly determined by the rate of growth of the economy, but rapid growth itself may depend upon certain government spending, e.g. on transport and communications. Here long-term planning

is essential so that the development of the essential infra-
structure anticipates, rather than lags behind, demand.

Thirdly, the government may feel that the economy should
develop certain industries, e.g. electronics and computers,
which are likely to be 'key' industries in the future. Either
through lack of capital, too small a scale of enterprise, or
insufficient skilled labour and components, the rate at which
such industries develop may be too slow under private enterprise. Measures to accelerate the growth of such industries can
be incorporated in the planning.

Lastly, regular meetings between the government and the
private sector for purposes of co-operation can have favourable
effects on business confidence and expectations.

II. INPUT–OUTPUT ANALYSIS

The need to 'disaggregate'

In analysing short-period changes in the level of income,
we were able to simplify by considering broad economic
aggregates – total consumer's expenditure, total investment
expenditure, total imports, and so on.

When it comes to dovetailing the individual plans of different
sectors of the economy, however, more detailed information is
necessary. The government, for instance, may want to know
the implications for the balance of payments of a certain growth
rate. To what extent will imports rise as the economy purchases
raw materials and semi-manufactures? To answer such a
question, it will need information about the dependence of
domestic production upon imported materials and also about
the inter-dependence of domestic industries. An increase in the
output of cars, for example, necessitates increased steel production, and thus more iron-ore imports.

For such problems, blanket categories, like 'consumption
expenditure', are no longer adequate. We need to disaggregate
– to break down the economy into much smaller sectors and
determine the relationships between them. This is the principle
of 'input–output' analysis.

A social accounting matrix

The principles of input–output analysis can be explained by

considering Fig. 13 (p. 45), where the economy consisted of firms, households and 'banks' (a capital market). The recorded (or ex-post) flows of Fig. 13 can be represented in a social accounting matrix (Table 11). In the matrix, the rows record the receipts of economic units, and the columns record the payments.

TABLE 11

A SOCIAL ACCOUNTING MATRIX
FOR THE FLOWS DEPICTED
IN FIG. 13

Payments / Receipts	Households	Firms	Banks	Total
Households	—	Y		Y
Firms	C	—	I	$C+I$
Banks	S		—	S
Total	$C+S$	Y	I	—

Payments / Receipts	Households	Firms	Banks	Total
Households	—	1,000		1,000
Firms	900	—	100	1,000
Banks	100		—	100
Total	1,000	1,000	100	—

The basis of the matrix is the 'double-entry' nature of all economic transactions. If A pays B a sum of money, £x, we can regard this either as a payment of £x by A or a receipt of £x by B. Provided we define our terms carefully and record all flows, the receipts of any unit must be exactly equal to its total payments.

For example, in the economy of Fig. 13, we have an income $Y = 1,000$ paid by firms and received by households, consumption expenditure $C=900$ paid by households and received by firms, saving $S=100$ paid by households and received by banks, and investment $I=100$ paid by banks and received by firms.

The matrix shows the following relationships:

(a) From the households' row and column:

$$Y = C + S.$$

This shows that the total income received by households was either spent on consumption or saved.

(b) From the firms' row and column:

$$C + I = Y.$$

This shows that the sum of consumption goods produced and investment equalled the total value of firms' output, Y.

(c) From the banks' row and column:

$$S = I.$$

An input–output matrix

It will be observed that the social accounting matrix above ignores transactions *within any one sector*. For example, firms are not shown as selling anything to, or buying anything from, other firms. This is because, in national income accounts, we are concerned only with the *final* output of firms and the sale of this output to households.

But when we disaggregate, we deliberately study the sales and purchases within sectors. Thus, for firms, we should note how much steel the car industry buys from the iron and steel industry and how many vehicles the iron and steel industry buys from the car industry. These transactions can be recorded as above in an *input–output* matrix.

The form of an input–output matrix can be illustrated by considering a simple economy which consists of households (who buy outputs and also supply labour services), and a productive sector 'disaggregated' into two – agriculture and manufacturing. Units are in unspecified real terms.

The analysis works on the basis that, in producing, one 'industry' requires inputs from the other two groups, and that its own output must go to the other two groups (Table 12). (We shall ignore the fact that an industry may sell part of its output to itself, the production of machines by manufacturing for instance, involving the use of machines.)

TABLE 12
AN INPUT–OUTPUT MATRIX

Input from: Output to:	Agriculture	Manufacturing	Labour/Consumers
Agriculture	0	40	60
Manufacturing	20	0	60
Labour/ Consumers	80	40	0

The table shows (reading across the rows) that agriculture uses 40 units from manufacturing and 60 units from labour in its production; that is, it uses units in the proportion of 2:3, manufacturing to labour. It also shows (reading down the columns) that its output goes to manufacturing (e.g. raw materials) and to consumers (e.g. foodstuffs) in the proportion of 1:4. We can deal similarly with manufacturing and labour.

The use of the matrix for planning

The importance of the table is that it allows us to trace the effect of a change in the output of any one group on the others, and the resulting feedback to the first group.

We make the following simplifying assumptions:

(1) Each industry uses its factors in fixed proportions, the output of agriculture always being produced by a combination of manufacturing inputs and labour inputs in the ratio of 2:3, and the output of manufacturing by the combination of agricultural inputs and labour inputs in the ratio of 1:3.

(2) There are constant returns to scale.

Suppose, for instance, that it is decided to increase the output of manufacturing by 25 per cent, that is, by 20 units. To achieve this, it will require a 25 per cent increase in its inputs from agriculture and labour, which will rise by 5 and 15 respectively. So far, so good; but the demand for extra inputs does not end there. Agriculture, in order to raise production by 5, will require extra inputs from manufacturing (2) and from labour

(5). The input-output table thus shows (and measures) the feedback to manufacturing from agriculture. Similarly we can discover the immediate extra demands on labour.

A process is therefore set in motion tending towards a new equilibrium at a higher output for manufacturing. Whether this new equilibrium is attainable depends upon whether resources are sufficient to fulfil the various requirements which a 25 per cent increase in manufacturing imposes.

We can apply the same reasoning (and measurement) for an overall growth rate in output. Let us suppose a growth rate of 4 per cent in agriculture and manufacturing is attainable. From the table we can trace out the demands this will make on all three groups – the extent to which agriculture, manufacturing and labour should expand so that they are in harmony with this 4 per cent growth. Alternatively, if it is estimated that demand was such that what was required was only a 2 per cent growth in agriculture but a 7 per cent growth in manufacturing, the necessary expansion of the three groups would be different.

Difficulties in making predictions in practice

Although simple, the above example serves to show the principles upon which the government can calculate the probable effects of certain rates of growth of selected key sectors or of the economy as a whole. In practice, however, such predictions must be used with considerable caution.

For one thing, allowance has to be made for the fact that industries may change the proportion in which they use factors of production at different levels of output; in other words, technical coefficients are not fixed. For another, there may be increasing returns to scale in certain industries, decreasing in others. Nor can we say with sufficient accuracy how the economy will behave at high levels of employment. We cannot always assume that supply responds to demand primarily in quantity terms. Unexpected bottlenecks and shortages may simply cause prices to rise, or firms may decide to lengthen order books. Above all, it takes a long time to collect the relevant statistics, and during this time important changes may be taking place in the structure of the economy and in the relevant technical coefficients of production. The result is that calculations and predictions may be based on out-of-date data.

Nevertheless, as research makes our knowledge more exact and as statistics improve in accuracy, so planning will play an increasingly important part in mixed economies.

III. A NOTE ON BRITAIN'S POST-WAR EXPERIENCE OF PLANNING

Having achieved a high level of employment since the war, Britain was able to switch her attention to the growth rate of the economy. One of the stimuli was the discovery that her growth rate was considerably lower than that achieved by many of her competitors, in particular Japan, Western Germany, France and Italy.

Economic planning was thus introduced by the government in the 1960s, first through the National Economic Development Council, later through the Department of Economic Affairs.

In 1965, the D.E.A. published a National Plan (Cmnd 2764) designed to raise the gross national product by 3·8 per cent per annum over the period 1964–70. The Plan showed the various changes which would be necessary to achieve this target. For example, it indicated a deficiency of about 370,000 workers, and suggested that this gap could be filled by raising productivity and by regional policies to reduce unemployment in areas where the rate was above the national average.

Although the Plan did have some side benefits – a new look at regional policy, increased training of the labour force, co-operation between employers and trade unions to improve productivity – its main aim failed dismally. During the first three years of the Plan, the average growth rate was less than 2 per cent. Eventually the Plan was buried in ridicule, and in 1969 the D.E.A. was wound up, its planning functions reverting to the Treasury.

What went wrong? At the outset, the Plan was too hastily prepared – in less than twelve months – and was probably too ambitious in its target. But its main fault was the assumption that, if only the Plan could get on the magic 3·8 per cent path, all other problems would fade away. What it failed to take account of was the basic weakness of the U.K.'s balance of payments. It overestimated the rate at which exports would grow; and with imports running at a high level, the balance of payments remained in serious deficit. Speculation against sterling increased the pressure on the slender reserves of convertible currencies. As a result the familiar 'stop' policy had to replace expansion and growth.

The fact is that any plan will have to take account of Britain's international trading position. Higher growth rates automatically increase stock-building and therefore a higher level of imports. If a deficit results, speculation against sterling may lead to a 'stop' policy. It seems, therefore, that the success of any future planning rests on Britain's being able to maintain a healthy balance of payments position with, if possible, a strengthening of her reserves. This means increasing the value of her exports. To some extent, exports depend upon the growth of world trade, over which she may have little control. But to a greater degree they depend upon being competitive in world markets as regards price, delivery dates, etc. Britain's great need, therefore, is to prevent her home price level rising faster than that of her competitors. Until she achieves this, planning for Britain will remain a mere theoretical concept.

SUGGESTED READING

W. I. Abraham, *National Income and Economic Accounting* (Prentice Hall, 1969) chs 1, 2, 5.

W. A. Lewis, *The Principles of Economic Planning*, 7th ed. (Allen & Unwin, 1952).

INDEX